# The Truth About Goldfish

## Discover the Answers to Goldfish Success

### By Meredith Clawson

# Disclaimer

*While all attempts have been made to verify information provided in this publication, neither the author nor the publisher assume any responsibility for errors, omissions, or contrary interpretation of the subject matter herein. Any perceived slights of specific persons or organizations are unintentional. The author neither makes nor attempts to make any diagnosis of your fish or cure or prevent any disease.*

*The publication is an informational product based on my own experience and research and is not aimed to replace any advice you may receive from a qualified veterinary practitioner. The author and the publisher assume no responsibility or liability whatsoever on the behalf of any purchaser or reader of these materials. The author is not a veterinarian nor claims to be.*

*As always, before applying any treatment or attempting anything mentioned in this book, or if you are in doubt, you should consult your veterinary practitioner and use your best judgment. If you fail to do so, you are acting at your own risk and the risk of your fish. The buyer and reader of this book assumes all risks for applying anything they learn from this book. The Truth About Goldfish, Pure Goldfish and the author are not liable or responsible for illness, health problem or death of your pet in the event that you should give up veterinary advice.*

*By choosing to use the information made available on The Truth About Goldfish and the official Pure Goldfish website and in this book, you agree to indemnify, defend and hold harmless Pure Goldfish and The Truth About Goldfish from all claims (whether valid or invalid), suits, judgment, proceedings, losses, damages, costs and expenses of any nature whatsoever (including reasonable attorney fees) for which Pure Goldfish and The Truth About Goldfish may become liable resulting from the use or misuse of any products recommended through the Pure Goldfish and The Truth About Goldfish websites.*

**Dedicated to my family**

for their encouragement in helping me to finish this book &
for their patience with my goldfish habit on a daily basis...
especially during water changes.

# Table of Contents

Introduction..................................................................................1

   Welcome Aboard!...........................................................1

   24 Hour Free Goldfish Support......................................1

The Truth About Goldfish Mini-Course..............................2

Section 1: Learning About Goldfish...................................5

   Parts of a Goldfish.........................................................5

     External Parts............................................................5

     Internal Parts............................................................8

   Sexing Goldfish............................................................10

   History of the Goldfish................................................12

     The Goldfish Evolves in China................................12

     The Goldfish Comes to Japan................................13

     The Goldfish Travels the Globe..............................14

   Types of Goldfish.........................................................14

     Goldfish Color Variations........................................15

     Goldfish Body Features...........................................16

     The Difference Between Goldfish and Koi.............18

   Slim-bodied Breeds......................................................19

   Fancy Breeds................................................................21

   Dorsalless Breeds.........................................................24

Section 2: General Care.....................................................26

   The Pillars of Goldfish Success...................................26

   Housing and Stocking..................................................28

     Stunting....................................................................28

     Stocking...................................................................29

     Housing in Aquariums.............................................32

Housing in Bowls.................................................................................................32

Filtration, what is Best?.......................................................................................34

Hang on Back (HOB) Power Filters ...................................................................35

Canister Filters...................................................................................................36

Undergravel Filters: Coming Full Circle ...........................................................37

The Wet-Dry Filter Method: A (Possibly) Very Maintenance-Reducing Filter.........39

Sponge Filters...................................................................................................42

Notes on Using Other Filters .............................................................................43

Natural Filtration ...............................................................................................43

Current ..............................................................................................................47

Aeration.............................................................................................................47

UV Sterilization...................................................................................................48

Low-Tech Goldfish Keeping .............................................................................49

What to Do for Cloudy Water ...........................................................................49

Lighting ...............................................................................................................51

Temperature.......................................................................................................52

Benefits of Warm Water ....................................................................................52

Outdoor Goldfish & Temperature ....................................................................53

Decorations & Plants .........................................................................................54

Rocks .................................................................................................................54

Plants .................................................................................................................55

Substrate.............................................................................................................57

Gravel ................................................................................................................57

Sand ..................................................................................................................59

Clay-bottom ......................................................................................................61

Bare-bottom ......................................................................................................61

Setting Up Your Goldfish Tank ...........................................................................63

Water Quality......................................................................................................65

Ammonia ....................................................................................... 65

Nitrite .......................................................................................... 66

PH ................................................................................................ 66

Nitrate ......................................................................................... 66

KH ................................................................................................ 69

GH ................................................................................................ 70

Water Conditioners ..................................................................... 71

Seachem Prime ........................................................................... 71

ATM Paradigm ............................................................................ 71

The Nitrogen Cycle ...................................................................... 72

Cycling Your Tank ....................................................................... 72

Secret Cycling Shortcuts ........................................................... 75

Bacteria: The Double-Edged Sword ........................................... 77

Good Bacteria ............................................................................. 77

Bad Bacteria ............................................................................... 77

Tank Maintenance ....................................................................... 79

Water Changes ........................................................................... 79

Probiotic Bacteria Supplementation ......................................... 85

Cleaning the Filter ..................................................................... 86

Dealing with Algae ..................................................................... 87

Feeding ........................................................................................ 90

What kind of food should you feed? .......................................... 90

Choosing a Quality Staple Food ................................................ 92

Adding the Supplements ............................................................ 94

How Often Do You Feed? ........................................................... 95

How Much to Feed? ..................................................................... 97

Overfeeding and Sick Fish ......................................................... 97

Vacation Feeding ........................................................................ 98

Growing Your Goldfish ..............................................................................99

Goldfish Lifespan .................................................................................. 101

Section 3: Collecting Goldfish................................................................. 102

    Where to Get Your Goldfish? ............................................................. 102

How to Purchase Healthy Goldfish ......................................................... 104

Choosing Your Type of Fish.................................................................... 105

Acclimating New Fish............................................................................. 106

Quarantining New Fish........................................................................... 107

Goldfish Communities & Aggression........................................................ 113

Section 4: Dangers to Goldfish Health ..................................................... 115

Water Poisoning .................................................................................... 117

    Ammonia Poisoning.......................................................................... 117

    Nitrite Poisoning .............................................................................. 118

    Nitrate Poisoning ............................................................................. 118

    Low PH or PH Crash......................................................................... 119

    Oxygen Deprivation (Anoxia) ............................................................ 120

    High pH or pH Spike......................................................................... 120

    Supersaturated Gas Poisoning .......................................................... 120

    Hydrogen Sulfide ............................................................................. 121

    Heavy Metals................................................................................... 121

    Salinity............................................................................................ 122

    High Dissolved Organics ................................................................... 122

    Chemical Contamination.................................................................... 122

Other Miscellaneous Dangers................................................................. 124

    Temperature Swings ......................................................................... 124

    Aeromonas Alley (Outdoor Fish) ........................................................ 124

    Jumping Out .................................................................................... 125

    Getting Dropped............................................................................... 125

Electrocution ...................................................................................................... 126

Injury ...................................................................................................................... 127

Rock Blockage ...................................................................................................... 127

Aggressive Tank Mates ...................................................................................... 128

Egg Binding .......................................................................................................... 128

Section 5: Health Issues & Disease ....................................................................... 130

Diagnostic Techniques ............................................................................................ 130

The Goldfish Physical ......................................................................................... 130

Microscopy ............................................................................................................ 131

The Hospital Tank ..................................................................................................... 134

Sudden Death ............................................................................................................ 135

Sterilization ................................................................................................................ 136

Parasitic Infections ................................................................................................... 137

Internal Parasites ................................................................................................. 138

External Parasites ................................................................................................ 139

Bacterial Infections .................................................................................................. 149

Bacterial Gill Infection ........................................................................................ 151

Ulcers ...................................................................................................................... 152

Pop Eye ................................................................................................................... 153

Fin Rot ..................................................................................................................... 153

Mouth Rot ............................................................................................................... 154

Columnaris (Cotton Wool Disease) .................................................................. 154

Mycobacterial Diseases ...................................................................................... 155

Dropsy ..................................................................................................................... 157

Fungal Infections ...................................................................................................... 160

Saprolegnia ............................................................................................................ 160

Branchiomyces ...................................................................................................... 160

Viruses ........................................................................................................................ 161

Carp Pox ........................................................................................ 161

IHN Virus ...................................................................................... 161

Lymphocystis .................................................................................. 161

SVC (Spring Viraemia of Carp) ......................................................... 161

GHV (Goldfish Herpes Virus) ............................................................ 162

Tumors ............................................................................................ 163

Swim Bladder Disorder ..................................................................... 165

Treatment Index .................................................................................. 168

Choosing the Right Treatment ........................................................... 168

The Medicine Cabinet ...................................................................... 169

Natural Treatments ............................................................................. 170

Aloe Vera ...................................................................................... 170

Chlorophyll .................................................................................... 170

Colloidal Silver .............................................................................. 171

Epsom Salts ................................................................................... 171

Garlic ........................................................................................... 172

Heat ............................................................................................. 172

Apricot Kernals .............................................................................. 173

3% Hydrogen Peroxide .................................................................... 173

KoiZyme ....................................................................................... 174

Melafix ......................................................................................... 174

Microbe-Lift Artemiss ..................................................................... 175

Microbe-Lift Herbtana ..................................................................... 175

MinnFinn ....................................................................................... 176

Pimafix ......................................................................................... 176

Salt .............................................................................................. 177

Tank Transfer Method (TTM) ............................................................ 179

Vitamin C ...................................................................................... 179

Wild Oil of Oregano ...................................................................... 180

Commercial Medications ................................................................. 182

    Copper ............................................................................... 183

    Cyromazine ......................................................................... 183

    E.M. Erythromycin ............................................................... 184

    Furan 2 ............................................................................... 184

    Formalin + Malachite Green .................................................. 184

    Kanamycin ........................................................................... 185

    Metronidazole ..................................................................... 185

    Neomycin Sulfate ................................................................. 185

    Sulfathiazole ........................................................................ 186

Euthanasia ...................................................................................... 187

Symptom Lookup & Solutions .......................................................... 189

    Bent Back ............................................................................ 189

    Black Patches ....................................................................... 189

    Bloating ............................................................................... 190

    Bloody Veins ........................................................................ 191

    Bottom Sitting ..................................................................... 192

    Clamped Fins ....................................................................... 193

    Cloudy Eyes ......................................................................... 193

    Color Loss or Pale Skin ......................................................... 194

    Coughing ............................................................................. 194

    Curling or Folding in Half ...................................................... 194

    Eating Bubbles ..................................................................... 195

    Filmy Skin, Milky White Patches ............................................ 195

    Flashing & Itching ................................................................ 196

    Floating Upside Down ........................................................... 196

    Gasping for Air ..................................................................... 196

Gills Flared Out ........................................................................................... 197

Gills Pale .................................................................................................... 197

Green Dots .................................................................................................. 197

Hanging at the Surface ................................................................................ 198

Head Standing ............................................................................................. 198

Holes in Gill Covers ..................................................................................... 198

Holes in Fins ............................................................................................... 199

Jerking ........................................................................................................ 199

Jumping Out ................................................................................................ 199

Labored Breathing ....................................................................................... 200

Leaning to One Side ..................................................................................... 200

Lumps ......................................................................................................... 200

Missing Scales ............................................................................................. 201

Mouth Red or Rotting .................................................................................. 201

Mouth Stuck Open ....................................................................................... 202

Mushy Belly ................................................................................................. 202

Pale Color .................................................................................................... 202

Popped out Eye/s ......................................................................................... 202

Pineconing Scales ........................................................................................ 203

Red Anal Port or Prolapsed Anal Port ........................................................... 203

Red Belly ..................................................................................................... 203

Red Hole in the Head ................................................................................... 204

Red Spots .................................................................................................... 204

Shredded Fins .............................................................................................. 204

Sores ........................................................................................................... 205

Spitting out Food ......................................................................................... 205

Splits in Fins ................................................................................................ 205

Swimming in Circles ..................................................................................... 206

Tail Standing ........................................................................................................... 206

Wasting/Weight Loss ........................................................................................... 206

Warts ......................................................................................................................... 207

White Edge on Fins ............................................................................................... 207

White Fuzzy Patches ............................................................................................. 207

White Spots ............................................................................................................. 208

White Spots in Wen ............................................................................................... 208

White, Long Stool .................................................................................................. 208

Won't Eat ................................................................................................................. 209

Worms on Body ..................................................................................................... 209

Yawning .................................................................................................................... 209

Yellow Speckles ...................................................................................................... 210

Sources List ................................................................................................................. 211

Further Reading ..................................................................................................... 211

Websites ................................................................................................................... 211

Conclusion .................................................................................................................. 212

# Introduction

## Welcome Aboard!

Hello fellow goldfish lover, and congratulations on getting the manual of wisdom you need to become a goldfish expert.

No matter where you are at in your journey, the methods contained in *The Truth About Goldfish* are the proven techniques everyone needs to know to enjoy a stress-free and rewarding relationship with your finned friends!

My goal in writing this book was to help you reach YOUR goal – healthy, happy pets that bring you entertainment for years to come. It was written from the perspective that goldfish keeping should be fun and simple, something that brings both you and your fish happiness.

By following the instructions contained in this book, the heartbreaking cycle of buying a new fish, watching helplessly as they slowly deteriorate and die within a short time, then getting more fish to replace them (only to watch them die too) can be stopped. Now is the time to open the door to a life with healthy goldfish.

*Puregoldfish.com (scan this code with a QR code reading app on your phone)*

*The Truth About Goldfish* was written by a real goldfish owner like you who spent nearly 20 years seeking these answers. While I don't claim to know everything there is to know about these fascinating creatures, and there will be some subjectivity to some of the information in this work (what works for one person might not always work for another), providing you with the facts you need to give your goldfish the best care possible has been my mission. This book isn't perfect, and never will be despite the updates I make regularly as I learn new things (yes, I'm always learning too!). But I'm sharing with you the best of what I know and have found to work in my own experience and in my discussions with other goldfish keepers. Feel free to use what you find useful and leave what you don't. I hope it helps push you to the next level of goldfish!

## 24 Hour Free Goldfish Support

As a buyer of this book, you have complete and unlimited access to the exclusive Pure Goldfish support system, including personal guidance and quality advice.

*Goldfish Support*

If you ever need some one-on-one help, don't hesitate to email your question. I look forward to hearing from you!

# The Truth About Goldfish Mini-Course

For those who want a quick low-down and don't have the time or desire to read through everything in this book... here are the key points packed into 7 simple steps:

## 1. Clean water

Clean water is foundational to the health of a goldfish. Goldfish are constantly excreting toxins from their waste and respiration, and unless those toxins are removed, the fish can end up poisoning themselves.

In water that does not contain enough aquatic plants or filtration from a store-bought/homemade filter, it is necessary to change the water much more frequently to replenish the oxygen content of the water while removing these toxic byproducts.

## 2. Feeding

Goldfish are grazers and live to eat. Always ensure your fish has access to foraging material – fresh, leafy veggies such as spinach, kale, and lettuce – so they don't always feel hungry. Uneaten veggies should be removed after 24 hours. In addition to veggies, feed once daily your healthy protein staple diet of choice (worms, pellets or gel food) as much as the fish can eat in 30 seconds. Goldfish need to be fed this richer food very sparingly in order to maintain healthy organs and so the tank does not get dirty so quickly.

If your fish aren't well or you suspect a problem, withhold all food. It won't starve. Goldfish can live for weeks without food. It is not advisable to feed if the fish does not want to eat as it will only foul the water.

## 3. Water changes

Water changing is pretty simple. Nitrates should not be allowed to rise above 30ppm, so if the levels are creeping up it is time to perform a water change.

If water changes are necessary to remove ammonia or nitrite, the tank may not have finished cycling OR the filtration may be inadequate.

If nitrates are consistently below 10ppm and evaporation top-offs alone are required, only maintaining proper mineralization is necessary. This can be done through the use of aragonite/crushed coral in moderate amounts, or soil below the substrate.

It is up to the hobbyist to decide if they prefer larger or smaller water changes. Larger water changes promote more growth of the fish, but smaller ones minimize the risk of drastic shifts in water conditions and are easier to execute.

## 4. Filtration

Filtration is what you rely on in between water changes, or sometimes completely, to keep the water clean. You may have heard that there are 3 types of filtration: biological, chemical and mechanical. I say there are 4, as filters relying on bacteria are far different than plant-based filtration.

- Filter bacteria typically live on some kind of sponge or porous media. If you rely on bacteria to keep your water clean, it will take time for the tank to become safe for your goldfish (unless you can obtain used filter media). It takes an average of 4-6 weeks for your colony to build up and your tank is safe for fish, unless you jump start things with a good liquid supplement or the addition of soil to the substrate.
- Chemical filtration depends on charcoal or resins to trap toxins. It eventually wears out and needs to be replaced, but it works quickly to instantly help give you a fish-safe aquarium and can be very useful in some situations.
- Mechanical filtration traps solids on floss, batting or a sponge. This alone will not remove the toxins and make the water safe for fish.
- Plant filtration harnesses the power of nature to purify the water. Plants eagerly absorb toxic ammonia, nitrite and often nitrate and use it as food to grow.

Without filtration, as stated, water changes are required to maintain clean water.

## 5. Substrate

The easiest substrate to clean would be none at all, but having one amuses the fish.

- **Sand** is easy to add, looks great and is not messy when installed correctly. It also affords you a place to plant non-demanding live plants in. A great option for beginners.
- **Gravel** alone can be used, but care must be taken that the fish won't choke on the grains of the rock. The pieces should not be able to fit inside their mouth. It requires frequent cleaning or nasty stuff sometimes builds up, which can be hurtful to the fish. Using an undergravel filter can help prevent this.
- **Soil-capped Gravel** is a natural option if you want a lush planted tank. You can add an inch of potting mix beneath the gravel first. This has a unique set of advantages, including jump-starting the cycling process. Soil does discolor the water and, unless you sift it first,

can release random pieces of wood or other additives. It can also gas off a lot of ammonia/nitrite initially in some cases, which is good for the cycle but harmful to the fish. Hydrogen sulfide can also be an issue until the plants really throw out their roots.

- **Clay**-based substrates do not supply nutrients to the plants directly, but have a very large surface area for bacteria to grow and can assist the plants by helping deliver surrounding nutrients to the roots.
- **Baked soil** substrates are also an option, as they are not as messy and nourish plants. Maintenance is similar to that of gravel.

## 6. Tank mates

Goldfish, for the most part, do very well with their own kind. A single goldfish can be kept happily by itself or you can add friends. Mixing other species of fish with goldfish has mixed results; in some cases it can be a nightmare, in others it can be a peaceful arrangement. Slim-bodied fish are the most versatile, as they are fast enough to escape being nipped at by most fish. Larger goldfish will eat any fish that fits in its mouth. Some tropical fish are not good tank mates under any circumstance as they will be too aggressive.

## 7. Quarantine

Proper quarantine procedures will help you with getting off to a good start with your new goldfish. If you bought your fish from a seller who thoroughly treats their fish prophylactically before making them available for sale, you will only have to isolate them for 2-4 weeks before adding them with your other fish. If you got your fish from a pet store or from a seller who does not "clean" their fish, you will need to do this yourself over a minimum of a 4 week period of time with the recommended treatments.

# Section 1: Learning About Goldfish

It's time to learn about goldfish!  Having a basic understanding of how the goldfish is "put together" will help deepen your knowledge of the species and may come in useful when diagnosing an illness or simply wondering if something is normal or not.

## Parts of a Goldfish

As a species that lives entirely underwater all of its life, goldfish are structured very differently than most pets.  They have their own set of features to deal with their environment.  It is useful to understand the anatomy of a goldfish, whether you are first getting started in goldfish keeping or you want to brush up on your facts.  This can help you distinguish between normal and abnormal behavior, as well as choose healthy goldfish when the time comes for you to add fish to your aquarium.

### External Parts

**Mouth:**  A goldfish's mouth is at the front of its body, and is the part of its body used to draw in food to its digestive system.  Surprisingly enough, goldfish have taste buds around the outside of their mouths, which they use to test the many surfaces they peck on as they scavenge for food.  That goldfish do not have teeth is a myth; their teeth are located in the back of their mouths and help in grinding up food before digestion occurs. These teeth are not spikey like shark teeth, but flatter and fall out occasionally to be replaced by new teeth.  They are called Pharyngeal teeth because of their location.

**Eyes:**  If you have ever watched a baby goldfish develop from the time of its hatching, one of the first features you will notice are the two tiny black dots which are its eyes.  From its early stages of life, the eyes of a goldfish are important to its survival.  Young fry rely to a large extent on their vision in order to hunt for food in the water.  Scientists say that the eyes of a goldfish are polarized, meaning that they have a specialized form of vision which allows them to see more contrast.  This helps them find food suspended in the water.  Goldfish can indeed see color, and it is estimated that they can perceive more colors than a human eye can!  (Not only that, but they are able to differentiate between colors, shapes and even human faces!)  A goldfish that catches sight of the person who feeds them will probably get more excited to see them than just anyone.

On more hybridized goldfish, you might see unusual eye characteristics, such as upturned eyes on a Celestial eye, protruding eyes on a Telescope, or even huge, balloon-like sacks of fluid on a Bubble Eye goldfish.  These goldfish are not able to see as well as varieties that have not been so inbred.  You may have noticed that goldfish have different colored eyes on the larger rim outside of their pupil.  Blue eyes, gold eyes, red eyes and black eyes are among some of the variations you may spot.  Albino goldfish have whitish eyes with red pupils and have an unusual look.

**Nose:**  The nose of a goldfish is located right above its mouth and is identified by the two protruding outside "nares" which are like nostrils.  Unlike with humans, a goldfish's nose is not connected to its mouth.  It smells by raising a flap *underneath the nostril* to allow water into a tiny pouch, where thousands of tiny hairs then sense a smell.

A goldfish's sense of smell is even more acute than a human's, and they can tell the difference between sweet, salty and sour smells.  They can also smell nearby predators or sense when it is breeding season.

In varieties such as the Pom Pom, the nares are intentionally bred to be far larger and fluffier than normal for a unique appearance.  Such goldfish sometimes lose a nare as the result of an injury, but it can grow back.

**Gill Covers (Operculum):**  The gill covers, which are also called the operculum, are a hard shell that protects the delicate gill filaments inside.  They may be flared out unintentionally through genetic mutations, or intentionally flared out if they are on a Curl-gill goldfish. They may also be covered in tiny white dots called breeding tubercles if they are on a male goldfish.

**Lateral Line**:  One amazing part of a goldfish's body is its unique structure called a lateral line, which is located on the sides of the goldfish.  It runs from the top of the gills down to the base of the tail, and close up it looks like a series of small spots all in a row a little darker than the color of the goldfish's body.  Some goldfish owners have been concerned about them, wondering if they are some kind of a scratch or an injury, but rest assured that they are a normal part of their anatomy and are "built in" to the goldfish for a specific purpose.

The lateral line is actually an organ that is able to detect movement, currents and vibrations in the water.  It helps the goldfish orient itself in relation to where it is in the water and navigate through its environment.  This enables it to school with other goldfish in a group, hunt for food, evade predators and control its location.

**Fins:**  As you probably have observed, goldfish don't have legs!  They rely very heavily on their fins for movement and stabilization in the water.  All goldfish have at least 2 pairs of fins, but slim-bodied varieties such as the Common and Comet goldfish do not have a pair of anal fins and lack a double tail, both of which fancy varieties have.  The fins of a slim-bodied goldfish are actually made of a double-layer, which is separated in fancy goldfish.  The fins are made of very thin rays that are covered by skin.  They also have the remarkable ability to repair themselves, as long as the rays themselves have not been damaged badly.

- The **pectoral fins** of the goldfish are located right under the gills and are paired.  They are the fins that are closest to the head of the goldfish and are used to help the fish swim forwards and backwards.  You will notice that these fins are almost constantly moving, helping the goldfish to navigate and keep its balance.
- The **pelvic fins** are the fins directly under the belly of the goldfish, positioned approximately in the middle of its body.  These are generally thicker than the pectoral fins and are used to stabilize and brake as the goldfish swims.
- The **anal fins** (also called the ventral fins) are positioned underneath the base of the tail.  In fancy goldfish that have paired anal fins, these fins are mostly present for decoration and do not aid much in swimming, though they do help to keep the goldfish upright.  However, the anal fin in a slim-bodied goldfish has more functionality.
- The **dorsal fin** is the tall fin on top of the goldfish's body that stands up or flexes down as the fish stops or brakes.  This fin is particularly useful in determining if the goldfish is feeling well or not; it will often stand straight up on a well fish but remain flattened down when the fish is not normal.
- The **tail fin** (or fins, in a fancy goldfish) is the strongest fin of the goldfish and is maneuvered by the muscles in the caudal peduncle and the sides of the fish.

**Skin:**  The goldfish's body is covered in a thin layer of skin, scientifically known as the epidermis.  The skin is covered in thousands of little pores that secrete mucus to cover the goldfish in slime.  You may observe, after handling a goldfish, that your hands have a residue of this slime that isn't sticky to the touch but is much like the slime of a snail.  This is goldfish mucus, which is produced in order to help the fish glide more swiftly through the water and escape the grasp of predators.  It also helps protect the fish from bacteria.  You will not be able to see this slime on a healthy goldfish as it swims through the water.

**Scales:**  Goldfish scales are always transparent.  They are given their color by the skin *underneath* them, but depending on the fish you may observe varying degrees of reflection, the most common being metallic.  Because of this, a fish may change color several times over its life, but it will never change its reflectivity.  Metallic scales are highly reflective, much like aluminum foil.  There are also matte-scaled goldfish, who have no reflectivity in their scales and are therefore not shiny at all.  A good example of a goldfish with matte scales is a Black Moor.  They have more of a velvety appearance because of their low reflectivity.  There are also pearl scales, which are elevated because of deposits of calcium carbonate on the scale itself.

What causes the scales to be shiny or not is actually based on the level of guanine, which is a substance in the scale itself.  Like the fins, they also have the ability to regenerate after being lost.

**Body:**  The unique shape of the body depends on the goldfish it belongs to, but each one is used to contain the internal organs of the fish.  Slim-bodied goldfish have more streamlined bodies and are generally thinner from side to side, whereas fancies are much rounder and deeper in the belly.  Because of this, they are much slower swimmers while the single-tails are zippier in the water.

**Vent:**  The vent of the goldfish is located just before the anal fin.  It is the opening that aids in both ridding the body of solid waste and reproduction.  The shape of the vent helps tell the difference between male and female goldfish.

## Internal Parts

**Brain:**  Goldfish do have a brain, and it processes all sensory information and regulates the body's function, such as breathing and decision-making.

**Ears:**  You can't see them, but goldfish do have ears.  They are inner ears located inside the skull, which allow the goldfish to perceive vibrations in the water and stay level as they swim.

**Pharynx:**  The Pharynx is the place inside the goldfish directly behind the mouth where the goldfish grinds up its food.  This is why the teeth of the goldfish are called "*Pharyn*geal Teeth."  The upper surface of the Pharynx is hard, and the lower teeth use it to help break up food.

**Gills:** The gills of the goldfish are used for respiration, which goldfish must do in order to live.  Interestingly enough, goldfish must have oxygen in order to live just like people, but they get their oxygen through the water and not through the air directly.  Unlike Siamese fighting fish (also called betta fish), goldfish are not surface breathers.  They breathe by taking water into their mouths and pass it through the gills, allowing it to go over their gill rakers where the oxygen is absorbed into the bloodstream.  The covers of the gills protect the gill rakers, which are shaped like spikes.  These rakes project forward and strain out particles of debris, supported by the gill arches, which are a hard bony structure.  The gills themselves are a made of conductive tissue that take in much needed oxygen from the surrounding water.

**Heart:**  The heart of the goldfish has two thick-walled, muscular chambers, a ventricle to receive blood and an atrium to pump it out.  It helps the goldfish live by pumping blood to the gills to get oxygenated, and to the rest of the body so it will function properly.

**Liver:**  A vital organ of the goldfish, the liver has many responsibilities.  It aids in detoxification, protein synthesis, and helps produce digestive enzymes.  It also stores fats and carbohydrates for the goldfish.

**Spleen:** This somewhat elongated organ is primarily a filter for the blood. It houses blood and reuses old blood cells.

**Stomach:** Contrary to popular belief, goldfish DO in fact have a stomach, though it is relatively small – approximately the size of the goldfish's eye. They use it to hold recently ingested food, break down the food through enzymes and help out with the digestive process. Because goldfish naturally feed in small amounts throughout the day, they do not need a large organ capable of housing a big meal. By the time the food has reached the stomach, most of it has already been broken down, so a large stomach is not necessary.

**Intestines:** Goldfish have two main intestines: the intestinal bulb, which temporarily stores food and absorbs fats from them, and the smaller caudal intestine, which absorbs proteins.

**Swim Bladder:** The swim bladder is an important organ for goldfish owners to understand, as the diets of fancy goldfish should be prepared with it in mind for many reasons. It is basically a gas-filled organ that controls the fish's buoyancy (where the fish sits in the water). They are pearly-white and are located at the top of the goldfish's abdomen. It has two lobes. One lobe is located near the tail (called the caudal sac) and the other, smaller one (called the anterior sac) is directly in front of it. Under normal circumstances, the sack fills with air or expels air as the fish wants to rise or descend in the water. The expressed air will either be pushed out through the esophagus (which is connected to the swim bladder through a duct) or passed through.

**Gonad(s):** These are the reproductive organs of the goldfish located inside its body. If the fish is a male, it will have testes that produce milt for spawning, and if it is a female it will have one ovary that produces eggs to release for spawning.

# Sexing Goldfish

Being able to tell if your goldfish is a boy or a girl is always helpful to know when you are trying to decide what to name it. After all, it would be a shame to name your female "Buster" only to find out later that she should have been called "Bella." Also, if you are planning on trying to spawn your goldfish and want to make sure you get one of each, knowing their sex can come in really handy.

So, how do you tell what gender your fish is? Unfortunately, it isn't very easy, and only experienced breeders really can tell at a glance – and even they can mess up! But when you know what to look for and the goldfish are in breeding condition, you might be able to come up with an (almost) certain answer.

If your goldfish is still very young (under 6 months old) then it is probably not sexually mature yet. In that case, you will have to wait a bit, and typically you can't tell until 9 to 12 months of age. The rate that goldfish mature sexually depends upon several factors, including where they are housed, how healthy they are and what they are fed. Pond-raised goldfish mature faster than those housed indoors in tanks. Here are some things you can look for to determine what gender your fish is.

## Signs your goldfish is a Male:

- **Breeding tubercles**: These are little white dots or "pimples" that appear on the gill covers and pectoral fin rays when the goldfish is in breeding condition. They may even appear on the head and face or patterned on the scales of the goldfish as well. Some owners mistakenly identify them as the parasite ich, but ich usually shows up on the surface of the fins and on the body in irregular sprinkles. Breeding tubercles are rough to the touch, like sandpaper.

- **Longer, narrower body shape:** When viewed from above, the body of a male is symmetrical and may have a ridge running down the middle of the abdomen. This method can sometimes be useful but isn't really enough alone to determine the gender of the fish.
- **Longer, thicker fins:** The leading ridges on the male's pectoral fins are thicker than those of females and are typically longer overall.
- **Aggressive behavior:** If you happen to spot a goldfish (or a couple of goldfish) ruthlessly pursuing another around its environment, chances are it is a heated male seeking to spawn with a female.

Signs your goldfish is a Female:

- **No breeding tubercles:** You won't find those tiny white sprays of breeding stars on a female's gill plates or fins! (In rare cases, however, a female goldfish may have breeding tubercles).
- **Rounder, shorter body shape:** Female goldfish are typically stockier and wider around the middle. They may also be asymmetrical when viewed from above, as the eggs may fill the abdomen and cause her to bulge more on one side.
- **Rounder, shorter fin shape:** Instead of having the slender pectoral fins of the male, a female goldfish's front fins are thicker and stubbier. The arch is more drastic as well.
- **Being chased rather than chasing:** The fish who is the victim of the pursuit is most likely the female.

All of these methods can help to determine the sex of your goldfish, but perhaps the most reliable method is examining the anal vent of the goldfish. The male's vent is thinner and more sunken in (concave), whereas the female's vent is oval and visibly protrudes (convex) when viewed from the side. I have always had success with this method in sexing my own goldfish.

# History of the Goldfish

The goldfish, as we know it today, are thought to have originated in ancient China with the humble, greenish-colored carp ancestor. Whether the variation of carp was the Prussian carp (also known as the Gibel carp) or the Crucian carp is a subject of debate. Because more recent research indicates that the Prussian carp is the wild form of the goldfish, it is becoming now more commonly understood who the true "daddy" of the goldfish was.

The Prussian carp, once regarded as a subspecies of the goldfish, strongly resembles the Common goldfish, but is deep-bellied with a taller back and shorter fins. Its tail is more deeply forked than that of the Crucian carp with larger scales. In the wild, it is a silvery green hue, though will sometimes show more yellow or even red variations. It reaches a length between 4 and 14 inches long.

## The Goldfish Evolves in China

Considered to be the oldest domesticated fish, the goldfish has a colorful history spanning 1700 years of careful, selective breeding and husbandry. For hundreds of years, they were kept only in Asia.

The first goldfish was bred in captivity during the Jin dynasty in China, around 265-420 AD, when the gold color was first documented. The Chinese word for goldfish is *jin yü*.

Keeping carp in ponds was popular during the Tang dynasty (618-907), and the yellowish gold coloring continued to be seen in these ponds at Buddhist monasteries. It was at this time that selective breeding started – the yellow color being preferred over the silver. Small containers became the first way of displaying the fish at special occasions for short periods of time, such as when company came over. They were returned to their ponds after the guests left.

The Song dynasty of 920-1279 marked an especially "regal" time in the history of the goldfish, as its empress commanded in 1162 that a pond be made to put all of the yellow and gold varieties in. Commoners were now banned from owning these colors of fish, as *yellow represented the imperial family*. Interestingly enough, yellow goldfish are actually easier to breed because of their genetics, but because of this decree there are now more orange goldfish than yellow as people sought to get around the rule (who wants to be banned from owning goldfish, after all?).

The goldfish really saw an increase in popularity during the Ming dynasty of 1368-1644. Instead of having their homes solely in ponds, owners began bringing them inside to keep them in clay jars. Much time and effort were invested in producing what we know as the fancy goldfish, with their stouter bodies, paired tail and anal fins, and varieties without dorsal fins.  More color selections were noted in 1276.

## The Goldfish Comes to Japan

The goldfish was introduced into Japan in 1502, a little over five hundred years ago.  They first landed in trading ports near the area of Osaka in western Japan, where business exchanges with China took place.  What did those goldfish look like that were first brought there?  Some people think that they were similar in appearance to the Wakin goldfish.

During the next few hundreds of years, goldfish became a wanted luxury item.  They were very expensive and mostly a commodity of the well-to-do, such as rich merchants and upper class warriors (called samurai).  It was in Japan that goldfish were first called goldfish, or *kingyo*, which means "golden fish."  Even fish that were silver or white were called this, just like today.

The late 1600s saw the expansion of the goldfish across the Japanese country, as its major cities welcomed them with excitement as precious treasures.  At this time in history, Japan was very closed off from the rest of the world as far as trade was concerned, but they were still able to receive some shipments of goldfish from China, and probably Korea (who had received the goldfish along with other neighboring countries before the Japanese).  A dorsalless variety was brought over, which the Japanese turned into the Ranchu.  Another kind was later developed into the Ryukin, which was named after the Ryuku Islands there (a trading center).  And the Oranda came also, which was allegedly sold to them by the Dutch on their way from China.  The Tosakin and Tamasaba also found their origins in Japan.  Other types of goldfish were bred there as well, but soon died out.

Because they were so valuable, goldfish were often used among nobles as a sort of "bribe" to help gain social status or a service.  They were so prized that their government outlawed anyone from keeping goldfish and seized every goldfish they could find for themselves!  As time went on, however, this wealthy ruling class began to lose their riches and had to turn to the people to fund them by breeding goldfish.  This meant that goldfish could now become more widely available.

It is thought that heavy breeding of goldfish in Japan didn't happen until the eighteenth century, and it wasn't until 1853 that the Telescope Eye goldfish landed on Japanese shores from China.  These, too, were received with excitement and cross-bred with other varieties to create new and interesting breeds.  To these, the Japanese goldfish breeders added the more obscure Tamasaba, dorsalless Pompom and Shukin.  Later on during the early 1900s, the Celestial and Bubble Eye goldfish were shipped in.  But it wasn't until after World War II that new color patterns and breeds such as the Pearlscale and Butterfly Tail arrived.

## The Goldfish Travels the Globe

The goldfish first reached European shores in 1665 when they landed in Portugal. In the middle of the century they began to be kept in ponds. From Portugal, they spread throughout the surrounding areas in the mid-1700s, including Russia, Germany, Holland and France. They arrived in England in 1780. But it wasn't until the 1800s that Australia and New Zealand were introduced to the goldfish. As European trade increased, goldfish became stylish gifts and popular pets. They truly made their grand appearance at the first public aquarium in the *London Zoo* during 1853.

In 1874, goldfish landed in the United States. It didn't take long before they became admired, and only took a few decades after their arrival in the New World for the Comet goldfish to be bred in Washington, D.C. The Comet was the only goldfish breed contributed by America. They continued to grow in popularity in the States, and the first goldfish farm was established in the late 1800s in Maryland.

During the 1900s, more varieties and fancier strains continued to develop. Britain produced the Bristol Shubunkin, and a rare strain of Veiltail Black Moors appeared there during the 1930s. While there for a while it appeared they had died out, more recent efforts have made to revive the beautiful breed.

## Types of Goldfish

The goldfish has come a very long way from its simple beginnings. Because of much selective breeding and even creativity on the part of goldfish breeders throughout the centuries, the average person can now enjoy a wide selection of goldfish types – from the more basic, natural kinds to the more unusual varieties. Like snowflakes, no two goldfish are ever the same. Each one has its own set of fascinating features and personalities as diverse (or perhaps even more) as the range of types you can find.

**Did You Know?**

There are over 125 different types of goldfish in the world today! Some have never left their homelands.

Why is it important for you to know the distinction between different breeds, especially if you are just getting started with the hobby? Knowing your varieties is actually very helpful in fish keeping – especially when it comes to understanding each one's unique needs. It can also help you find the best match for you when it comes to choosing which one (or ones) to own.

## Goldfish Color Variations

When goldfish are very young, they are a drab brown until at least 2 months old, when they start to get their coloring.  The color of the fish depends, in a large part, upon the genetics of the parents.  The more similar the parents are to each other, the more likely the babies are to have the color of their parents.  A wide variety of colors may be found in goldfish that have very different parents.  Color isn't solely based on mommy and daddy fish, though.  Lighting, feeding and overall health can also cause goldfish to be a certain color.

As you have just learned from the anatomy section, the scales of the goldfish do not have any color themselves.  They are transparent, and simply let the color underneath show through.  Among goldfish, there is a wide range of different color variations and patterns.  They fall into two main categories: solid (also called self-colored) and multicolored.

As far as solid colors go, you will commonly see goldfish that come in:

- **Yellow**.  Yellow is called the *only true gold*, meaning that orange fish are not considered "gold" fish in the sense of the word.
- **Orange.**  Also called red, orange is the most common color found among goldfish.
- **Black**.  Black is a color that is especially changeable in goldfish.  An orange or red goldfish may have some black markings in one environment, but upon being moved to another environment it may totally fade away!  Keeping the black color of a goldfish that is entirely black is still difficult, and many have been known to lose it to orange as they age.
- **Brown**.  Also called chocolate, this coloration may be more cool-toned with hints of gray or warmer, often with gold on the underbelly.
- **White.**  This can either be an opalescent/metallic, shiny tone, or matte, meaning it lacks shininess.  Sometimes white goldfish can almost look pink or yellow.  Just because your goldfish is white does not mean it is an albino, though!  Albino goldfish are very, very rare, and are different from more common white goldfish that have blue eyes or red eyes by their strikingly pink pupils.  White, too, is a changeable color and will often become variegated in older fish.
- **Blue.**  Also called silver or lilac, this particular shade sometimes verges on green.

Goldfish come in multicolored patterns, too.  They are:

- **Tricolor**:  Tricolor is a mixture of usually 3 colors: black, white and red (orange), though it sometimes may include blue or brown.  Most of the time they have a mix of both matte and metallic scales (nacreous).

- **Nacreous**: This pattern is relatively common among many goldfish breeds. It is often referred to as calico. Nacreous isn't itself a coloration, but rather a pattern of scale types – the matte and the metallic combined. Matte scales are scales which contain no reflectivity, meaning they aren't shiny. They are the opposite of metallic scales, which are highly reflective. Nacreous goldfish aren't just metallic scaled or matte scaled – they are a mixture of both! A nacreous goldfish can come in any color (but is often black, white and orange) and can be completely matte, sometimes white with the occasional shiny scale. Some nacreous goldfish may be entirely white with no shiny scales. A fish like this will often read "pink" to the eye. Pink gill plates are common with this color pattern. A calico goldfish usually retains its black. An orange and white nacreous goldfish is called Sakura, while another variant, called Kirin, displays gray or "dirty" black patches with white and orange or rust.
- **Tancho/Red Crane**: This is a fish that is all white with a red spot, ideally a circle, covering the top of its head, like a cap. This is a relatively stable color pattern.
- **Panda:** A panda patterned goldfish is now found in many different breeds. The fish is mostly white with black around the eyes and black fins. The black may also extend onto the body a bit in some fish. This pattern has caused much frustration for owners of fish that are panda colored, because the black (being very unstable) tends to fade and leave the fish white and red. It is considered to be a juvenile state coloration that the fish will most likely outgrow.
- **Mottled.** Mottled goldfish are metallic goldfish that are a mixture of more than one color. A good example would be a red and white goldfish. Two-toned goldfish and tri-colored are both considered mottled.
- **Sarasa.** This color pattern is a Japanese word describing a mottled red and white pattern.
- **12 Reds.** This coloration, considered to be unstable, includes red spots in 12 places: the lips, dorsal fin, tail fin, pectoral fins, pelvic fins, anal fins and gill covers. While it sometimes has been created by literally plucking away any red scales on the body while the fish is young, leaving only white with red tips, careful selective breeding can also produce it naturally. It is usually found on the Jikin, Butterfly and Ryukin goldfish. These fish command a higher price due to their rarity.
- **Jade seal.** This is used to describe a goldfish with an oval shaped marking on the top of the head, like a seal.

## Goldfish Body Features

There is certainly a huge assortment of different characteristics that goldfish have today.

- **Wen**: The wen is a fleshy growth, sometimes jokingly called a brain, that is located on the top of a goldfish's head.  In some fish, it may extend over the entire head and gill covers.  The fish is called a "tiger head" when this happens.  Two chubby cheeks on either side of the fish's mouth are a result of wen growth, giving them a puppy-dog look.  As the goldfish ages, the wen usually grows.  Large wens are coveted by many goldfish breeders, and they have different tactics to try to get the wen to grow as full as possible on their goldfish.  Some fish even have their eyesight obscured by the excess wen growth, though the wen has no nerves and can be trimmed painlessly, like hair.
- **Crown:**  This is made up of one or two bubble-like domes that are located on top of the goldfish's head.  Fish that have these are sometimes called high-head.
- **Bubble Eye:**  These are huge, jiggling, fluid-filled sacks located underneath and around the eyes, which is usually pointed upwards in fish that have them.
- **Celestial Eye:**  This is a type of eye that is very shiny and opalescent around the pupil.  They are also pointed skyward.
- **Pom Pom:**  A goldfish that has these will look like it has two carnations growing from its nostrils.  Also called "narial bouquets," these are basically exaggerated nostrils similar to the wen in texture.  They continue to grow as the fish gets older.
- **Telescope Eye:**  A telescope eye is projected outwards mounted on a cone-shaped stalk.  It may be opalescent, like the celestial eye, or solid colored.  They can be up to ¾ inch long!
- **Curled gill:**  Also called "outturned operculum," flared gills are where the gill covers are slightly turned out at the ends.  This feature isn't commonly found on fish within the US.
- **Double tails/fantail:**  Fantails are tails that have 4 lobes.  They cleft down the middle from the tip to the caudal peduncle.
- **Triple tail:**  This is a tail that has three lobes, the top two being fused together, creating a triangular shape when viewed from the top… also known as "tripod."
- **Ribbon tail:**  A long and narrow quadruple tail with a deep lobe is called a ribbon tail.
- **Fringe tail:**  Fringe tails are what they sound like – their edges are serrated and drape behind the fish.
- **Veiltail:**  This tail type is extra wide and long.  It has no lobes but rather is squared off at the end.  The other fins of the fish are long also.
- **Broadtail:**  Broadtail and Veiltail finnage are similar, but not identical.  The Broadtail has shorter, very squared-off fins that may wrap around the fish.  It is set higher on the fish and does not hang down as much.
- **Butterfly tail:**  This is set horizontally on the fish and is shaped like a butterfly's 4 wings when viewed from above.  In older fish, the fins may tend to droop.

## The Difference Between Goldfish and Koi

Because young slim-bodied goldfish (*Carassius aratus aratus*) and koi (*Cyprinus carpio*) are both similar in body shape, they are often mistaken for one another by beginning aquarists. Both do quite well in ponds, but they are actually not the same. They are able to interbreed with one another, but the offspring are infertile. Here are some ways to tell the difference between a goldfish and a koi:

- **Barbels:** Perhaps the easiest way to differentiate between the two fish are the presence of barbels near the mouth of the koi. They are like small whiskers on either side of the fish's jaw. Infertile hybrids will have them too though.
- **Size:** While Common and Comet goldfish (and other slim-bodied varieties) will grow very large, (up to 12 inches long), koi can triple that. As they grow, this distinction will become very obvious.
- **Coloration:** Koi come in a more unusual variety of colors than goldfish do.

**Body Structure:** Less obvious ways to distinguish between the two kinds of fish are looking at the structure of the fish and observing subtle differences. In koi, the jaw line underneath the head is flatter and the farthest edge of the dorsal fin is fused to the back at the base.

Many wild characteristics have been produced that help to make each breed very unique, but all goldfish regardless of all of their "bells and whistles" fall into two main categories.

| Slim-bodied Goldfish | Fancy Goldfish |
|---|---|
| Long, slender, "flat" body shape | Stocky, compact, "egg" body shape |
| Single anal fin | Usually have paired anal fins |
| Typically, one tail with 2 forked lobes | Two tails with 4 lobes, may be forked |
| Hardy | Generally more delicate |
| Fast swimmers | Slow swimmers |

# Slim-bodied Breeds

Slim-bodied goldfish are also called *flat-bodied* goldfish or *single-tailed* goldfish.

## Common

As the name implies, this goldfish is the easiest to find.  They are most commonly found in bright metallic red (orange), though they can come in any color.  It has stiff fins that don't drape and a long body.  The edge of the dorsal fin, when held upright, indents slightly.  Its singular tail is slightly forked and the lobes are short and round.  It is the most similar to the ancestor of all goldfish, the Prussian carp.  You will often see small Commons packed together in a tank at the pet store, sold very cheaply.  They are often used as "feeders," typically for reptiles.  The price often is the main reason people buy them for pets.  Few people know that these little guys grow to a length of 12 inches long!

## Comet

The Comet goldfish is very similar to the Common in body shape – the main difference between the two is that the Comet has longer fins, especially the tail (which is singular).  It can grow to be almost the same length as the body!  This goldfish breed is the only one to have originated in the States.  The tail lobes are deeply indented and do not fold over.  Usually it is found in metallic red, but can come in a wide variety of other colorations and patterns as well.  It too is a very hardy strain that reaches up to a foot in length.

## Shubunkin

This goldfish is another slim-bodied goldfish, differing mostly from the Common and Comet in coloration.  It almost always comes in calico coloring with nacreous scales.  A good specimen has a lot of blue mixed in with its red, white and black tones.  There are three main types of Shubunkins: the *American*, which has a long, pointed, deeply indented tail, the *Bristol*, known for its very large, slightly forked tail with round lobes (shaped like a B) and the *London*, which has a shorter, rounder tail like the Common.  Shubunkin goldfish are very hardy and reach up to 12 inches long.

## Wakin

The Wakin goldfish is very similar to the Common goldfish in its more streamlined body but has a quadruple tail cleft down the middle to the base of the caudal peduncle – classifying it as a fancy goldfish (even though it is in all other respects most like the single tails).  It usually has red or red and white (sarasa) coloring, a sturdy build and can reach up to a foot in length.

## Jikin

Jikin goldfish are a rarer variety, kind of like the Wakin, but aren't usually found outside of Japan. What makes them distinct from other breeds is their unique 12 Reds coloring. Their bodies naturally have some red scales on top of the white, but in order to maintain the 12 Reds coloring, they are plucked off by hand while they are little. While they are considered a slim-bodied breed, they aren't as hardy when it comes to colder temperatures. They will grow to be a little under a foot in length.

**Watonai**

Pronounced "wah-town-eye," this breed of goldfish is best described as a long-bodied fantail. They are actually a cross between the Ryukin and the Wakin. Extremely hardy, they make great pond fish and grow to be up to a foot long.

## Fancy Breeds

**Fantail**

This is probably one of the most popular of the fancy goldfish varieties – probably because it is one of the hardiest and easy to breed. The Fantail's tail has 3 or 4 lobes, split down the middle to the base of the tail in good specimens.  They come in a variety of colors and patterns, the most common being a metallic orange or nacreous calico.  The Fantail reaches an average length of 6 to 8 inches.

**Ryukin**

Ryukin goldfish, like the Fantail, are hardy and grow up to 8 inches long.  They are distinguished by their high back (shaped like a hump behind the head), very deep body and pointed snout.  Bred to be viewed from the side, they are most often found in solid red or red and white coloration (though they also come in far more color patterns).  They have a 3 or 4 lobed double tail and short body.

**Tamasaba**

While considered to be a slim-bodied goldfish, the Tosakin is kind of a mixture of the two categories of goldfish types.  It only has one tail – long and flowing – with a deep, compact body shape nearly identical to the Ryukin goldfish.  Fast swimmers for their body shapes, they are very hardy and can reach 6 to 8 inches in length.

**Telescope Eye**

There are many names for the Telescope Eye goldfish, including the *Popeye*, *Demekin* (Japanese name) and *Dragon Eye* (Chinese name).  It is most recognized by its amazing eyes, which are large and circular or cone-shaped, depending on the fish.  Surprisingly, they do not see any better because of their large eyes; their vision is actually more impaired.  Because they stick out so far, they are also prone to injury and have been known to come off completely.  They have an egg-shaped body and triple or quadruple tail, and come in a wide range of colors – the solid black, non-metallic variety is called the Black Moor, and the white with black points is called the Panda Moor.  Black is usually a very unstable color, but it is most stable on the Black Moor.  Panda Moors, however, often lose their black coloring.

**Veiltail**

The name of this goldfish accurately describes the most beautiful feature of this kind of goldfish. It is known for its flowing fins and squared-off tail that has no lobes or indentation and is quite long. The dorsal fin is very high and drapes to the side on some fish. The pectoral, pelvic and anal fins on this fish are especially long and may even drag along the bottom of the tank as the fish swims. There are some Veiltail varieties that have telescope eyes, though these are less common. The Veiltail is one of the more delicate strains of goldfish and comes in a wide range of color and patterns. At one point in time, a strain of Veiltail called the Philadelphia Veiltail had almost become extinct in the US, but thanks to hardworking breeders it was saved in 1970's. The Veiltail usually reaches a total length of 6 to 8 inches long.

## Oranda

One of the most popular goldfish varieties, the Oranda is characterized by its wen growth that gives it a tall head, and in many cases, large cheeks. The head of the Oranda is typically wider than other goldfish. There are many varieties of Oranda, including a Pom Pom, Veiltail and Telescope Eye mix. They come in many colors, some common ones being self-colored reds and oranges, red and white, calico, blue and chocolate. It is relatively hardy and grows very large – it was actually an Oranda that set the record for the world's largest goldfish! It is the exception to the rule when it comes to the typical size of fancies. They can reach up to 12 inches long!

## Tosakin

This delicate breed of goldfish is rarely available in the US, and is native to Japan. Similar to the Ryukin in body shape, what sets the Tosakin apart is its unique tail – set horizontally, unforked, and twisted gracefully once or even twice at the two front ends. It is usually found in red and white, self-colored red, self-colored white and even black. Like other Japanese varieties of goldfish, it is bred to be viewed from above. It will reach a length of around 6 inches.

## Pearlscale

What is most striking about the Pearlscale is its round, elevated scales shaped like beads and arranged in rows along the fish's body. These are made of calcium carbonate deposits on each individual scale. The Pearlscale's body is short, round and shaped like an orange. Generally, the older the fish grows, the wider its belly becomes... to the point where the fish looks like a softball. It may not have any headgrowth, have a wen on its head, or have one or two "bubbles" on its head – in which case it is called a Crown Pearlscale, High Head or *Hama Nishiki*. It comes in all colors, the most common being red and white or calico, and reaches 6 to 8 inches in length.

## Pompom

The defining characteristic of the Pompom are the flowery-shaped "nares" or nostril flaps that have been exaggerated more than any other feature of this fish. Pompoms have the body confirmation of a Fantail.  The pompoms can come off if torn, but are able to grow back with clean water.  Common colors are chocolate with orange pompoms or solid metallic orange.  They reach 6-8 inches in length.

## Dorsalless Breeds

Dorsalless goldfish are considered fancy goldfish, but lack a top fin.

### Lionhead

As the name implies, this breed of goldfish seems to have a mane. Its wen covers its entire head (tiger head), giving it a puffy face – in fact, they were bred by the Chinese to resemble the Pekingese dog! The Lionhead has no dorsal fin – the slope of its back is flat and smooth (in good specimens). It has a short double tail and all of its fins are paired. You can find Lionheads of almost every color and pattern variety. They grow anywhere from 6 to 8 inches long.

### Ranchu

Beloved by the Japanese for hundreds of years, the Ranchu was perhaps the most expensive variety of goldfish for some time. In recent years, it has become more affordable and available to the average goldfish keeper. Its name literally means "king of fish." Very similar to the Lionhead, the Ranchu differs by its sloping, rounded back (without a dorsal fin) and tighter tail tuck. It, too, comes in a wide variety of colors and will reach 6 to 8 inches.

### Phoenix Tail

This variety of goldfish is a rare egg-shaped fish similar to the Lionhead, but with a long flowing tail and a wenless head. It, too, lacks a dorsal fin. Developed in China, it is not usually found in the United States. Their rarity can make good specimens very expensive. It comes in a wide variety of colors and scale types and grows anywhere from 6 to 8 inches in length.

### Bubble Eye

What catches your eye about this kind of goldfish is its striking sacks of fluid that bulge from underneath its eyes. They jiggle like jelly as the fish moves through the water, and enlarge the older the fish gets. Definitely one of the more delicate varieties, the Bubble Eye doesn't grow quite as large as other fancy goldfish – not usually more than 6 inches. Their lifespan is typically shorter too.

### Celestial Eye

Another dorsalless variety, the delicate Celestial Eye goldfish is known to the Chinese as the stargazer – and for good reason. It began in China with eyes that were able to move slightly, but after the Japanese worked on developing the breed, its eyes (which are opalescent) became permanently fixed heavenwards.  It is most commonly found in metallic red or orange, though black is growing in popularity.  Like the Bubble Eye, it will reach a length of 6 inches.

**Izumo Nankin**

The Izumo Nankin is a small, rare breed of goldfish originating from Japan with a small, pointed head, no dorsal fin and a hump behind the head.  It is thought to have been developed around 1750.  It is one of the more difficult goldfish to keep and breed due to its delicate nature.  It is mostly found in red and white coloration and often viewed from the top.

# Section 2: General Care
## The Pillars of Goldfish Success

The artist has his painting. The musician has his opus. The chef has his soufflé. As goldfish owners, our masterpiece is our aquarium. We are all working towards an aesthetic on some level. Perhaps you just want a pet you can have for companionship or amusement. Maybe it's a beautiful, relaxing aquarium you can sit and watch after a long day. Or it could be as simple as just wanting to keep this fish alive so your child can enjoy it. There are many reasons why we have found ourselves in this situation, and it can seem overwhelming to think we must learn an art form, but the truth is that it really is one. Goldfish are not easy fish to keep, and that is what makes it a rewarding challenge. It is not a one time, set-it-and-forget-it thing. It is a journey. There are ups and downs along the way, but this book is here to guide you through the process to make it easier for you. It is here to be your recipe, your instructor and your guide to pave the way for your hobby so you don't have to make as many mistakes.

Keeping goldfish is an art; a detailed science that follows a careful formula. There are many daily life activities and other hobbies that are actually an art too – health, fitness, business, raising children. Once you realize that you probably are already an artist, it becomes less intimidating to undertake goldfish keeping!

Nobody picks up a paintbrush for the first time without any experience and create the next museum-worthy piece (unless you have an incredible amount of natural talent). To become proficient in any art requires practice, dedication, patience and a bit of skill. But the result of this is something beautiful.

It is interesting to note that the principles below, in whole or in part, are also are applied to goldfish themselves when it comes to judging, showing and culling.

You will always be learning. I am still learning too after all of these years, and still do not claim to know everything.  But my goal is to impart what I've learned to you to help your fish thrive.

While there is room for variation, creativity and originality between enthusiasts that still afford a good result, successful artists all have common core principles that ensure healthy, happy fish and a hobby they can not only enjoy themselves, but something that brings delight to others. The fundamentals must be mastered in order to achieve excellence.

**1. Natural**

The closer we mimic the natural life of the goldfish (or, to be more accurate, their granddaddy the Carp) in the wild, the healthier they will be. This is because things are as similar as possible to the intended state of the fish. The further off we get from this design (in nearly every aspect of our fishkeeping), the harder it becomes. Unnatural conditions are more likely to lead to sick fish.

*"Goldfish do best when their environment is most like the one their ancestors have in the wild."*

## 2. Balance & Unity

Every part of the aquarium – fish included – works together to form one whole system. When one thing is not right, it will have a "domino effect." Seemingly unrelated aspects of the aquarium are all interconnected. It is important to see the goldfish tank in this light as it will help us become better fish keepers with a deeper understanding of why things work the way they do.

## 3. Stability and Consistency

There is something to be said for the role of stability in a happy goldfish. Sudden changes may pose risks of stress and shock, even if they are in a better direction, simply because of this principle as it relates to fish. Instability can lead to sick fish.

Goldfish do best when their environment is most like the one their ancestors have in the wild. This is true in just about every aspect of their care, be it feeding or their living space. If you want your goldfish to flourish, they need conditions as close as possible to what they would have out in nature. Goldfish may look quite modified compared to their granddaddies, but really they are just domesticated carp. Understanding this principal will make everything in goldfish keeping much easier.

## Housing and Stocking

The first step in deciding how to house your goldfish is to figure out if you want to keep them indoors or outdoors – or perhaps both. There are advantages and disadvantages in each case, but I am going to focus primarily on indoor housing in this section.

Larger aquariums are very popular among goldfish keepers and certainly have their own set of advantages (i.e. large goldfish have proper swimming area and the tank can be outfitted with certain filtration styles too powerful for a smaller tank). Large tanks are typically more expensive, but those who want and have the skill to make their own out of glass or acrylic using different sealants can do so.

Of course, there are thousands of people who cannot afford larger aquariums or simply don't have the space, but still can enjoy the hobby on a smaller scale and keep healthy, happy fish.

### Stunting

Though goldfish *can* grow to be quite large (given the right environmental conditions and genetic blueprint), they can also thrive for decades at a smaller size as is evidenced by the goldfish that hold world records for their old age – all of which are stunted little fair (common/comet) goldfish.

Goldfish secrete a hormone called *somatostatin* which inhibits their growth when allowed to accumulate in the water. This hormone is not removed by regular biological bacteria-based filtration, and though some evidence exists that activated carbon can aid in its removal, water changes are the most effective method for its removal, thus allowing the goldfish to continue growing (if other factors are in place, such as genetic predisposition and nutrition). This is why goldfish breeders trying to get their fish to grow faster and bigger advocate large, frequent water changes as one of the best ways to help the fish attain a large size. Goldfish raised in ponds are often among the largest specimens, as the growth inhibiting hormone is diluted by the sheer volume of water in their environment.

Retaining this hormone in the water should not come at the expense of the overall water quality (and consequently, the health of the fish), and fortunately it does not have to. Utilizing biological and/or plant filtration, in conjunction with small water changes if necessary, allows most of the hormone to remain in the water and the fish stays much smaller as a result. Smaller aquaria concentrate this hormone as well. In such an environment they do grow some, but their growth is so slow it is hardly noticeable. This slow rate of growth coupled with unheated water (and consequently a lower metabolism) may explain why such environmentally stunted goldfish, given proper care, are the consistently the most long-lived.

Common misconceptions about stocking are that it is cruel to the fish causing suffering and disfiguration, but this conclusion seems unsupported by any research or available case studies of stunted fish.  It also appears from the current data available that tank size does not have a direct relation on the growth of the fish when water quality is maintained separately, as is evidenced by the growth of channel catfish in a controlled study where clean water was continually flushed through the systems and the fish continued to grow until they could not physically turn around.

That all goldfish in the right conditions will get large and given proper care by their owners is simply incorrect. A goldfish that is a genetic runt will never be able to attain the same size as one of its siblings, no matter how much space and clean water it is given.  This does not mean this fish is inferior in any way or that its quality of life will be affected, it is just smaller.  Many pet store goldfish are stunted, as they have been intentionally kept small by suppliers in order to time the distribution of a certain size and type of fish.  A goldfish does most of its growing in the first year of life.  If certain conditions don't favor rapid growth during that time (i.e. colder water, less water changes, lighter feeding), it also may never get big no matter how much clean water, food and space it is given in later years.

## Stocking

It is true that the smaller the space, the faster toxins build up in the water.  Larger volumes of water dilute these toxins, which can allow more time between water changes.  But regardless of water volume, toxins will build up to lethal levels if no filtration or water change protocol is employed – it is only a matter of time.  If the water quality in either a small or a large tank is insufficient, dangerous ammonia or nitrite spikes can result.

**Swimming Space** is arguably an important part of long-term goldfish health as well.  A goldfish kept in a tank too small for it to turn around in easily, but with 100% perfect water conditions, is at likely at risk for muscle atrophy.  That said, adequate swimming space is a term that at present lacks a scientific definition for goldfish in particular, and would greatly depend on the size and variety of goldfish in question. This in addition to lack of any short or long-term controlled studies on the topic makes finding an evidence-based guideline founded on swimming space alone challenging.  I would only encourage goldfish owners to provide, at a minimum, enough space for their fish for it to comfortably swim around in, as well as consider how many other fish and decorations are in with it that could restrict movement.

**Muscle atrophy** in fish has clinically been linked to stressors such as capture, transport and handling, overcrowding at the expense of water quality, aggression, temperature extremes (though the carp species seems to be more resistant to this), hypoxia, salinity, malnutrition and water contaminants.[1] Most healthy goldfish seem able to handle some limited short-term stress without harmful long term effects, but continual long-term stress will ultimately lead to illness and/or premature death. It is therefore logical to conclude that a fish that have lived exceptionally long lives have not been subjected to continual long-term stress to experience these and other repercussions.

So this brings us to the question, what size tank do you need? It really depends on many factors:

- How frequently you want to do water changes
- Whether or not you keep live plants, how many and what kind
- Your choice of substrate
- How many fish you want to keep
- The size of the fish to begin with
- Your goals for the fish's growth
- Surface are and oxygenation
- Feeding frequency and amount
- Filtration style, size and effectiveness

As you can see, there are far too many variables to be able to give a broad-brush, one-size-fits-all rule for the size of a goldfish's tank.

What is a legitimate, one-size-fits-all rule and is backed by many studies is that goldfish must have good quality water that cannot be polluted with toxins in order to live a long, healthy life. Regardless of the size or style of container you choose to house your fish in, the ammonia and nitrite must always be at 0, the water not allowed to become too acidic and the nitrates below 30ppm.

Some think if you have trouble with maintaining good water quality, it means you need to get a bigger tank, or perhaps that all small tanks will have water quality issues if used to house messy goldfish. However, bigger tanks are not exempt from water quality issues; they simply slow things down a bit, and well-equipped (and correctly cared for) small tanks can maintain proper water parameters in order to provide a suitable living environment for the fish.

It is true that the smaller the space, the faster toxins build up in the water. Larger volumes of water dilute these toxins, which can allow more time between water changes. But regardless of water volume, toxins will build up to lethal levels if no filtration or water change protocol is

---

[1] Morphologic Effects of the Stress Response in Fish, https://watermark.silverchair.com/ilar-50-387.pdf

employed – it is only a matter of time.  If the water quality in either a small or a large tank is insufficient, dangerous ammonia or nitrite spikes can result.

**Swimming Space** is arguably an important part of long-term goldfish health as well.  A goldfish kept in a tank too small for it to turn around in easily, but with 100% perfect water conditions, is at likely at risk for muscle atrophy.  That said, adequate swimming space is a term that at present lacks a scientific definition for goldfish in particular, and would greatly depend on the size and variety of goldfish in question. This in addition to lack of any short or long-term controlled studies on the topic makes finding an evidence-based guideline founded on swimming space alone challenging.  I would only encourage goldfish owners to provide, at a minimum, enough space for their fish for it to comfortably swim around in, as well as consider how many other fish and decorations are in with it that could restrict movement.

**Muscle atrophy** in fish has clinically been linked to stressors such as capture, transport and handling, overcrowding at the expense of water quality, aggression, temperature extremes (though the carp species seems to be more resistant to this), hypoxia, salinity, malnutrition and water contaminants.[2]  Most healthy goldfish seem able to handle some limited short-term stress without harmful long term effects, but continual long-term stress will ultimately lead to illness and/or premature death. It is therefore logical to conclude that a fish that have lived exceptionally long lives have not been subjected to continual long-term stress to experience these and other repercussions.

So this brings us to the question, what size tank do you need? It really depends on many factors:

- How frequently you want to do water changes
- Whether or not you keep live plants, how many and what kind
- Your choice of substrate
- How many fish you want to keep
- The size of the fish to begin with
- Your goals for the fish's growth
- Surface are and oxygenation
- Feeding frequency and amount
- Filtration style, size and effectiveness

As you can see, there are far too many variables to be able to give a broad-brush, one-size-fits-all rule for the size of a goldfish's tank.

---

[2] Morphologic Effects of the Stress Response in Fish, https://watermark.silverchair.com/ilar-50-387.pdf

What is a legitimate, one-size-fits-all rule and is backed by many studies is that goldfish must have good quality water that cannot be polluted with toxins in order to live a long, healthy life. Regardless of the size or style of container you choose to house your fish in, the ammonia and nitrite must always be at 0, the water not allowed to become too acidic and the nitrates below 30ppm.

Some think if you have trouble with maintaining good water quality, it means you need to get a bigger tank, or perhaps that all small tanks will have water quality issues if used to house messy goldfish.  However, bigger tanks are not exempt from water quality issues; they simply slow things down a bit, and well-equipped (and correctly cared for) small tanks can maintain proper water parameters in order to provide a suitable living environment for the fish.

## Housing in Aquariums

For what it's worth, my favorite kind of aquarium for goldfish is the Seaclear line of acrylic aquariums.  They look absolutely stunning and are far stronger (and lighter) than glass.  I've never received so many compliments on my tanks as when I switched from glass to SeaClear.

*Seaclear Aquariums*

Speaking of big tanks, now is a good time to point out that you can still provide a spacious habitat for your goldfish without investing in a pricy aquarium if you are short on extra cash.  Other containers are just as suitable if you aren't as worried about the appearance.  Some goldfish owners have had success housing their goldfish in Tupperware bins, wooden barrels, horse troughs or even tall garbage cans.  As long as the plastic of the container doesn't leech chemicals into the water, the goldfish won't mind.  These kinds of containers are especially suited to a garage or unfinished basement where decorating isn't as much of an issue.

Occasionally, Petco has something called their "dollar-per-gallon" sale that rolls around each year. This is can be a great opportunity, if you catch them at the right time. When all else fails, you can try secondhand stores or even Craigslist.

## Housing in Bowls

Many people (myself included) were introduced to the goldfish hobby with a simple bowl and a fair fish won as a prize for a game, and the goldfish bowl continues to be an attraction that draws young children and adults alike into the fantastic world of goldfish keeping.  There is also an abundance of "feeder goldfish" that are sold as bait, which some people would have pity on and for a few dimes spare them from certain death.  While these reasons would not justify their use if they were harmful to goldfish, there seems to be much evidence to the contrary.

Admittedly at one time I never thought I would have included a section on bowls in this book other than for the sole purpose of discouraging their use, but many hours of further research and my own tests have led me to conclude that these can be safe homes for goldfish – if set up and maintained correctly.

The oldest goldfish in the world, named Tish, lived to 43 years old in a bowl. Understanding that the more concentrated growth hormones in the water can enable the fish to stay small, and even live for many years – perhaps even longer than goldfish who are grown to a larger size.  Please know that larger goldfish need more space to move comfortably and small bowls are not a good option for them.

*Learn more about fishbowls*

It is true that a goldfish may live a very short life in a bowl, if it is not supplied with means of removing the toxins constantly produced by the fish.  The same holds true in larger tanks.  Frequent water changes can be done to dilute the toxins, but determining how much and how often requires frequent testing.  For this reason, it is a good idea to ensure the bowl is outfitted with either an electric filter (with either a carbon cartridge or biological media such as a sponge) or live plants, which help to take care of the waste byproducts produced by fish and convert them into plant mass. More information on setting up and maintaining a fishbowl is discussed on the web page on bowls on the Pure Goldfish website.

# Filtration, what is Best?

We've covered how to properly house goldfish as far as their tank size and stocking goes. Now, let's talk about another important element of housing: filtering your tank.

Filtration does three critical things:

1. It helps increase oxygen levels.
2. It helps breaks down organic waste & can trap some so you can remove it easier.
3. It keeps the water clear and pretty (well, maybe not critical).

Because your goldfish eats, it obviously also produces waste on a regular basis – the byproducts of which are toxic to them. In the wild, the ratio of waste to water would be so small that those toxins wouldn't be significant. A tank is different in that it is a closed system. And it is thousands of times smaller than they would have in the wild. Ordinarily the water isn't moving out and new water isn't coming in constantly. This means that unless we do something, the waste will build up until your fish get sick and die! Filtration is a VITAL part of all aquarium setups in nearly every situation. You can remove the waste manually each day, but that will take a lot of time and having a filter ensures that those toxins are broken down faster and works to make the water safe for your fish 24/7. In most cases, to keep the aquarium running smoothly, you will need some kind of a filter.

Many different kinds of electricity-operated filters are available on the market today, including:

- Hang on back filters (HOB filters)
- Power filters
- Canister filters
- Internal cartridge filters
- Undergravel filters
- Sponge filters
- Bio wheels
- Fluidized filters
- Wet/dry filters
- Box filters
- Aquaponic filters
- Sumps

It can seem overwhelming at times trying to choose the best one, but at the end of the day it depends on what you want to accomplish, your budget and how much time you want to spend maintaining it.

Like most people, I am pretty busy most of the time and the less time I spend on tank maintenance, the better. A good filter will not only keep the fish healthy and happy but minimize the need for water changes.

Prefilters are usually comprised of a sponge or piece of polyfiber media designed for mechanical filtration. Utilizing prefilters can help make tank maintenance easier. Rather than trapping solid waste inside the filter (which can occupy important space for biological filtration and be more difficult to access), prefilters used on the intakes of HOB, canister, wet/dry pumps and even undergravel filters can be very useful, especially if you have filter media particles smaller than a golf ball. Frequently cleaning the prefilter (every 1-2 weeks) will allow for best water flow and may help prevent high nitrates.

## Hang on Back (HOB) Power Filters

Hang on back filters are probably the most commonly available filter for aquariums. They all offer the advantages of being relatively quiet, inconspicuous and affordable. They also are extremely easy to clean and maintain.

There are two main weaknesses with most HOB filters, especially for use with goldfish.

- The first is that most HOB filters require a very high water turnover rate to convert ammonia to nitrite and then to nitrate. This is because they are rather small with completely submerged media. The high turnover of the water can lead to a strong current in the water, which is not ideal for fancy goldfish that have exaggerated finnage or eyes. The strong water flow can blow them around, causing stress.
- The second main problem which most HOB filters is that they are usually less efficient at dealing with a heavy waste load (goldfish produce a lot of waste). When all the media is submerged underwater rather than exposed to any oxygen, it can't perform as effectively as a wet/dry filter. Some HOB filter makers have tried, rather unsuccessfully, to overcome this by adding a biowheel or a plastic grid layer that is alternately exposed to water and air, but these appear, according to the tests, to perform no more effectively than conventional HOB filters. The majority of designs do not make much room for holding biological media, so high porosity media can really help in compensating for the lack of compartment space.
- They must be cleaned regularly to avoid overflowing, but this should be done for the health of the tank.

Because of these problems, in the past I have not recommended them to goldfish keepers. But a promising new hang on back filter has recently entered the market that has attempted to address these issues, and that is the Fluval C power filter.

*Fluval C*

Instead of relying on a high water turnover to maximize efficiency, this filter maximizes surface area dwell time within the filter itself, recirculating the water multiple times when the adjustable flow rate is reduced. That helps with the first problem of having to have a strong current to complete nitrification.

In order to increase efficiency by harnessing the power of media exposed to oxygen, the Fluval C accommodates a wet/dry trickle compartment inside that allows the water to "rain" over the media. Essentially you have your own mini wet/dry filter inside your HOB filter, along with room for submerged media.

The mechanical filter includes an indicator to let you know when it is clogged. If you choose to utilize the mechanical filtration aspect, I would not recommend waiting to clean the mechanical filter until the point the alert is popping up, but at least once weekly. Goldfish can quickly foul the mechanical filter if it is let be too long.

*Nitrate reducing filter media*

I would also personally recommend replacing the C-nodes (their biological media that comes included with the filter for the trickle chamber) with filter media that can also remove nitrate. It also provides a greater surface area for bacteria to colonize in the core, rather than just on the surface of the media, giving your bacteria greater room. The activated carbon area can also be converted to house more biological filter media (carbon is usually not necessary unless you are trying to remove medications or chlorine from your water). After all, with one of the greatest limitations of the HOB filter being its size, it's a good idea to maximize what space you have.

*Pothos*

Some have found that adding Pothos to their HOB filter aids in nitrate removal and nutrient absorption, while adding a layer of aesthetic interest. I have also found adding some land moss (the kind that grows on rocks just above the waterline at a river) to the flow output is a nice way of silencing the return sound while helping to aid in additional nutrient export.

## Canister Filters

Canister filters are the filter of choice among most aquascapers, as they offer considerable space for biological media and can be situated under the tank in order to be inconspicuous. They are usually very quiet, the only sound usually consisting of the vibration of the return pump, unless the water is allowed to fall back into the tank. The canister itself can hold a larger amount of filter

*Canister filters*

media, such as large golf ball-sized media.  In fact, it is easy to put just about any kind of filter media or mechanical filtration sponges or pads in a canister filter.  It doesn't matter if the media is unattractive, and the unit is usually situated in an inconspicuous area in a tank cabinet.  An in-line UV sterilizer can be connected above the return pup.  A spray bar extension can allow for better oxygenation of the water, or the return pipe can be elevated to allow the water to "trickle" back in.

There are a few functionality drawbacks to canisters, the first of which is that the media is totally submerged in water.  This makes the bacteria perform less efficiently than bacteria that can come in contact with air and water in a wet/dry system.  This can be overcome, at least in part, by adding more media or media with a larger surface area.  They can also be a bit tricky to deal with when it comes to performing maintenance, as water may end up leaking when the canister is opened.  Finally, larger canister filters can produce significant water current, which may stress goldfish with more modified body types.

*Golf Ball Sized Filter Media*

Those who use canister filters often keep it in a plastic bin or on a towel to help with accidental spills and try to find way to reduce the current to avoid stressing the fish.  A water alarm is never a bad idea to detect leaks early.

There are even methods of connecting a canister filter to an undergravel filter to greatly enhance the biological surface area while prefiltering the water.

## Undergravel Filters: Coming Full Circle

*Undergravel Filters*

Undergravel (UG) filters are generally considered "old school" as far as aquarium technology goes as they have been around since the 1950's.  In recent years they have received considerable criticism.  But I believe they shouldn't be dismissed as some amateur, outdated filtration method – in fact, there are fishkeepers who have used them for years that really like them, and, provided they are set up in a way that is safe for the fish, they can be a great option for the hobbyist.

UG filtration offers the benefits of a massively unsurpassed surface colonization area for bacteria to grow on (the entire tank bottom) while giving the tank bottom some aesthetic interest.  Because the filter plates or tubes are concealed beneath the substrate, they are relatively unobtrusive in the tank.  They are even more efficient when used with foraging fish like goldfish, who "clean" the biofilm (layer of beneficial bacteria that forms on the surface) which allows the old bacteria to be removed, keeping it from getting overgrown with old bacteria.  UG filters outfitted with airstones allow for significant oxygenation of the water, though pump-driven UG filters may be a better option (more on that later).

An overlooked advantage of a UG filter is the fact that the flow rate is very slow. This is potentially great for goldfish, as they seem to favor slower-moving water.

The conventional filter works by pulling water through the substrate and in doing so provides mechanical and biological filtration. Undergravel filtration usually functions as secondary filtration, as goldfish produce a lot of waste and they aren't the normally most powerful filter on the market. They are often combined with HOB filtration (one that incorporates wet/dry filtration would be ideal). However, they can provide sufficient filtration all by themselves, provided you use the optimal setup. Some find that they can even be as effective as wet/dry filters.

They are not ideal for a planted tank, unless you plan on keeping your plants in containers. Though some report success with plants such as Swords, other plants may suffer from too much water movement around the roots.

**Addressing Concerns about UG filters**

A legitimate area of concern with Undergravel filters for goldfish is that the traditional pea-sized gravel can pose a choking hazard. This is true, but there are workarounds. For larger goldfish (over 4"), it is recommended to use ½ - ¾" (or greater) size substrate for the bottom in order to keep your goldfish safe. River pebbles are ideal for this. If you want to go really advanced, you could even use hydroton (or other sinking biomedia, preferably spherical to avoid trapping debris) which will provide maximum surface area for the bacteria, in addition to an environment where nitrate reduction can occur.

Hydroton is an expanded clay pellet that is spherical in shape and commonly used in aquaponics systems. Hydroton is like a mini version of the more typical nitrate reducing biomedia. It has an excellent surface area for beneficial bacteria to grow, in addition to a nice dark core that good anaerobic bacteria like, and the shape makes it easier to clean than gravel and better allows water to be drawn through

*Hydroton*

the substrate. They are red-brown in color. Sometimes it can take several days for the pellets to become waterlogged and sink to the bottom. If a pellet doesn't sink after that then it should be removed as it means the surface is not porous to the center of the pellet. It might not look that great though.

Another legitimate objection to UG filters is that Undergravel filters set up the typical way, even with nitrate-reducing substrate, can be trickier to keep clean than a tank with a bare or sand bottom. This is because all the waste is forced down and pushed to the bottom, becoming trapped in the substrate and underneath it. It is important to regularly clean them to prevent health issues in your fish. These should be vacuumed regularly (weekly is best) to prevent toxic

*Probiotic Bacteria Supplement*

anaerobic pockets from forming as the debris accumulates between the substrate cracks.  Using a probiotic bacteria supplement is highly recommended if you use a UG to help fight sludge buildup, as it can get really disgusting underneath the filter plate – especially if not cleaned regularly.  Some periodically remove the substrate and plate to thoroughly clean it out, which can be a huge chore.  Others have found you can insert the siphon into the lifter tube to remove the trapped waste under the plates.  Even regular vacuuming may still leave some amount of debris trapped underneath, depending on your substrate choice.

*Reverse-Flow Powerhead & Prefilter*

That said, there is a "secret" to preventing nasty sludge buildup and having to clean it all out some fishkeepers use, and that is to *reverse the flow*.  One can direct the flow of the submersible water pump down the uplift tubes with a reverse flow powerhead, forcing the water to go up through the substrate instead of being sucked toward the tank bottom.  You can use a sponge prefilter on the power filter (recommended, as it prevents waste from going underneath and possibly trapped into the substrate) which is much easier to clean (recommended to do at least once weekly), and you don't get nearly the nasty buildup as when it is used the other way.  Prefilters can be rinsed off in the sink or with a garden hose; they are only serving as mechanical filtration.  You get the benefits of a massive surface area for bacteria colonization without the pain and hazards of trapped waste underneath it.  Vacuuming frequency can be greatly reduced.  Using a powerhead also prevents having to regularly replace the airstones.  The airstones aren't very powerful anyway.  To ensure enough oxygen is present after removing the airstones, something like a bubble wall can be installed underneath the substrate if desired.

*Bubble Wall*

It is worth noting that spreading rooting plants probably should not be used with UG filters, as they will restrict areas of water flow over time.  You can always plant them in pots if desired.

UG filters can be a tried-and-true option for filtering your aquarium efficiently, while providing a layer of aesthetic interest at the bottom of the tank.

## The Wet-Dry Filter Method: A (Possibly) Very Maintenance-Reducing Filter

A little-known filtration style, the wet-dry filter is extremely efficient, and while not quite as easy to conceal without some effort, the reduction in tank maintenance is totally worth it.

Benefits over other filtration methods are numerous:

- Wet-dry filters (also called trickle filters) can remove nitrates when packed with the right kind of media (and in the right conditions).
- Conversion from ammonia to nitrite to nitrate is far more efficient because the media is wet without being completely submerged. This amplifies its abilities to keep your tank well-filtered. We'll touch on nitrate reduction later.

*Wet-Dry Filter*

- They offer a massive surface area for beneficial bacteria to colonize and work, reducing maintenance. Goldfish produce a lot of waste and a very biologically powerful filter is required to efficiently keep up with them. They cycle very quickly in my experience.
- If your nitrates hit 0, you can actually do water changes once a month instead of once a week, and even then, the water change is just enough to remove the debris from the bottom of the tank. If you want to feed your fish more (such as if you are trying to grow out young fish quickly), or have higher stocking levels than normal you will need to do more maintenance. Of course, it is a good idea to test your water to ensure your filter is established enough to perform.
- The filter itself only needs to be cleaned every 6-12 months because it isn't functioning to debris and muck; it is only functioning for the nitrogen cycle.

I think most people agree that they have other things to do or would rather spend the time just watching their fish. Depending on large, frequent water changes for long-term maintenance can be challenging for many because it requires nearly the same volume of aged, aerated water that is in the main aquarium – and not everyone has space for that. A powerful filtration setup can pull up the slack and keep the fish in the environment it needs longer for good health.

How does it work? Water is pushed by a submersible pump at the bottom of the tank through a tube and then through a rain bar, which then flows through the perforated boxes (for box-style wet/dry filters), into a tray and back through a return outlet. The returning water is very rich in oxygen, eliminating the need for additional aeration. Wet/dry filters make a "trickling" sound while operating that sounds like rain. The more media fills the boxes, the quieter the sound. The boxes can be filled with whatever media you would like, be it chemical, mechanical or biological filtration. That said, I only use porous media in the boxes as I am not fond of carbon chemical filtration (carbon particles are linked to lateral line disease) and find mechanical filtration difficult to clean regularly (I prefer siphoning the bottom to remove particles).

*Submersible Pump*

There are two main kinds of wet/dry filters:

1) Wet/dry filters can be configured **underneath the tank** (sump style) or above the tank. Setting them up below the tank has the advantages of keeping the apparatus out of site if

the tank sits on a closed cabinet.  The filter can usually accommodate a greater water volume, adding to the gallonage of the overall system (which can be very useful for heavily stocked aquariums).  In order to operate a below-tank wet/dry filter, there are some precautionary steps that have to be taken to ensure the unit does not overflow during a power outage or during maintenance.  Unless you drill the tank, it is recommended to make use of an overflow box to prevent disaster.  This setup isn't the cheapest when you buy everything premade.  For those who have the desire and technical capability to do so, there are DIY versions of this that can be built and installed without detracting from the aesthetics of the tank (assuming the filter is concealed).

2) Wet/dry filters can be configured **above the tank.** DIY versions can be a bit of an eyesore. (Actually, all of them can, sorry 😦) Manufactured ones may be hard to find at your local pet store but can offer a more attractive solution if you know where to look.  This is probably the most feasible option for most hobbyists.  There are several styles to choose from, depending on your design preference.  The stackable box style allows for the use of more vertical space, giving you more room for your biological media and increasing your bioload capacity of the tank, whereas the long, compact style is best for those who prefer a less obtrusive unit.

## Nitrate Reduction

*Nitrate reducing filter media*

How does this filter remove nitrates? Certain forms of nitrate reducing media can be added.  This kind of media is quite porous. The surface of the pellets is perfect for growing beneficial bacteria, and the dark core actually provides a perfect home for beneficial anaerobic bacteria that actually remove nitrate. When this filter media is exposed to water while not being completely submerged, this creates the perfect environment for a high-powered good anaerobic biological colony.  A wet/dry filter is the most effective biological filter.

It is not recommended to use a thick layer of small media in your filter, which traps debris and can become very nasty and dangerous for your goldfish. Instead, I highly advise opting for media that not only has a rough texture for bacteria colonies on the surface but is completely porous through to the core so that nitrate removing bacteria can get in there and set up shop. A solid rock won't provide home for good anaerobic bacteria. That is the environment they like; in that dark core. Large chunks of coral are a fantastic option, and will buffer the water a bit, but it can be difficult to obtain. If you live near the beach you can probably find this for free. Ceramic or mineral-based media is easily available on the market for the rest of us. It usually comes in white. I also like bio filtration stones for a more natural look.  I recommend if it is under the size of a golf ball, be sure not to use more than one layer of the media and space it out a little bit so it won't trap debris.

**Plants in the Wet/Dry Filter**

Growing plants in the top boxes is another way to aid in further nitrate removal and purify the water.  Their roots spreading through the media helps prevent pockets of debris buildup and utilize nutrients from fish waste.  Not only that, but trailing plants can help to cover the apparatus above the tank for those who find it less than pleasing to the eye.  Pothos are a good choice, as they are fast growers, hardy and can grow well in water.  They are great for the "brown thumb" gardener. You simply snip a stem of about 5 leaves off of an existing plant (cut at an angle) and leave the snipped end in water.  It will start to develop roots in a week or two if all goes well.  The plant can then be transferred to the top chambers of the filter.  Another way is to buy a full plant and then remove all the soil from the roots (important), transferring it directly to the tank or filter.  The leaves should be left in the open air and the roots submerged.

*Pothos*

## Sponge Filters

Sponge filters offer the advantages of having a low current, providing good aeration with the bubbles, very affordable and relatively easy to clean.  They are excellent for baby fry as they do not produce a lot of current and won't suck up small fish.

*Sponge filters*     In the past I've used sponge filters exclusively on all my tanks, but they have a few disadvantages. They do not offer nitrate reduction. They can become covered with particles of waste and crud which restricts the ability of the beneficial bacteria to do their job. In my experience they required more frequent, larger volume water changes to remove all the nitrates they create.

There are a few things to be aware of when using a sponge filter.  The main drawback is that they must be cleaned very frequently, as they quickly become covered in debris (suffocating the beneficial bacteria).  At that point they are little more than just a mechanical filter.  As a primary filter, they do not offer the ability to perform nitrate reduction.  And they do take up space inside the tank itself, which aesthetically can be undesirable.

I do like sponge filters and use them in various applications, but feel they are best for everyday use when employed to provide oxygenation and mechanical filtration along with another filter (essentially as a prefilter).

Another possibility is to convert the sponge filter into a moving bed filter with the biological media (usually K1 Kaldnes filter media) housed in a plastic bottle, which will allow the beneficial bacteria to live separately from the waste-trapping sponge.  There are videos on how to do this online when you search for "DIY Kaldnes K1 sponge filter."  You can also use other filter media inside the bottle, such as hydroton, for a static bed.  The main drawback of this kind of filter is that it can become a nitrate factory, and you may need to consider other ways of reducing those nitrates such as growing Pothos or performing more frequent water changes (though this may offset the cost of starting with a more efficient filter).

*Hydroton*

## Notes on Using Other Filters

As you can see, the type of filter you use and how it is filled will greatly affect your water change schedule.  Each filter will have a different level of efficiency at pushing your system through the nitrogen cycle.  The most reliable way to know how often to change your water for your particular filter is to test the water.  When the nitrates start getting between 20-30ppm, it is time for a water change.  They should not be allowed to go above 30ppm.

If you do opt to use some kind of particle-trapping mechanical filtration in your filter, it is a good idea to frequently clean the filtration media out.  This is because collected waste that has water running through it quickly is a perfect place for nasty bacteria to grow and cause sickness for your fish.  The recommended cleaning schedule for it would be at least once weekly, preferably twice a week or more.  This also applies to sponge filters, which are primarily mechanical.  Cleaning mechanical filtration less frequently can be possible when using a probiotic bacteria supplement in your water on a weekly basis.

*Probiotic Bacteria Supplement*

## Natural Filtration

The filters above can all keep your aquarium safe for goldfish.  They can even be the most ideal solution in some cases, especially when keeping live plants is not possible or practical in a certain setup.  That said, filtration that depends on electricity has some drawbacks.  What will you do during a power outage?  The more heavily stocked your tank is, the greater the danger that you could have a problem with water quality or oxygen deprivation when that filter stops running – unless you have some battery backup plan.  Then there is the cost to operate them, which is a continual expense and is not the most environmentally friendly.  Also, (though not a major issue for most) they can look unsightly.  Most filters are hard to conceal.  And most require some form of continual maintenance to function properly, compounding your workload.

Goldfish keeping has been around for hundreds of years – before electricity. If everyone relied solely on constant water changes to remove toxins and keep their pets alive, the hobby might not still be around. So, what are their secrets?

Enter **natural filtration**.

**Live Plants**

Most of us tend to underestimate the power of plants and natural biological processes to purify water. But back in the days before modern access to electricity, it was understood that you couldn't keep fish without them:

> "Hence the reason why we cannot keep fish any length of time in an ornamental basin or in any piece of water where there are not vegetables growing. You may keep gold-fish in water exposed to the air, but although the air has free access to it, you are obliged to frequently change the water, for it soon becomes so far charged with carbonic acid as to be unfit for the respiration of the fish. And in regard to streams and natural sources of water [without plants], the fish will soon die, in consequence of there being nothing to take up the carbonic acid which they throw off, and which ultimately poisons them."[3]

Healthy, growing plants simultaneously purify the water of toxins that goldfish produce while providing oxygen.

It's important to choose plants that goldfish won't eat, as stems won't help much in purifying the water 😊 You also need a sufficient amount of plants, as well as the right kind. It is recommended to have at least 50% of the substrate planted. Generally speaking, slow-growing plants are less useful in purifying the water, as are unhealthy ones.

The drawbacks are that it may take a bit of finesse to create a balanced, natural, thriving tank, rather than a mess of rotting plants and cloudy water that is harmful to the fish. Plants have their own set of requirements to remain healthy, such as nutrients and a source of carbon. But with the right materials, you can set up a planted tank that provides lush growth and clean water for your pets.

Plants readily consume ammonia and nitrite. In fact, they prefer them to nitrate. But this means that plants and aerobic filter bacteria compete with each other for ammonia and nitrate. In a

---

[3] *Professor Brand's Lectures at the Royal Institution* (Leicester Journal – Friday 21 July 1843)

planted tank, minimizing biological filtration can yield better plant growth.  Another option is to provide these nutrients in soil.

**Deep Sand Bed Filters**

This type of filtration is more well-known among saltwater reef keepers, where low level of nitrates are very important.  But the same principles apply in freshwater, and they basically work the same way.  It turns the substrate into a living ecosystem that effectively processes the toxins created by the fish, sometimes referred to as "nutrient recycling."  Fish waste is broken down – first by smaller creatures in the food chain such as snails and worms, then by microscopic bacteria – and finally taken up in the roots of the plants to be used for growth.  Fish waste contains lots of beneficial elements needed for plants, but this is only usable if the waste can reach the roots.  It takes the help of burrowing creatures to deliver the waste to the roots in a deep sand bed.

Benefits:

- Lower nitrates without water changes
- Eliminate tedious gravel vacuuming
- Enhanced plant growth
- Minimize or eliminate reliance on electrical filtration
- Neutralize hydrogen sulfide
- Boost CO2

*More on Deep Sand Bed Filters*

The deep sand bed filter utilizes zones for both aerobic and anaerobic respiration.  A layer of larger-grain sand of about 3" is placed on the bottom of the tank, which provides massive surface area for bacteria to grow.  The larger grain size allows mulm to quickly penetrate into the lower layers, where it is used as a fertilizer for plants.  Sharp-grained sands are not recommended.  CaribSea makes an ideal sand for this called Crystal River. You can also use their Peace River gravel/sand which is slightly larger (larger grains may require a deeper bed to get effective denitrification conditions).  The top 1" becomes a breeding ground for beneficial bacteria that convert ammonia into nitrite and into nitrate, while the lower portion is suitable for growing bacteria that utilize the nitrate.

(Adding some sand from an established tank on top of the new sand is a good way to kickstart the bacteria.)

A key ingredient for a successful DSB is utilizing burrowing creatures that dig down below the substrate's surface.  These diffuse nutrients from mulm within the sand bed and increase substrate aeration.  These may include Malaysian Trumpet Snails (easy to acquire), California blackworms (can be purchased at some local fish stores) and even clams. The more burrowing action you have in your DSB, the more powerful of a filter you will have. You can skip on having burrowers and just have live plants, but this will reduce the effectiveness of the filter.

Rooting plants are essential. The roots of the plants penetrate into the deepest parts of your DSB (where other creatures won't go) preventing the sand from compacting and buildup of hydrogen sulfide. Good choices for goldfish include:

- Amazon Swords
- Cabomba
- Ludwegia
- Rotala
- Pennywort
- Water Sprite

Many folks with freshwater DSB also intentionally add "digging fish." But since you plan on keeping goldfish, you have instant diggers who will do the job of churning up the top layer for you!

By adding creatures such as worms, scuds etc. you are supplying the tank with a food source for your fish. This will make your goldfish's life so much more interesting as it has an exciting activity to do (that it would be doing in the wild), which is foraging for tasty little critters! Some find they need to replenish the burrowers periodically. Others find they can create hiding places using rocks, old biomedia or other weighted objects and it creates a hiding place to keep some alive without the need to do so. Continually replenishing when needed is a good idea to keep the filter working in good shape. You can even culture these yourself in a separate tank or a hang-on breeding box (just don't let the flow of the box create splashing. The breeding box can replace the internal filter or pump.

Adding a (very small) internal power filter or submersible pump will be the extent of electrical filtration needed. Its purpose is to provide water circulation and oxygen (and, if desired, mechanical filtration). No aerators or filters should be used to keep the carbon dioxide from gassing off.

Allowing a few days for the plants to start growing in and the burrowing creatures to settle in is recommended, though overnight is the bare minimum.

Maintenance is greatly reduced. Mulm that is more than ¼" deep sitting on the substrate's surface should be siphoned off as needed (without vacuuming the sand).

Avoid frequently disturbing the substrate yourself as much as possible. When plants require replanting, those that can tolerate it should be cut off at the base and the root systems left in place to decay. This decay plays a valuable role in the health of the DSB in its release of CO2 which is used by other plants. The more you disrupt the substrate, the less powerful it will be due to disrupting the bacterial functions. Greatly disrupting a large area of substrate and in the presence of your fish can possibly result in harm to your livestock due to the release of hydrogen sulfide. This is generally more of a danger in tanks where nutrient diffusion is inadequate, such as those made of fine sand.

## Current

While we are on the subject of filtration, something probably should be said for water current in your aquarium. The carp originally lives in slow to moderately moving waters. Especially for fancy goldfish, a very strong current can cause stress as their large fins catch the current and get blown around in the water. This can lead to a fish that is in a state of continual stress. They usually will get exhausted and hide in an area in the tank where there is the least amount of current (the main indication of too much water movement).

One tip that has been offered is tying a string to a penny. If the penny is dipped in the water and is moving around, that can indicate too much current. Some tips for diffusing the current include:

- Aiming the water flow towards the closest wall of the tank (usually makes a small difference)
- Blocking the intake or output area with a sponge
- Using a rain bar type diffuser
- Drilling small holes in the return outlet to distribute the water flow

## Aeration

If you use a wet/dry filter, aeration is not likely a problem for your tank as the returning water is heavily oxygenated. However, some filters (such as most hang on back filters or canister filters) do not do much to oxygenate the water.

*Bubble Wall*

Oxygen is necessary for aquatic life (including your beneficial bacteria) and helping to break down waste. Water with low dissolved oxygen is not good for goldfish as it can, among other things, increase the risk of sickness. Low dissolved oxygen is increasingly prevalent at warmer temperatures. Lack of live plants will also reduce oxygen in the water.

For such tanks, using an airstone is recommended. The bubbles greatly help to oxygenate the water. 1 airstone per 10 gallons is recommended for tanks where supplemental aeration is necessary. Some find a bubble wall positioned along the back of the tank makes aerating the tank aesthetically pleasing and functional for their aquarium.

## UV Sterilization

There are many conflicting opinions on the use of UV sterilizers for goldfish aquariums. The invention is designed to kill microorganisms – without the use of chemicals – by use of a strong ultraviolet light. It has been used for reducing suspended algae and the bacteria count in the water. Very high-powered UV sterilizers can also kill viruses and larger pathogens such as ich. They are sometimes used for sick fish as they can take additional load off the immune system.

UV sterilization has some compelling benefits:

- Proponents of UV sterilization advocate the method as a way to help with water clarity and fish health. In the wild and in ponds, sunlight helps reduce microorganisms. Most aquariums do not have much (if any) natural sunlight. This can lead to a higher bacteria count in the water. With goldfish, there is a balance: not enough bacteria in the water can cause stress. Too much can lead to disease. UV sterilization behaves like germicidal sunlight in your aquarium. Some fish keepers prefer to keep it on only for a short amount of time each day.
- Some find increased longevity in fish tanks that use a UV sterilizer over those that do not.
- Algae reduction, especially suspended algae, or cloudy water can be clarified.
- By killing bacteria in the water, some water-born bacterial diseases have been known to reverse. Considering the mass of research on the prevalence of diseases such as Fish TB, it is safe to say that most tanks have bacteria in the water and in biofilms that can cause disease in people. Though it is rare for that to happen, having a UV sterilizer can help you feel more comfortable about putting your hands in the water.
- Some long-finned goldfish struggle with chronic redness in fins. UV sterilizers may help alleviate this.

There are some drawbacks to UV sterilizers:

- The bulb does not last forever. It must be replaced every 8-12 months if used continuously, a recurring expense.
- The quartz glass sleeves are not cheap and can be difficult to clean (they require frequent cleaning). They can accidentally break during the cleaning process.
- The bulbs can also break easily and burn your eyes if you look at them.
- Knowing exactly how effective the UV sterilizer is can be difficult to calculate when it comes to killing parasites.

- Parasites can only be killed by passing through the sterilizer in their free-swimming stage, but spend most of their time on the bottom or on the fish.  10X the strength of the bulb used for killing algae is needed to kill parasites.

**Choosing a UV Sterilizer**

*UV Sterilizer*

Not all UV sterilizers are created equal.  Many do little more than just clarify the water and do not have the means to harm microorganisms.  The microwatts (not wattage) are what kill bacteria. 28,000 minimum is recommended.  The exposure (or dwell) time should be at least 4 seconds.

## Low-Tech Goldfish Keeping

On the other hand, goldfish have been kept for hundreds of years as pets indoors – without modern technology.  Water changes, well-controlled feeding and the periodic removal of dissolved organic matter have been used as a time-tested way to control high bacteria loads.

Not only that, but algae-rich green water has often been not only tolerated – but actually encouraged – as a nutrient source for goldfish by even serious, modern-day hobbyists for its benefits to the fish.  Green water provides a nutrient source to the fish which, hobbyists report, results in better growth and brighter colors for the fish.  The exact intensity of green can be controlled with water changes.

For these setups, it is a delicate balance of being able to view the fish well while still providing the environmental benefits of green water.  In fact, green water can offer the benefits ammonia and nitrite control as the algae feed on goldfish waste products.  In some setups, the filter is replaced (yes, completely eliminated) with airstones and weekly water changes of 50-75% are used to take care of what the algae won't.

## What to Do for Cloudy Water

Often times people opt to get UV sterilizer are trying to battle with cloudy water.

*Probiotic Bacteria Supplement*

Water that looks "milky" is often due to a bacterial bloom, most common occurring in new systems.  This water has high bacteria counts and may pose health risks to the fish.  Partial water changes may not prove effective, as the remaining bacteria will continue to multiply.  Adding a liquid probiotic bacteria supplement to jumpstart the filter can really help at outcompeting the bacteria that cause the bloom.  The good news is that with time, good husbandry and a bit of patience, the issue will eventually resolve.

For established systems, accumulating debris in the tank may be the cause of the bacterial bloom. Overfeeding fish or feeding poor quality food can also lead to cloudy water as the food or undigested carbohydrates dissolves in the aquarium.

*Caribsea Supernaturals Aquarium Sand*

Many kinds of sands can cause persistent cloudiness in the water (that's a major reason why I use Caribsea Supernaturals aquarium sand. I had no issues with persistent cloudiness, unlike with other kinds).

Water that looks tinted (like tea) is usually so from tannins that are leaching into it from driftwood or dead leaves. Tannins can lower the pH.

Cloudy green water can be caused by excess light and nutrients, but may also be due to high phosphates in the tap water. As stated, some goldfish owners actually put considerable effort into cultivating green water for its benefits to the fish. Those who do not want it may attempt to reduce the amount of light exposure to the tank, phosphate reducers, clarifying filter pads and more frequent water changes and tank maintenance. If all else fails, a UV sterilizer might be the way to go.

## Lighting

*Full-spectrum Aquarium Light*

Ensuring that your goldfish tank is well lit is, in fact, an important part of their general environment and health.  Goldfish kept in the dark for a very long time will turn completely white as they gradually lose their pigmentation.  Not only does light promote the growth of green algae (which goldfish enjoy snacking on), but it gives your goldfish Vitamin D and promotes good coloring.  Good, full-spectrum lighting also helps boost their immune system, helping them to fend off sickness easier.

Sunlight is very beneficial for goldfish coloration and health.  However, placing the tank near a window can result in excess algae.  This isn't necessarily a bad thing if you want to promote good color in the fish and maybe a bit of foraging material, but it does mean extra scrubbing periodically if algae are undesirable aesthetically for the fishkeeper.  Many fish keepers prefer to cultivate as much algae as aesthetically possible for its benefits to the fish.  The main reason not to keep a tank where it can get direct sunlight is that the temperature can rapidly spike and fall.  The smaller the volume of water, the more quickly it will overheat.  This can cause stress to the goldfish, so it is a good idea to avoid placing the tank underneath south-facing windows or east/west facing windows that do not have blinds.

Artificial lighting can be put in place and is probably necessary if the aquarium does not get much indirect natural light or you keep high-light demanding plants in the tank.  It is probably worth noting that the two plants most goldfish won't eat are both low light plants.  But without providing a full-spectrum light source, vitamin deficiencies can result in the fish not growing properly or having a poor immune system.  One additional benefit of an aquarium light is how it makes the tank and the fish look quite stunning.

If you do choose this option, the lights should be kept on for no more than 15 hours a day.  Goldfish shouldn't have the lights on all the time.  Darkness is also as important as light for them – it provides a better sleeping environment for them at night and helps mimic the natural day-and-night cycle that they would have outdoors if they lived in the wild.

The amount of light a goldfish gets in the wild throughout the year depends on the season, with winter days generally being shorter and springtime days growing longer and longer until summer.  Goldfish who are allowed to sleep in the dark get more rest than those who don't, which also helps to keep their immune system strong.

# Temperature

Goldfish can tolerate the perhaps widest range of temperatures than almost any other aquarium fish. While generally considered a coldwater fish, there is mounting evidence that fancy varieties, which are more delicate than hardy pond-dwelling breeds, do much better in warmer waters – especially the delicate fancy kinds.

There is also much evidence to suggest that goldfish are actually not coldwater fish at all and benefit from warmer temperatures. True coldwater fish, such as trout, cannot thrive in warm water, which is untrue of goldfish. Coldwater fish are very stressed in warm water, leading to sickness and even death. Where goldfish are found naturally in the wild, near the equator and in tropical Asian areas, is also where many tropical fish species are found.

While goldfish will not die in cold water, it should probably be considered less than ideal for fancies.

## Benefits of Warm Water

- **Better Health** – Warmer water has been shown to decrease the chances of disease and help them live longer over time. This is likely because there is still ample bacteria in the water, but fewer pathogenic bacteria. For every 10 degrees the temperature goes up (until dissolved oxygen starts decreasing around 82 degrees), the immune system of the fish doubles.
- **Enough Oxygen** – Water with temperatures between 75 and 80 degrees Fahrenheit still has enough oxygen for goldfish to breathe comfortably.
- **Improved Growth** – In Asia, some owners find that keeping their goldfish at a constant temperature of 82 degrees F yields the most growth.
- **Greater Lifespan** – There is also evidence that goldfish do not spawn at this temperature, and that reducing spawning behavior can lengthen the lifespan of the goldfish.
- **Better Coloration** – One study found that fish kept in waters at 78 degrees F and higher had more vibrant coloring, an indicator of good health
- **Induce Spawning** – The change from cooler water temperatures to warmer temperatures can trigger spawning in goldfish. Artificially changing the temperature is one way to do this.

A heater is a great way to have complete control over the water temperature. Newer heaters may incorporate shatter-resistant glass, helping to protect your tank from disaster. If the goldfish are kept in a basement or garage where the temperature rises and falls quite a bit or is a bit chilly, a heater is probably

*Shatter-Resistant Aquarium Heater*

mandatory, and even for average aquariums it is highly recommended.  Most goldfish have been imported from areas such as Hong Kong and Thailand, where they were born and raised in tropical temperatures all their lives and may not do as well when kept in cooler, air-conditioned homes.

I generally keep my fancy goldfish aquariums at room temperature, unless I have a spawning, fry grow-out or quarantine tank set up, or maybe if I have a fish that needs a little special attention in the health department.  This saves on electrical costs.  In the wintertime when the basement gets colder I may add a heater in with my delicate fancy goldfish if I don't intend to spawn them.

## Outdoor Goldfish & Temperature

Most fancy goldfish do best kept indoors in a heated environment.  While some varieties such as Black Moors, Orandas and Fantails have been kept outside over winter, the cold weather carries some risks that seem to be associated with swim bladder issues.  Shorter-bodied fish are more prone to such problems and, though some have had success keeping them outside all winter, other experts have found that the fish tend to decline year after year and may live a much shorter life.  In my experience I have found that the harder the winter, the more likely the fish will encounter trouble.  By using a heater to keep the temperatures between 45-55 degrees F, this can help mitigate some of the extreme cold that can be detrimental to delicate fish.  I've found that keeping fish in the garage can be much easier than keeping them in the great outdoors, as you have access to electricity and can shelter them from predators and extreme weather.

If you do want to keep goldfish in a pond, long-bodied varieties such as the Common, Comet, Shubunkin, Wakin and Watonai are the best options as they are the most equipped to deal with outdoor life and the temperature swings that come with it.

# Decorations & Plants

Most animals need a place to feel sheltered within their home, and goldfish are no exception. And not only do decorations and plants provide that, they also enhance the beauty of your tank. Let's face it – an empty aquarium isn't all that interesting to look at. It also helps to mimic the environment a goldfish would have in nature.

Studies have shown that more complex environments can actually lengthen the lifespan of the fish!

Fish tank decorations come in all colors, shapes and sizes – architectural inspired coliseums, castles and ships are popular. There is usually something for everyone's personal taste. These can provide amusement for the goldfish as they swim through them, hunting for food or playing, provided they do not pose a safety hazard. Some designs help afford shelter where the fish can rest in the shade if it likes. Generally, the larger the item the more expensive it is.

It is really important to make sure what you get is goldfish-proof with no sharp edges. It is worth noting that some ornaments sold at pet stores are often painted with chemicals that may gradually leach into the tank. You can even make your own ornaments using fired glazed clay (food safe) or even waterproof cement and stones. Purchasing ornaments (usually resin) may save a good bit of time and some prefer the details and/or colors from a storebought piece.

Some use driftwood in their goldfish tanks, but it is important to make sure there are no sharp points on it that can hurt your fish. Personally, I am wary of driftwood causing injury and choose not to use it with my fancy goldies and only use it in tanks with my agile slim-bodied fish.

## Rocks

Rocks add a very natural and realistic aspect to any aquarium. They provide a more interesting environment for goldfish to explore, which is important for animals kept in closed confinement like goldfish.

Hunting for rocks for your aquarium is a fun pastime. You can use rocks you find around where you live, provided they will not alter the pH and do not have any contaminants from them that will hurt your fish (such as roadside chemicals, pesticides, weed spray, etc.). Smooth pieces of granite, river rock, slate and shale, quartz, basalt and even petrified wood are all suitable. On the other hand, limestone, marble, sandstone and pyrite should probably be avoided because they will either alter the pH, leach metals or minerals or disintegrate.

Here are a few tips for the hardscape in a natural aquarium:

- Use odd numbers.  In nature, objects often appear in groups of 3, 5, 7, etc.
- Have a "focal point" that draws the eye, usually off-centered.
- Use a variety of stone sizes.  It looks realistic to have a mix of large and small stones instead of having them all be the same size.
- Stagger the hardscape to show depth. Instead of putting all objects on the same plane, you may consider putting some closer to the front and others closer to the back.

Obviously, these suggestions are totally optional.  It is your tank and your rules, and sometimes the unconventional can look beautiful as well.

## Plants

Plants are a great way to decorate your tank.  They also can provide protection for goldfish eggs during breeding season.  Plastic plants are also usually cheaper the smaller they are and can often be found in assortments.  While they mostly come in organic shades of green, some companies have gotten creative and made theirs in every color of the rainbow.  Now they even have glow in the dark aquarium plants that shine at night.  Not all artificial plants are plastic though – silk plants are somewhat softer to the touch, though they do fade over time and they eventually fall apart.  Plastic or fibrous plants have some advantages.  Generally speaking, artificial plants of both cloth and plastic last for a long time without getting eaten by your goldfish.  You don't have to feed them with root fertilizer or worry about leaving them out of the water too long, either.  It won't bother them to have the goldfish digging up the substrate around the bottom.  One nice thing too is that they won't introduce harmful pathogens into your tank, which is a concern for some fish keepers.  They are quite difficult to kill.  😊

But not having live plants makes you miss out on more than you think.

- Live plants are a home for beneficial bacteria
- They suck out toxins from the water (including ammonia, nitrite and nitrate)
- They remove heavy metals
- They provide shelter for eggs and fry

Live plants, however, never have that "fake" look.  While there are quite a variety of them, most live plants that would do just fine in a tank full of tropical fish won't last a day in your goldfish tank.  Be that as it may, there are still some kinds that goldfish won't go for and they can still help out when it comes to keeping the water clean.  Sometimes goldfish owners will purposely buy plants that goldfish eat to provide them with a little snack.  In some ways they can be messy, but in others they can prove very helpful.  For that, *duckweed* or *Elodea* are fantastic grazing plants.  They both float at the surface and give the fish something to do like they would in the wild.  Duckweed especially grows quickly, which is important because you don't want your fish to eat it all right away. You must have a rather large ratio of edible plants to fish or it will all be devoured in a matter of days.

That goldfish actually care about artificial plants is questionable. I put off buying live plants for a long time and finally got sick of having to replace the plastic ones and clean them and deal with those annoying marbles falling out from the base I used to weigh them down with. Plus, they are extremely tedious to clean. Algae grows on them like crazy and the colors typically fade after a few months. Go natural is my advice – it is more like what fish are used to and your whole tank will benefit from it as a result.

*Anubias*

*Java Fern*

The two top plants that have any chance of withstanding goldfish long-term are Anubias and Java fern. This is because they are some of the few that goldfish won't eat due to how tough the leaves are. Best of all, both don't need a substrate to survive – simply affix them to a hard surface (wood or rock) with plant glue – I use Seachem Flourish glue. I like to use small pieces of quartz to weigh them down because they are all over the place where I live, but there are other fish-safe rocks you can find as well for the job. Anubias is especially fail-proof and comes in many sub-varieties and sizes, offering lots of room for creativity. Java fern can be a bit pickier in my experience, but if you have a green thumb it can make a great addition to the tank. You can get one huge plant or tons of little ones or a mix of both. Go

*Seachem Flourish Glue*

crazy, your fish will love you and your tank will look great.

Sterilizing live plants can be done using bleach, but I you can also use hydrogen peroxide at 1 part peroxide to 3 parts water dipped for 6 seconds. This will effectively knock off any hitchhikers as well as clean the plants of debris before placing them in your tank.

## Substrate

### Gravel

Gravel can be a fantastic substrate for goldfish – and for you – when set up the right way.

I don't recommend plain aquarium gravel (meaning gravel with no filter or no soil underlayer) at all for goldfish for two reasons:

1) **It can be a choking hazard.** The typical aquarium gravel sold in stores is the perfect size to get stuck in the mouth of goldfish.   Young fish may not be able to fit their mouths around gravel, but as they grow that can change.

2) **It can trap toxic waste with no way to break it down**.  Debris or uneaten food works its way down through the many cracks between the gravel and can develop toxic pockets of anaerobic bacteria.  This can seriously harm fish once disturbed during siphoning.  These pockets can also leach nasty stuff (toxic hydrogen sulfide) into the water over time, making your fish sick.  Gravel must be constantly cleaned to prevent this from happening.  The rotting debris in the gravel will lower the pH of the water, killing the beneficial bacteria and leading to a dangerous cycle crash.

If you have gravel and would like to remove it or redo, it is probably a good idea to do so gradually as bacteria grows on the gravel surface and avoid throwing off your cycle.  Some recommend removing it one handful a day until it is all gone.

If you believe your fish are sick due to hydrogen sulfide poisoning from your gravel, it is recommended to relocate them to a bucket, remove all gravel at once and do a 100% water change.  Removing handfuls of gravel bit by bit that have anaerobic bacteria growing in it can release more hydrogen sulfide all at once, causing sickness or even death.  The gravel should then be thoroughly cleaned in dechlorinated water or the tank water before returning it to the tank.  Proceed to remove it handful by handful each day afterwards.

But in the right situation, gravel can be a great substrate.  There is more than one way to utilize gravel to create a safe and natural aquarium bottom.

**Gravel Types**

There are many styles of gravel.  Most colored gravel (and even most black or white gravel) is coated with paint.  This can flake off over time.  While the paint may be labeled non-toxic to aquatic life, there is no way to know exactly what it is leaching into the aquarium over time.

Some gravel is coated with a layer of clear acrylic to prevent shifts in the pH and give it a polished appearance in the bag.  This is generally harmless, though I prefer using gravel that does help boost the pH a bit as it can help counteract the tendency of the water to go acidic and some of the acidity in the soil (if you are using soil underneath it).

Smooth gemstone or colored glass chips about the size of regular gravel can be used for a naturally colorful substrate with added luster. These are inert and are ideal for smaller tanks or fishbowls for most people as they can be more costly. Most crystals are made of quartz, and the minerals are bound up in the structure of the stone. Sometimes you can score a big bag of these at a garage sale or goodwill.

In general, the best size of gravel for goldfish with a big mouth is either very small – almost a course sand (roughly 2mm and under) to oversize (roughly 10mm and above). Small goldfish do just fine with standard ¼" pea gravel. You can also mix a shallow layer (¼" deep or so) of gravel with sand, if desired. Gravel smaller than 2mm can be used with all goldfish.

Please note that fish housed with gravel should, in most cases, be fed with floating foods or sinking foods placed on a dish to avoid food getting trapped between the rocks and rotting. However, the addition of some Malaysian trumpet snails can work their way around in the gravel cleaning up any uneaten food. If you are able to figure out another way to feed sinking foods so they don't rot in the substrate, more power to you 😊

## Undergravel Filters

The first method is to use an undergravel filter. Undergravel filters help to prevent anaerobic bacteria from building up by circulating water through the substrate. However, may aquarium plants do not do well planted in a well aerated substrate. If live plants are desired, it may be a good idea to keep them in containers.

It is a very good idea to use a prefilter on your reverse flow UG filter to prevent waste from being pushed up into the substrate and getting trapped there. Prefilters should be cleaned as often as any other mechanical filtration media. Vacuuming the substrate may still need to be done occasionally, but the workload should be much reduced with the reverse flow setup.

## Soil Base Gravel

When first setting up the tank (no water yet!), 1" of dry soil can be added below ½" of gravel. Add water slowly to a depth of 2" by pouring the water onto a plastic bag or other diffuser. Gently poke plants into soil layer with tweezers. Carefully add remaining gravel so you get 1" total of gravel to cover the soil areas. Drain off cloudy water fill with fresh water, if necessary. The final water should be clear. Let the tank run overnight with heater and filter before adding fish that evening or the next morning. This method can also used in any aquarium, from a fishbowl to pond.

Soil takes 2 months to become fully stable. During that time, it is necessary to monitor ammonia and nitrites, water change, add a water conditioner that removes heavy metals, aerate water, and run charcoal if you think the dirt has pesticides in it. Plants grow well in freshly submerged soil but even better in soil soaked 6+ weeks (though I don't bother to presoak it myself). Aquatic plants grow better in sediment/soil better than sand.

No need to wait 6 weeks to add full fish load, soil starts protecting fish in days.  Monitor the water quality and perform water changes as necessary.  Freshly submerged soil may or may not gas off some initial ammonia/nitrite before you see nitrates.  In some cases there is no ammonia/nitrite spike and you see nitrates within days.

If you see a lot of bubbles floating up from the soil, you can poke overly anaerobic and gaseous soils with a chopstick to release the air bubbles.

It is worth noting that eventually the soil will run out of nutrients to feed your plants with.  There is some debate about how long soil lasts or if it ever needs replacing.  Diana Walstad, author of *Ecology of the Planted Aquarium*, does not replace the soil.  She relies on soil to get the plants off to a good head start while supplying important beneficial bacteria to the tank – and then on nutrients from fish waste and mulm to continually feed the plants.  Some of her soil-based aquariums are over a decade old and have never been replaced.  The good news is goldfish are excellent waste producers and can help fertilize the plants.

## Sand

Simply from a purely aesthetic view, sand is quite beautiful.  Aquascapers almost always use sand exclusively, as the smaller grain size gives the illusion of the tank being larger than it really is.  There is a wide variety of sand styles and colors to choose from.

Goldfish are foraging creatures by nature and seem to really enjoy the activity of searching for food in the substrate.  A bare-bottom tank is potentially depriving them of this natural behavior.  Sand also lends a lovely, natural effect at the bottom of the tank and helps deflect some of the glare from the lights above.

Sand is superior to gravel in that it has a far greater surface area for beneficial bacteria to grow.  Finer sands do not allow nearly as much debris to get trapped inside.  A shallow layer (½" or so) with regular vacuuming is the most common.  Most live plants with finer roots like to root in sand.  But sand does not supply any nutrients to the plants.

**Soil & Sand**

As with gravel, soil can also be added underneath sand in a goldfish tank to provide a host of benefits to plants and fish.  Most tropical fishkeepers use 1" sand cap on 1" gravel.  But goldfish are digging fish and large goldfish can easily pop a cap of 1".  I recommend using 2.5" of fine sand or 2-3" of course sand over the soil if that is the case.  But on its own, a 2" fine sand cap can impede water flow and waste penetration to the soil where it can be processed.  Adding Malaysian trumpet snails, rooting plants and blackworms can overcome this problem – essentially merging a Walstad substrate with a freshwater deep sand bed. 3" of course sand is useful to protect the soil from larger digging goldfish. More can be used if needed for very large digging goldfish. For small goldfish, 1.5" of fine sand, with or without burrowing creatures, over the soil should be plenty. The biggest issue I've found with using sand and soil is that when you need to pull up a plant to move it, it mixes the soil in with the sand and can make the substrate look unpleasant.

A deep sand bed can also be used without soil. Please see the section on freshwater deep sand beds for more information.

Some speculate that goldfish could possibly be ingesting the sand at the bottom. Over time, this may accumulate inside their abdomen. There are anecdotal reports of goldfish that have been necropsied and found to have sand inside them. Some say that it is good for goldfish to eat sand because it helps keep their digestive system working. Is it beneficial, or harmful? There is unfortunately a lack of any long-term studies done on fish longevity with a sand substrate, so it is difficult to say one way or another. Each fish owner must do what they think is best for the fish when choosing to keep sand or not and weigh the pros with the potential cons. That said, fish in the wild (including the goldfish's ancestor, the carp) spend most of their lives foraging at the bottom of a body of water that is often comprised of sand without any known problems from such activity. My personal opinion is that, as long as the sand has a large enough grain, the goldfish are able to spit it out easily and do not swallow it. I have found that larger-grain sand is also far more easier to not suck up in a siphon (Crystal River by Caribsea is great). Finer sands will have some initial cloudiness regardless of quality, but this can be remedied by rinsing the sand first and then running a sponge filter for 8-12 hours with periodic squeezing (if needed; as it often isn't).

Sand comes in several colors. White sand offers a bright, fresh look, though it may get a bit dingy over time due to foreign particles mixing in with it – as well as require more frequent vacuuming. Some find that using a tan or neutral colored sand or mixing half black sand with the white is a good way to overcome this (the mixed bottom looks like a stony gray).

I personally recommend avoiding polymer coated sand or sand that has been chemically colored with paints to prevent these contaminants from leaching into the water over time.

For a river-bottom effect, a goldfish-safe and aesthetically interesting option could be to mix in some small pebbles (about dime-sized, or bigger than the goldfish could pick up in its mouth) in with the sand. As long as there is enough sand to prevent waste getting trapped in between the rocks, this kind of mixed substrate could be an interesting and natural-looking bottom for the tank. Some fish, especially older ones with heavily modified body types, may spend a good bit of time sitting at the bottom of the tank.  The courser, quartz-based sands can be a bit abrasive on their stomachs.  By adding a single layer of smooth pebbles pushed about halfway into the sand, this abrasiveness can be reduced – or by only using a soft, fine-grain sand instead.

## Clay-bottom

A clay/mud-bottom aquarium would be much closer to the most natural goldfish substrate. It is what the ancestor of the carp would have in the wild.  There are concerns with the fish creating a very cloudy tank as they constantly suck around through the mud looking for food.  Part of why we keep fish is to watch them – not to see a cloudy mess for a tank!  One might be able to place some pebbles (NOT gravel) mostly submerged in the mud to help hold it down, and though this would interfere with the foraging behavior of the fish, cleaning would still be simple – no gunk would build up between the pebbles (provided there is enough mud between them).  The pebbles should all be larger than the fish's mouth.  The mud would also leach beneficial minerals into the water with time.  This route would primarily be for aesthetics and long-term health of the fish rather than enabling foraging behavior.  Calcium bentonite is an economical, mineral-rich, fish friendly substrate that is widely used as a pond sealant.  It can be obtained from pond suppliers in large quantities and will not harm the fish's gill or digestive function.  Fish kept in ponds with calcium bentonite clay bottoms have been shown to have superior coloration, likely due to the minerals it supplies to the water column.  I have not personally tried this method but feel it is worth mentioning.

Perhaps a more accessible bottom that utilizes the benefits of clay is a fractured volcanic clay substrate.  Products such as CaribSea's Eco-complete or Seachem's Flourite are made of clay, which has a much higher surface area than gravel or even sand.  Clay substrates support a strong colony of beneficial bacteria and can support the development of bacteria that remove nitrates.  The clay sand supports finer roots and does not trap the debris like the gravel kind.  Denitrification has been an advantage I have found from the sands as well.

## Bare-bottom

Bare-bottom is the simplest (and most affordable) of all substrate methods.  Vacuuming it is incredibly easy and if you ever need to medicate the whole tank, your plants (if you have any) will probably be removable and you won't have to worry about anything lingering in your substrate.  You will probably want to do separate mineral supplementation in some form, either by adding it directly to the water column or using a mud refugium.

The cons are it doesn't have that same natural "look" as a substrate.  Part of why we keep goldfish is to enjoy looking at the beautiful setup.  Also, goldfish don't get to exercise much of their natural sifting behaviors, so there is that drawback.  The maintenance advantages can result in easier cleaning, making for a very healthy aquarium.

I recommend bare-bottom tanks to be reserved for breeding, fry-raising or hospital tanks.

## Setting Up Your Goldfish Tank

Gathering the supplies you will need ahead of time can save you time and, in some cases, money. Planning ahead and getting ready to own goldfish before you buy them can save you stress and impromptu trips to the pet store.

**Locating your tank** is important both for you and your fish.  Placing it near a window or in direct sunlight can result in an abundance of algae in the tank, and also a more fluctuation in temperature as the water heats up.  This is just something to be aware of and isn't necessarily bad. Natural window light is free and helps boost plant growth.  Placing the tank in an area that receives a lot of traffic can disturb the goldfish.  Make sure you place it in an area that can tolerate a water spill – even very meticulous fish keepers still have accidents.  Having a stand for your tank is not absolutely necessary, but it can make it easier to view your fish and require less stooping during feeding and tank cleaning.  It can be difficult to get a siphon started with a tank set on the floor, unless you use a kit that connects to the sink or a battery-operated vacuum siphon.  Most stands also offer concealed storage space as well; an added benefit.  You will be surprised how fast it fills up.  A good thing to remember is that the combined weight of a tank filled with water and the stand can be hundreds of pounds, so it is not easy to move and does put strain on the floor. Corners of the room offer more stability.  Some small tanks do not need a special stand and can be placed on a desk or nightstand.

In general, aquariums are best placed near a north or east-facing window.  On hot days it may be necessary to cover the side of the aquarium closest to the light source.  Utilizing natural window light is beneficial for both fish and plants and can even help save your electricity bill by reducing your dependence on artificial lighting.  If your tank is located near a south or west window, it's a good idea to draw the blinds to prevent the tank from overheating.

*Backgrounds*

As far as appearance goes, tanks themselves come in a variety of looks.  For glass aquariums, the most common trim is black plastic rimming, but wood or rimless are also available.  Both the trim and the stand can be primed and painted with special paint for the specific surface material, if you want.  The back and bottom of the tank can also be painted (on the outside!) to minimize the glare if you are not using some kind of a substrate, but this is permanent so you have to be certain that is what you want before doing it.  I personally would rather use a layer of black paper underneath cut to size.  For a look that is a little more flexible but still colorful, you can back the tank with commercially available backgrounds.  For a clean look that helps conceal any cords or tubing trailing behind the tank, I've had success using frost static-cling window film.  Because it's static-cling you can always remove it later, and it's super easy to put on. It adds a very high-end touch that professional aquascapers use.

Something really should be said for the use of acrylic aquariums. These are ideal option for those who want something shatter-proof. Acrylic is 5 times stronger than glass, lighter in weight and can withstand extreme temperatures, making it an ideal material for outdoor or garage tanks. I

own several acrylic aquariums and find them to look exceptionally nice.

*Seaclear Aquariums*

Any tank you buy, whether new or used (but especially used) should be rinsed out thoroughly before use. A used tank should always be sterilized. Particles from the factory or dirt and mineral deposits from previous owners can be easily washed out and dried with a paper towel. As long as the paper towel comes out stained, you need to keep cleaning so you can start with a fresh slate. Some like to brine new tanks (add enough salt so no more dissolves) for 24 hours before using them.

Place the tank on the stand where you have decided to put your aquarium. Be sure you have access to an outlet for electricity. Water is very heavy, so you must be sure the stand will hold up to the challenge.

There are literally dozens of ways to set up a goldfish tank, and there is no one right way. You may find you want to adjust your setup every 6 months or so, or even completely redo things. Your fish tank is your canvas to paint the masterpiece. In the sections on tank size, substrate, plants, filtration and decorations, I've just attempted to show you the paints ☺

# Water Quality

There is probably no aspect of goldfish keeping more overlooked by the general public as water quality, which is really unfortunate because there is probably no other factor nearly as important. Clean water is as critical to goldfish as clean air is to people.  When the quality of the water is off, everything else will get thrown off as well, causing a "domino effect."  I maintain that while good water quality isn't the only element necessary for goldfish care, *it is the most fundamental.*

You don't have to guess if your water is safe for goldfish – it's easy to know exactly what is going on with easy tests.  Testing the water regularly doesn't require you to leave the house every time; you can do it right by your tank!  Kits are available at most pet stores or online and are well worth the price.  There are strip tests, liquid tests and constant detection tests.  Papers strip tests seem to be the most affordable at first glance but there are fewer of them; liquid tests will give you more bang for your buck and are more accurate, but it can be trickier to read the results depending on the lighting and/or your unique color perception.  Liquid test kits are also often comprised of toxic chemicals which should not be disposed of into the environment (not down the drain).  They also take a bit of time to mix up and process.  For those reasons, I recommend using a test strip kit for weekly monitoring of pH nitrite, nitrate, KH and GH.  Ammonia will need a separate kit.  I like using Seachem's ammonia and pH alert pack for constant readings.

A quick word of advice... tests never trump the goldfish themselves. If the fish is not looking or acting like it should yet the tests read fine, don't assume they are accurate.  Fluctuations can happen.  And the tests themselves are not always very accurate because the scientific grade test kits – which are 30 times more accurate than

*Alert Pack*  *Test Strips*

commercially available ones – are much more expensive, too expensive to sell to pet stores for the average hobbyist.  Water tests also will not inform you of the count of bad bacteria or dissolved organic matter (rotting debris).  What I am saying is there are other things at play in your water, but testing parameters is the right place to start.

Anyone who wants to own goldfish should still have a test kit that covers these parameters (in order of importance):

## Ammonia

What is ammonia anyway?  Ammonia is the byproduct of goldfish waste.  Goldfish produce 25% of their ammonia through solid waste, and the other 75% as they breathe (respiration).  This means that trying to suck every little particle of goldfish poo will not be enough to take out all of the ammonia, and even very little fish produce large volumes of it.  Fortunately, there are natural processes that remove ammonia from your tank, which we will cover in depth later. More than any other killer of all aquarium fish worldwide, ammonia is the most deadly. How much ammonia is acceptable in the goldfish tank? The answer is, none. 0 ppm is what you want to see on the test. If you can detect it, your fish aren't safe. When there is ammonia building up in the water, the goldfish cannot release it properly and it poisons them. We will get into the symptoms of this kind of poisoning later on.

50% daily water changes are recommended to protect a tank suffering from ammonia until it consistently tests negative.

## Nitrite

Nitrite is a converted form of ammonia. Though slightly less deadly, it is still dangerous to goldfish health and should not ever be detected. Levels over 0 ppm can start causing problems in your tank. For goldfish, it irritates the skin and gills and makes it difficult for the goldfish's blood system to work properly.

If you have a nitrite spike, performing daily water changes of 50% for 2-3 weeks is recommended until the crisis is over.

## PH

The pH of the water tells you how acidic or alkaline your water is. It comes on a scale of 0 to 14, with 0 being the most acidic, 14 being the most alkaline and 7 being neutral. A high pH (7.8 to 8.5) can hurt your fish indirectly by making the toxins in the water stronger than they already are, while a low pH can hurt your goldfish directly by burning them. For goldfish, the most ideal pH is 7.4 – the same pH as human blood.

If your pH is on the high end, I would not recommend trying to bring it down unless it is over 9 or you suspect it is causing problems for your goldfish. This can cause more stress than needed. Instead, focus on ensuring that the water is free of ammonia and nitrite.

If your pH is on the low end out of the tap, a buffer may be necessary. Crushed coral can help to naturally stabilize the pH in a safe range for goldfish. The pH of an aquarium naturally drops over time and can be disastrous if your KH is on the low end (more on that later).

*Crushed Coral*

## Nitrate

Nitrate is the converted form of nitrite and is harmless to fish in levels under 30 ppm. It is a kind of fertilizer for the plants in the tank and really contributes to algae growth.

It used to be thought that nitrate in any quantity was safe for goldfish, but that has been proven false, as high levels of nitrate suppress the immune system and cause other health issues. Nitrates will only show up once the tank has cycled. It is best to try to keep your nitrates under 20ppm on a regular basis.

These are the most critical parameters to keep track of in your goldfish tank, though there are others that can provide more information about the conditions and stability of your goldfish's water.

## Tips for Lower Nitrates

Nitrate control is important for maintaining a healthy tank. But most aquarium filters will be producing nitrates if they are working properly. The average hobbyist is faced with the task of performing regular partial water changes in an effort to keep it within the acceptable range. But water changes may have their own set of drawbacks. The most obvious one is the workload. Spending time maintaining the tank is not as enjoyable as spending time watching it. The more tanks you have the greater your burden becomes.

There is also a line of thinking that tanks that chronically have nitrate levels that must be maintained via water changes have not achieved a "full cycle." I tend to agree.

So, is there a way to avoid becoming a slave to your nitrate levels and keep them under control without water changes? Good news: there is. And not just one.

**1. Utilize Nitrate Reducing Filter Media**

Certain types of filter media can support the growth of good anaerobic bacteria that consume nitrate. To work properly, you usually need to have a lot of it and pair it with a very slow flow rate. Stronger flows are better for aerobic respiration (better suited for bacteria converting ammonia to nitrite). It is worth noting that water conditioners that bind nitrate (i.e. Prime) can prevent this kind of bacteria from multiplying. It's important to note that not everyone who tries this method experiences a full cycle, due to various factors in their tank, and that some report more success with the addition of a carbon source. Bacteria that consume nitrate without creating nitrite may be slow to develop. It may take up to 4-6 months for this to happen.

**2. Utilizing Live Plants**

Very heavily planted tanks often keep nitrate levels very low naturally. While not their preferred food source (live plants prefer ammonia and nitrite to nitrate) they will feast on it if the other two aren't available. Floating plants are better at exporting nutrients than submersible ones. However, **live plants alone do not seem to be enough to totally remove all nitrates** in many cases.

Many people have heavily planted tanks full of lush growth that still have chronic nitrate issues. Sumps that contain a refugium with a large plant or algae mass have been demonstrated to effectively control nitrates, as well as a tank with an aquaponic filtration system.

Live plants can also be used to remove nitrates in an **aquaponics setup**. As an added bonus, your fish help grow your food! It is rewarding in many ways. Please note that live plants growing in an aquaponic setup are not only effective in removing nitrates – they can also absorb growth inhibiting hormones, allowing the fish to grow to full size even in a tank without water changes.

## 3. Utilizing Substrate

Anaerobic bacterial activity in substrates can contribute to nitrate reduction. This includes deep sand beds and substrates that include soil or clay. The bacteria that consume nitrate may take a long time to populate, in my experience. I had a test fishbowl set up with a soil substrate that had consistent readings of 40ppm nitrate for about 3 or 4 months. I did not change the water at all during that time. Then out of the blue it started dropping rapidly until it hit 0 and has remained there ever since. The longer the tank has been established the better the chances of developing a full cycle. Another tank of mine had consistent weekly nitrate readings of 40ppm for nearly a year. I switched the substrate from a typical fine grain sand to a volcanic clay sand (Flourite black sand) of about 1.5-2" deep, and not long after (I believe it was only around 3 months) the nitrates started dropping until they hit 0 and stayed there. I was able to relinquish all water changes and top-off evaporation only each week.

A soil substrate offers the benefit of a source of organic carbon. Carbon is a very important energy source for plants. By feeding the plants, you enable them to better consume nitrates. Live plants and a carbon-rich substrate can work together for effective nitrate removal. Some folks that keep a dirted aquarium experience the benefits of consistently low or no nitrates.

A deep sand substrate can facilitate denitrification, and when set up properly poses no ill effects to the fish from hydrogen sulfide. Deep sand beds are popular among saltwater fishkeepers. I'll talk more about deep sand beds later on in more detail.

Smaller grain clay-based substrates have an extremely high surface area for bacteria to grow (far greater than regular sand), which means you can use a shallower substrate while still benefiting from anaerobic respiration. A 1.5" layer of clay sand such as Flourite black sand can function as a denitrifying medium without interfering as much with the swimming space of the fish.

## 4. Utilizing Algae

Certain types of algae readily consume nitrate and can even act in place of the primary filter in certain setups, eating up ammonia, nitrite and nitrate. But not everyone wants to have a tank covered in green slime – though the fish seem to enjoy it as they feast on it throughout the day. (An algae-rich diet coupled with natural sunlight is a great way to get colorful, growing goldfish.)

Algae scrubbing filters can be used as a way to grow a concentrated mass of green algae in a concealed compartment. An additional benefit is that they can help out-compete nuisance algae from growing in the tank by eating their food. There are DIY versions, or you can opt for a pre-made solution.

*Algae Scrubbers*

## 5. Avoid overfeeding

Excessive food translates into higher nitrates. By feeding the fish only what they need to sustain them and avoiding overfeeding, your nitrates will be easier to manage. Feeding more than required for survival is acceptable in certain situations, such as during conditioning for breeding or if trying to grow out smaller fish, but expect to perform more maintenance.

## KH

Carbonate Hardness (KH) helps to stabilize the pH. The ideal range is between 50 – 120 ppm. A low KH will result in a continually dipping or suddenly crashing pH, which is very dangerous to goldfish.

If your KH is under 100ppm, a slow-release buffer in the filter would be a good idea to keep your pH in check. Crushed coral (added to the filter in a mesh bag) is a great option, starting at ½ cup per 20 gallons. Keeping a buffer in your filter is a good "safety net" to prevent a pH dip or crash from happening and potentially harming or killing your beautiful collection even if your KH is between the recommended range.

On the other hand, distilled water (due to its lack of minerals) will do the opposite by lowering the KH. Generally goldfish like a high KH anyway, so there is usually no need to reduce it unless it is over 300ppm.

Together, GH and KH make up what we call "Hardness." Hard water has high KH and GH levels, and soft water has low KH and GH levels. Goldfish prefer hard water.

## GH

GH, or General Hardness, is the measure of all minerals in the water (including KH). If you want to know a measure of the mineral content of your water, you can subtract the KH from the GH reading. It is still possible to have a lot of minerals in the water but have a low pH because minerals alone do not affect it directly.

GH will let you know if your water is hard or soft. Hard waters have lots of dissolved minerals while soft water has less.

The ideal range for GH is 100 ppm to 300 ppm. A GH over 300 ppm is harmful to goldfish. Crushed coral contains minerals to help raise your GH. These minerals, such as calcium and magnesium, are also beneficial to goldfish health. Crushed coral should be replaced every few months.

**How often should you test your water?**

In new tanks (that have not been cycled) or in cycled tanks where fish have newly been added, the water should be tested daily before each water change.

*Alert Pack*

For a tank that is still cycling, this should be daily. For mature setups that have been around and stable for a few months, testing the water should be done at the end of every week. It is recommended to test the pH of your water on a daily basis. Because I don't want to manually run tests every day, I use the Seachem's ammonia and pH alert pack. It only requires one quick glance.

**Checking (and correcting) your water source**

The quality of the water you are starting with in your aquarium should not be overlooked. Most water contains chlorine and chloromines which need to be removed with a proper water conditioner. But that's not always the end of the story - some water sources have even more issues right out of the faucet. High nitrates, ammonia or nitrite levels, a low pH or a low alkalinity can make water changes worsen the situation rather than remedy it.

Testing your water source periodically is highly recommended so you know what you are working with and can make changes if needed prior to adding the water to the tank. The water authorities may change their methods of treating the water without warning, or a sudden runoff from an intensive agricultural area could lead to a big change in your water source that can negatively impact your fish. One benefit of aging and aerating your water allows you to check it or adjust it before adding it to the tank after it has sat for a bit. Finally, the temperature should also be matched to avoid placing undue stress on the fish.

## Water Conditioners

Nearly all water that comes from the tap contains chlorine and chloramines, which fish can't live in. That is why it is a must to have some kind of water conditioner which removes those deadly chemicals.  Fish placed in water that contains typical levels of chlorine will suffer from its toxicity and eventually die.  Some tap suppliers do add ammonia to their water, especially in the spring time, so it can be helpful to perform a complete water test on your tap water so you know what you are working with.

The kind of water conditioner you choose will depend upon the kind of water you have.  The most basic water conditioner is one that removes one or both of these.  Some may also detoxify ammonia and nitrite.  I like those kinds because they can also be used during a water quality emergency and also help during cycling the tank.

### Seachem Prime

Seachem Prime is one such water conditioner.  It eliminates chlorine, chloromines, ammonia, nitrite, and can also help with neutralizing some heavy metals.  However, it will not take out all contaminants from the water, such as pharmaceuticals and fluoride, which are sadly present in much tap water.  Some fishkeepers, such as myself, do not like having those contaminants in their fish's water (or their own).  It also will not remove copper and has the possibility to make copper more toxic because it is a reducing agent.  For this reason, it should not be used until after 48 hours when treating with copper treatements.  But, overall, it is an affordable and useful product. Because it binds nitrate, it may inhibit nitrate removal by certain bacteria.

*Seachem Prime*

### ATM Paradigm

If you want to use a water conditioner that removes chlorine and chloromines without chemicals, ATM Paradigm can be very useful.  The liquid is a shiny golden color and is made of Vitamin C.  Vitamin C plays an important role in boosting the immune system of the fish.  Using it on a weekly basis can help protect fish from disease.  It is not as concentrated as Prime and does not remove heavy metals, but it may not be necessary depending on your water source or if you keep a planted tank.

*Seachem Prime*

# The Nitrogen Cycle

Every fishkeeper should have a basic understanding of the nitrogen cycle if they want to be successful at keeping fish without live plants or carbon. As an overview, the nitrogen cycle is basically how the toxic waste goldfish produce never gets to a dangerous level. Here's how it works:

The cycle begins when goldfish are introduced into the tank. The fish food goes into the fish and comes out as waste. Then **ammonia** from that waste and their gills is released into the water. A kind of beneficial bacteria called *Nitrosomonas* comes along and eats the ammonia, turning it into **nitrite**. Nitrite is less deadly, but is still toxic and causes sick fish. Another beneficial bacteria comes along called *Nitrobacter*, which then takes the nitrite and turns it into **nitrate**. Nitrate is the final product of the nitrogen cycle, and is then used for plant nutrition or removed out with water changes. Best of all, it is way less toxic to fish than ammonia. Goldfish nibble on the plants, create more waste, and the cycle begins all over again.

The nitrogen cycle is necessary to keep the water clean – you can't do without it! And it can only take place normally in an aquarium that has gone through the complete cycle once. This is why every goldfish owner must cycle their tank before adding fish! If you put a fish in an uncycled tank, there is not enough ammonia-converting *Nitrosomonas* and nitrite-converting *Nitrobacter* to take away the toxins, and they just build and build until the goldfish becomes very sick and finally dies. This happens so frequently with first time goldfish owners that it has been dubbed **New Tank Syndrome**. The only way to avoid New Tank Syndrome is to totally cycle your tank, and I am going to tell you how to do that later.

## Cycling Your Tank

There is a lot of confusing information surrounding the matter of cycling the tank, some of which has been given out even by uninformed pet store workers. When I got my first fancy goldfish, I was told that it might be a good idea to set up the tank, add water and let it sit for a couple of days before putting in my fish but that it wasn't totally necessary. This advice may have worked if I used carbon in my filter or utilized live plants, but without either one of those there is nothing to take out the toxins. So I took home my fish that same day to the tank. Needless to say, I lost my fish within a month or so without understanding what had happened.

So what does cycling involve? It basically means you need to build up a colony of good bacteria who can work to remove the toxic waste that your goldfish will produce. They live mostly in the filter, but also cover the surfaces inside the tank. That is why having a filtration system in place

24/7 is not optional if you are going to keep fish – that is, unless you plan on doing a LOT of water changes to compensate.

To start the cycle, you will need three things: an aquarium filled with treated water, a running filter, and a source of ammonia. It is important to treat the water in your tank first because water straight from the tap contains chlorine added by the water company. Chlorine kills all bacteria – both good kinds and bad kinds – and that will prevent you from getting a colony started. But if you have well water, this step won't be necessary in most cases.

You will also need a bit of time for the bacteria to become established (if you don't introduce a bacteria source to start with). I know this is hard to take when you are really excited to get your goldfish, but if you rush things and run out and get a fish before the cycle has been completed, then the bacteria colony won't be built up strong enough to handle the waste load of your fish and your fish will suffer as a result (that is, unless you follow the secret cycling shortcut... keep reading to find out!). The fact is traditional fish tank cycling does not happen overnight. It doesn't even happen in a week. For a tank to become fully cycled and ready to receive fish, it usually takes up to 3 to 6 weeks starting from scratch. The process can be sped up by raising the temperature to about 82 degrees F.

The process can be kick started if you can get some beneficial bacteria from an already established tank's filter into your filter, but you would need a very trusted source because you could also bring disease into your tank that way.

As an ammonia source, some recommend using raw shrimp, fish food or feeder fish. One of the most common methods is to use liquid ammonia out of a bottle. This process is called the fishless cycle.

I recommend the fishless cycle because it really isn't necessary to expose any fish to the very dangerous toxins of an uncycled aquarium and other "disposable" fish can also introduce disease into your tank, which can spread to any future fish you get. Please don't do that. Feeder fish are known for harboring them because they are kept in very crowded conditions. Not only that, but you cannot control the amount of ammonia they produce at any given time. Raw shrimp can create ammonia, but it can also introduce nasty bacteria as it decays in the tank that lead to sickness in fish.

Some hobbyists like to use fish food to seed their filter. It takes about the same time as the liquid ammonia method (3-6 weeks). Ammonia should show up in the first 3 days. More food is needed if it doesn't. Rotting fish food may lead to an increase in heterotrophic bacteria that can favor disease.

The cycle will start immediately once liquid ammonia is added to the tank. With aquarium ammonia, you know how much ammonia has been put in the water from the beginning. For the pre-measured aquarium kind, 1 drop per gallon will give you exactly 2ppm of ammonia.

*Liquid Ammonia*

If you are using the household cleaning kind (must be unscented!) then you will have to use an eye dropper to gradually add a few drops of ammonia to the tank water, then use your test kit to test the water. This will have to be repeated a few times – ammonia, test, ammonia, test – until you have added 2 ppm of ammonia.

You will have to do this daily get the readings up to 2 ppm. Each day, test for ammonia and nitrite. When nitrite appears in the test readings that means the cycle is in progress. When nitrite and ammonia readings are finally 0 ppm and nitrates start showing up that means the tank has fully cycled and it is "safe" to add fish.

Some tips:

- Do not stop adding ammonia until you get the fish.
- The warmer you keep the water, the faster the cycle will complete. Without fish in the water, you can turn the heater up into the high eighties without worrying about hurting them – just make sure to *turn it down before putting in fish!*
- A higher oxygen concentration will also help the beneficial bacteria to multiply, so providing plenty of aeration can help with building your colony.

By waiting until the tank has cycled before getting your goldfish, you will ensure that they come to a safe environment to live. You will also be far less stressed by not having to constantly worry about a sudden high ammonia surge as the parameters struggle to remain balanced. And we could all use a bit less stress now, couldn't we?

Remember, even if you have made it through the fishless cycling process and have an ammonia reading of 0, things can still go wrong unless you do lots of large water changes and feed sparingly as the tank adjusts. The bacteria you have won't be very diverse at first, which is necessary to keep things under control. It's still a sensitive time for another few weeks. Testing the water daily for a few weeks is a wise course of action.

Now you know why introducing a goldfish to a tank which has not been cycled, has no carbon or plants and then following the ordinary recommended routine for regular tank maintenance will inevitably take your goldfish to bad health or death.  This is because there is no beneficial bacteria colony built up to handle the unexpected waste load of your fish, so the water parameters for deadly ammonia and nitrite will skyrocket.  When a fish is negatively affected by this (as will almost always happen) it manifests as New Tank Syndrome.  Avoiding New Tank Syndrome is critical when getting new fish.

## Secret Cycling Shortcuts

**Caring for an Uncycled Aquarium**

Sometimes fish keepers intentionally or accidentally end up with fish in a tank that has not been cycled. A filter is present, but the nitrogen cycle has not been completed. In this case, I recommend four things:

- **Water changes** are your best friend with an uncycled tank.  Doing them will slow the progress of the cycle but will protect your fish from dangerous toxins that can quickly and unexpectedly build up. 90% daily is ideal, but 50% every day to every other day is highly advised.  If you can age your water, great.  If not, the water change itself is more pressing.

*Seachem Prime*

- **Ammonia binders** can help protect the fish from surges in ammonia and perhaps nitrite, depending on the brand. Seachem Prime is an excellent product for this.
- **Beneficial bacteria supplements** are something that in the past I've dismissed, but after further research have concluded to be something that can be very useful during cycling with fish to speed up the process.  Not all bacterial supplements are created equal.  Many offer hit-and-miss results.  But ATM Colony Pro is the most probably the best of the commercial available bacteria supplements, consuming ammonia and nitrite.

*ATM Colony Pro*

- **Reduce or remove feed** to slow the accumulation of ammonia.  Food is quickly converted to ammonia, and reducing that will help in a large way.  Focus on providing leafy foraging materials for the fish almost exclusively so they don't feel hungry.  I would advise feeding protein food only twice weekly until things have evened out.
- **Salt** is beneficial to use to protect your fish when nitrites start showing up at 1 teaspoon per 5 gallons, and replace the removed salt each time you do a water change.

This method can help to prevent your fish from having to go through New Tank Syndrome and the cycle will mature "under the hood" as it would by cycling manually.  You will then be able to decrease the water changes and increase feeding to normal amounts.  Please note that it may take longer to establish a strong biofilter using this method than cycling with bottled ammonia beforehand, so more frequent water changes may be necessary in the first month or two.  Once nitrates start showing up, you are nearing the end of the cycle.  Watch for algae growth on the walls and decorations in the tank.   Once nitrates show up, you can gradually start to resume feeding to normal amounts.  Regularly testing the water after nitrates start showing up can help indicate how soon after a partial water change it rises to over 20ppm.  Once nitrates reach over 20ppm, a partial water change is in order.

It is best to avoid using any medications in the main tank as they can interfere with the bacteria as they establish their colony.

Did you know it is possible to completely, entirely *skip* the fish-free or fish-in cycling process altogether by utilizing enough live plants with or without a substrate with a soil layer?  (Both combined will give you the best results.)  That said, it is still important to test the water after adding new fish each day to ensure things are going smoothly.  If at any time ammonia or nitrite is detected, a water change may be in order.  Live plants use ammonia and nitrite as a food source, while the bacteria in soil quickly seeds your aquarium filter with nitrifying bacteria.

It is recommended to let the plants grow in for a week or so before adding fish.

# Bacteria: The Double-Edged Sword

In every established aquarium (meaning tanks that have cycled for several weeks) there are tiny little "bugs" too small to see. There are two kinds – good and bad.

## Good Bacteria

The good bacteria have a very important role to play in the tank. Their job is to break down waste and crud in the tank and convert it into a much safer form – and by doing so they get the meals they need to stay alive. It's a win-win situation.

When there is a lot of food available, they multiply. If there isn't enough, their numbers go down as they die off. This is how they regulate themselves. You don't have to get them in a bottle – they already exist in the water and the air, the fish and the plants. It's like they come out of nowhere.

So what do they eat? As we covered previously, this is the best part for you (and your fish)... ammonia and nitrite (the byproducts of fish waste and uneaten food) are their favorite foods. They take those dangerous toxins and turn them into the much safer nitrate, creating a cycled tank. They don't eat nitrate though. Plants and/or water changes remove nitrate, but water changes are important for more reasons than just reducing nitrate as we've already learned.

Without good bacteria, your tank wouldn't be able to sustain your fish for very long.

Where do they live? Beneficial bacteria live on surfaces in the tank, such as walls, the plants, and especially the surfaces in the filter. They cling to the filter media very tightly. They DON'T swim around in the water. Again, part of why it's a myth that too much filter cleaning will destroy them (more on that later). You can swish and squeeze your filter media all you want, but they won't come off. Only tap water will kill them.

## Bad Bacteria

This is where we really need to watch out. Bad bacteria are a very dangerous thing for goldfish, especially when the fish's immune system is weakened. You can't see them with the naked eye. A few of them can get a foothold on a goldfish whose immune system is already shot, and a large number of them can stress the immune system of a healthy goldfish until the fish is overcome.

As the name implies, bad bacteria (the most common being *"Aeromonas," "Pseudomonas"* or *"Columnaris"* for those who care) are the enemies of your tank. We're talking a big culprit for all manner of heinous aquarium crimes, including *body ulcers, pop eye, bloat, mouth rot* and more. In all these conditions they are eating your fish alive.

They will multiply and reproduce to the point when they are out of control, especially when:

- Oxygen is low
- There are high amounts of dissolved organics in the water
- There is a lot of rotting debris or mulm (gross crud, often whitish)
- There is built up waste from overfeeding or infrequent cleaning paired with a lack of nutrient recycling
- The water is stagnant in trapped pockets, such as in gravel or pebble beds

**Filters** should be cleaned whenever the flow becomes restricted.

**Some kinds of substrate** are also a perfect home for bad bacteria. In a bare-bottom tank, goldfish will stir up the bottom constantly looking for food. As they plow through the waste it prevents things from becoming stagnant and creating toxic gasses. But in a tank with a layer of gravel or pebbles only at the bottom, fish waste will fall in between the cracks where the fish can't get to it. It then gets trapped, and without the microorganisms needed to properly break it down it begins to decompose and release large amounts of toxic gasses into the pocket. If a fish or a fish keeper with a siphon should turn up the gravel where that is happening, a "mini-bomb" of toxic gas may be released into the tank. It can also slowly leach into the water around it as it festers undisturbed, which some theorize can cause disease.

The first thing to do if your tank has a bad bacteria problem is to clean everything thoroughly in old tank water and remove any layer of substrate you might have while doing 75% water changes daily, removing visible particles of crud. A course of treatment may be necessary for fish that have been infected and aren't improving with clean water over the course of a week or more – likely the fish is dealing with a secondary bacterial infection. You can read more about that in the treatments section.

# Tank Maintenance

Like every pet, goldfish need their aquariums to be taken care of. It isn't just a "set it up once and then you can sit back" kind of thing. They need you to be there for them to make sure things run smoothly. As a goldfish owner, their very lives depend on you to keep their environment steady and safe. What are some of the responsibilities you have as far as tank maintenance goes?

## Water Changes

In today's standard tank, periodic water changes are required to keep the system in balance – even after the cycling process has completed. Without them, minerals deplete and the pH starts to plummet. Nitrate continues to rise to dangerous levels. Waste builds up and leads to an increase in bad bacteria. Ammonia and nitrate may spike. The substrate can start to go overly anaerobic. Unless the hobbyist intervenes by performing a water change (which requires more than a top-off), the livestock can be wiped out – even overnight. Not long after the water change, these issues start building up again... requiring yet another water change. Rinse and repeat.

But being a slave to water changes for regular tank maintenance can take the joy out of fishkeeping. Most people live busy lives, and this chore can put more burden on them. So this caused me to question whether or not there is a way to overcome this dilemma, which not only reduces the labor of fishkeeping, but creates a more self-reliant aquarium that allows for greater stability and safety of the fish.

This means we need to ensure our tanks do the following in order to avoid the vicious water change cycle:

- **Replenish minerals & save the pH** – There are several ways to do this. One is simply to add some seashells or crushed coral to the tank. These replenish minerals and keep the pH from sagging. These should be replaced every 6 months or when water tests indicate. Another is to utilize soil in the substrate. Soil contains minerals as well which perform a similar function and keep the pH from dipping too low.
- **Breakdown waste naturally** – Natural processes can break down waste, including microorganisms and creatures that eat fish waste such as snails and aquatic worms. Soil contains a host of bacteria that break down the waste. You can do one method or the other or both. It's up to you.
- **Use live plants** – These help eat up excess ammonia and nitrite and can even be used as a primary filter.
- **Reduce nitrates naturally** – Please see the section on nitrates for suggestions.

**Aging & aerating water**

This may prove useful for those who perform large water changes. In general, it is not necessary to age or aerate the water when performing a water change under 30%. But in other cases, it may be useful to consider otherwise.

Many goldfish keepers and breeders, including those in Asia, routinely age and aerate their water as part of their husbandry practices.

Isn't simply dechlorinating the tap water enough, if there are no other water quality issues from the water supply? Initially it seems that having safe water parameters and no chlorine or chloromines means the water is perfect for goldfish. But there's one problem: this kind of water is not what goldfish are used to. In a healthy, established tank, there are in fact tons of microorganisms and bacteria that support the immune system of the fish. Suddenly replacing that with a large volume of "sterile" water completely void of life may lead to stress.

We have been told all our lives in many respects that "sterile" means healthy. Many methods have been developed to wipe out bacteria thinking we are getting rid of those nasty little "germs," but not all bacteria are bad. In fact, many are important and even essential for health. What we really want is water that is clean from waste and has a strong, healthy bacteria presence that keeps bad bacteria in check.

By letting the water go through an aging process prior to adding it to the tank, you are allowing microorganisms to start colonizing the water – organisms that goldfish would have if they lived in their native waters. However, admittedly not very many will be there compared to in an established tank or a lake. If you want your fish to live in a probiotic-rich environment, an aquarium that contains plants and soil with minimal water changes is ideal and easy. But in some cases such as breeding or fry raising tanks, such a setup is not desirable to many.

Do you have to add a water conditioner when aging the water? For most, the answer is probably yes. Chlorine will evaporate overnight, but chloromines will not. They will bind the chlorine and keep it from evaporating. Not only that, but heavy metals and other chemicals will remain unless neutralized by the proper water treatment.

Along with dechlorinating the water (and adjusting the pH or other parameters if necessary), aging and aerating the water for a few days is a recommended regular part of the water change routine for hobbyists that remove more than 20% of the water at a time with an aquarium siphon. If you follow what I teach regarding filtration and feeding, large water changes probably won't be necessary for your ordinary routine, unless you are trying to grow out a spawn of many small fish who will require more food and produce more waste – or have sick fish on your hands. If you simply do not have

*Aquarium Siphon*

*Pump*

room to age your water and your fish are sick from poor water quality, the water change itself is more important than aging it.

Aging water requires space, a large container (large garbage bins are sometimes used) or empty tank, and a pump with hosing to refill the aquarium.

Is aging your water mandatory?  That probably depends on the source of the water.  Aging your water is highly recommended:

- If you have well water
- If your fish have been having unexplained, mysterious health issues or deaths
- If you are trying to make your goldfish grow quickly
- If you are trying to induce spawning
- If you need to make pH adjustments straight from the water source
- If your water has dissolved gasses that cause bubbles that stick to the insides of surfaces in the tank (when the temperatures are matched) during a water change
- If your water has carbon dioxide that causes the pH to start low and quickly rise overnight
- If your goldfish show signs of stress during or following a large water change

If you simply do not have the space, desire or capability to age your water and the above does not apply, your fish may do just fine without the aging process.

For larger and/or bucket-free water changes, you can follow the below method for doing water changes.

**How to Do Larger Water Changes**

Large water changes can be very useful for goldfish.  Whether you need to remove medications from the water, are treating a sick fish, are doing a fish-in cycle or simply prefer to do larger water changes as part of your regular maintenance, there is a simple and relatively quick way to do so.

It is not necessary to take your goldfish out of the tank while performing a large water change, unless you remove all of the water.  This adds the stress of capture on them.  Instead of putting them in a bucket or another container while you change the water, in most cases you can simply leave them in while you do your thing and they'll do theirs.  Just try not to bang on the tank with the siphon or that might frighten them.  Most of the time it is not necessary to remove anything from the tank, whether plants or decorations – you can just scoot them around to get to the waste lodged underneath.

The following method requires no bucket-hauling. Here is how to perform a water change in 10 easy steps:

1. To perform a water change, you need to start by disconnecting your filter and heater. This is especially important because when the water level goes down, the heater may break (and this has happened to me before) and the filter (depending on the kind) will no longer be able to draw in water. Plus it's just a good safety measure.

2. Connect the end of your Python aquarium water change system to the nearest sink by removing the sink's aeration cap and attaching the brass adapter by screwing it onto the sink's threads. Make sure the green nozzle is in the "drain" position and turn on the water. This will create a vacuum pressure at the other end of the tube. You may need to adjust the water flow depending on how powerful the suction needs to be.

*Python Water Change System*

3. Depending on how small your fish is, you may want to put some netting over the end of the siphon, secured with a rubber band, to prevent your fish from getting sucked up (which *can* happen). Even adult goldfish might get curious and get stuck in the hose, so netting can be a very good idea. Remember that if there is ever an emergency (say you suck up a fish or the hosing snaps), there is a white switch on the hosing you can flip to temporarily stop the flow of the water from coming or going – but don't rely on it too long because the pressure will make it give!

4. Place the free end of the siphon into the water. The water will begin to be pulled out of the tank and go into the sink. You will want to lightly drag the opening of the siphon across the bottom of the tank, making sure to focus on the areas where debris builds up. Continue to vacuum the bottom of the tank until you have drained the percentage of water you want. You will want to spend the majority of the siphon time at the bottom of the tank where the debris are to make sure you really get the crud out.

5. Go to the sink and turn it off.

6. It is time to treat the aquarium with your water conditioner to prepare for the refill. You will want to dose the water that is left for the entire tank volume, not just the water that is there. Follow the directions on the water conditioner and pour in the amount needed.

7. Return to the sink and turn it on again (after reconnecting the adapter if using a separate hose for refilling). I recommend using a digital, waterproof thermometer to match the temperature within 2 degrees. Once it passes the test, turn the green nozzle to the "fill" position" and the water will flow from the sink to the tank. Don't forget to leave the other end of the python in the tank while you do this, or you will end up with a very big puddle on

*Digital Waterproof Thermometer*

the floor!  Don't stop filling the tank until the water has reached about a half an inch or so from the top.  There's no reason to not take advantage of the full volume of your tank and give your fish as much possible room to swim.

8.  You can either flip the white switch to stop the water flow until you get to the sink or just time it so you turn off the sink by hand without letting the tank overflow.

9.  After removing the siphon from the tank, you will need to once again pull the green nozzle into the "drain" position and turn it on to empty the extra water still sitting in the tube.

10. Once all the water has been pulled out, you can wind up the hose and store it away until the next use.

It is recommended to perform water changes slowly (especially if you are doing a large water change) to avoid undue stress on the fish and let them adjust to the new water, which may have compressed gasses.

It is also a good idea to use two hoses – one for removing dirty water from the tank and one for refilling the clean water.  This is because over time the fish tank water will cause dark mold to grow in the tubing, even when periodically cleaned, and this buildup is of questionable effect on the fish.

**How much water should you change and how often?**

Your water change schedule depends on three main factors:

- Your filtration setup and age
- Your stocking levels
- Your feeding regimen

All of these play a role in one thing: your water quality.

In an established system, it is important for you to change the water frequently enough so that your nitrate readings are consistently under 30ppm.  With the right feeding schedule and a wet/dry filtration setup, you shouldn't have to change the water more than once monthly to remove solid waste.  This should typically be about 20%. If you utilize a filtration method that does not reduce nitrates, this may need to be larger and more frequent. (Please note that if you have nitrates coming straight out of your water source before you ever test the tank water, you may need to use a nitrate reducer as excessive nitrates can harm fish.)

If you have the capability, time or desire to do more frequent or larger water changes with aged, aerated water to promote faster growth of your fish, more power to you.  I prefer to limit reliance on water changes for many reasons in most cases.

For therapeutic reasons, sick fish may require more frequent water changes to remove pathogens. An uncycled or very overstocked aquarium will also need more frequent water changes and should be tested daily prior to each water change. A biologically strong, established filter (such as the Wet/Dry filter) will reduce the need for as many water changes because it helps keep nitrates lower. The need for water changes depends, in a large part, on the levels of nitrate in the tank. Weekly testing can let you know if you are keeping your nitrates under the recommended level of no more than 30ppm.

*Aquarium Siphon*

In some cases, weekly or every other week water changes of 10-20% to remove the debris at the bottom is perfectly acceptable as well, if you feel like being more aggressive with your tank hygiene.

Changing any one of these factors outlined previously will most likely require a change in the frequency and/or amount of water changes.

It is probably worth mentioning that larger, more frequent water changes, provided they are done with aged, aerated water that has been properly treated, are rarely a bad thing for fish. They can even help with faster growth. The benefits of this must be weighted with the additional time required to perform them, as well as the additional expense reflected in the water bill.

A word of caution: if you already have goldfish but you haven't been doing large water changes, you do not want to start doing them abruptly unless there is a problem with the fish itself which requires more immediate intervention. This is because your fish can become used to high nitrates, but when the frequent water changes begin your nitrates will go way down. This could potentially shock your fish because they are not used to that big of a difference in that parameter.

**Signs You May Need to Do a Water Change...**

- Ammonia or nitrite readings
- High nitrate
- Foul or strong fishy smell
- Tinted water color (i.e. cloudy, yellowish, brownish or green)
- Excess suspended waste or large piles of waste on the bottom
- An overabundance of planarian worms (little white wriggling "strings")
- And, of course, sick or not quite right fish

**The role of minerals**

Once the water is dechlorinated, aged and aerated and there are beneficial microorganisms, there's only one last thing that could make it any better: essential minerals.

In the wild, minerals play a more significant role than we might expect. They are found in the mud bottoms of ponds. Koi (which are cousins of the goldfish) that are provided these trace minerals show brighter colors, better overall health and even the reversal of some diseases. Mineral deficiency can be a problem with fish that are kept confined in domesticity.

Remineralizing the water can be done through commercially available supplements. Perhaps the most ideal way is the most natural way: periodically adding a small amount of calcium bentonite clay, which contains the minerals found in the mud bottoms of rivers and ponds.

## Probiotic Bacteria Supplementation

I strongly advocate using a probiotic bacteria supplement in your aquarium as a part of routine maintenance. Adding a good quality probiotic bacteria supplement to your water on a weekly basis offers several advantages:

*Probiotic Bacteria Supplement*

- It reduces the need for water changes by digesting debris, waste, decaying plant matter and uneaten food. Waste-controlling bacteria have long been in use for septic systems as they are very effective at doing their job. Studies indicate that the difference can amount to as much as a 60% reduction in maintenance for filter cleaning and vacuuming.
- It is able to get to difficult to clean places to break down trapped waste.
- It can help to prevent disease naturally by providing a cleaner environment for your fish (without additional work on your part). This is an especially significant point. By outcompeting disease-causing strains of bacteria such as Aeromonas, Columnaris and pseudomonas, probiotic bacteria offer an approach to disease control that, in many cases, supersedes antibiotic medications by working to take the load off the fish's immune system for them rather than suppressing it. Every natural defense we hobbyists can use against bacterial infections in our goldfish should be seriously considered, especially given the prevalence of antibiotic resistant bacteria (many of which pose lethal threats to our pets) which is present in many home aquariums (along with the other previously mentioned strains). And, as I'm sure you agree, preventing disease is much better than trying to cure it.
- The healthier aquarium environment can lead to increased growth and a stronger immune system as stress on the fish is reduced.
- It improves the efficiency of your filter. This product does not contain nitrifying bacteria and does not compete with the bacteria in your filter. Instead, it helps the filter to work better by clearing away sludge that accumulates around it. It does not make your aquarium

cycle (this is not a nitrifying bacteria product), but it can help your filter to perform at its best.

- Clearer water can result as the probiotic bacteria out-compete the ones responsible for the cloudy, milky-looking water.
- Some find algae problems to be less aggressive.
- Odor reduction as a result of the disposal of decomposing organic and mulm is another plus.

It takes about a month to notice the difference, so results are not to be expected right away. But because there is little danger of overdose, some find that doubling the dose for the first month can help it work faster.

Other methods of ensuring your tank has a strong colony of beneficial probiotic bacteria to help outcompete disease include using a soil layer under your substrate, UV sterilization to reduce pathogenic free-floating bacteria, having large amounts of live plants and even using river water (that has been quarantined for 4 weeks minimum prior to use).

## Cleaning the Filter

Over time, even good, highly effective filters can become clogged with debris. This can result in impaired biological activity or even issues with the filter not working right. To prevent this from happening, regular cleaning is a good idea.

Filters that are intended to trap debris through mechanical filtration must be cleaned more frequently than those that aren't; at least on a weekly basis. This is because as time goes on, the trapped waste breaks down, creating toxins, which decompose and pollute the water even more quickly as the flow of the current passes over it, creating mulm.

Provided the filter is correctly cleaned, the beneficial bacteria will not be considerably harmed. Manual swishing is not enough to dislodge them. The good bacteria cling to the hard surface of the filter media and aggressive scrubbing or even tap pressure won't be enough to get rid of them (though the chlorine in tap will kill them).

That is why I do not recommend using tap water to clean your entire filter – you will destroy all of your hard-earned "good bugs" and cause your tank's cycle to be reset. This is doubtlessly dangerous to your goldfish. Using hot tap water to power-wash your mechanical filtration media (if you use it) is fine, provided you do not wash the biological media along with it. A bucket of tank water will be just what you need to rinse out your biological filter media a few times, swishing them rigorously through the water to get the particles out.

**Wet/Dry Filters**: Disassemble the filter and transfer the biological media into a bucket of old tank water, stirring to remove debris.  Wipe down the insides of the compartments with a dry, soft cloth.  Take apart the rain bar segments and use a bristle brush to clean the insides and holes free of buildup as needed (usually monthly).  Complete cleaning of the entire apparatus should be done every 6-12 months.  Pumps should be cleared from debris and backwashed monthly or more frequently if necessary.

**Sponge Filters**: Tap and rinse sponges well.  Squeezing the sponge can cause it to become limp in a shorter timeframe.  This should be done as needed.

**Hang on Back Filters**: Rinse the biological sponge media (if you have any) in tank water.  If you have a disposable cartridge that you plan on reusing, rinse that too.  This should be done when the filter flow is reduced.

**Canister Filters**: Disassemble the filter and clean each biological segment in old tank water.  This should be done every week if it contains mechanical filtration and every 2-3 months if it does not.  I prefer not to use mechanical filtration in canisters because they are so difficult to clean.  Instead, I use golf-ball sized ceramic media which does not trap debris and provides a home for nitrate removing bacteria.  If you would like to use mechanical filtration in your tank, the addition of a sponge filter as a standalone or prefilter can be an easier option to maintain.

*Jumbo Filter Media*

**Undergravel Filters**: There are many methods to clean an Undergravel filter.  The first – and possibly the easiest – is to insert your siphon down the uplift tube to remove debris trapped beneath the plates.  You can also clean this filter while siphoning the gravel on a weekly basis.  Lastly, you can break down the entire tank and rinse it out.  A reverse-flow UG filter with a prefilter can be vacuumed less frequently, and the prefilter rinsed in the sink or with a garden hose weekly.

## Dealing with Algae

Some owners are concerned with algae growth on the sides of the tank.  While not always the most attractive thing to look at, having certain types is actually beneficial to the fish.  Green algae (especially hair or string) is what is best for goldfish.  If it doesn't affect your ability to enjoy the tank too much, the walls of the tank can be left unscrubbed because beneficial bacteria do grow on them and just the "problem areas" on the front of the tank wiped down.  For algae removal on the front of the glass only, what you use will depend on your situation.  If it takes a while to accumulate, it probably isn't too much of a nuisance to wipe down every month or so, especially if the tank is shallow.

One truth worth noting is algae can kill live aquarium plants as they grow on the surface of their leaves, preventing the plants from taking in enough light.  Many kinds of algae can do this, including notorious black beard algae, green algae of various sorts and brown diatoms (which are not technically an algae, but behave like one to the aquarist.)

In the planted tank, the struggle is real – either the algae wins or the plants, unless something is done to keep the algae at bay.  The good news is healthy plants help inhibit algae by outcompeting them for nutrients.  Floating plants are especially useful, as they not only help provide shade to the aquarium and reduce available light to the algae, but are even more efficient at exporting excess nutrients than submerged plants.  But even in cases where there are enough healthy plants, sometimes algae still gets a foothold.

Many fishkeepers have been advised to get algae eating fish to deal with a nuisance algae outbreak.  The results of combining algae eating fish and goldfish are mixed.  Some keep them together for years without issue, others wake up to an injured goldfish.

Personally, I have found that snails are indispensable for keeping algae at bay.  In addition to helping break down fish waste, they happily feast on most types of problematic algae.  Nerite snails are great for cleaning flat surfaces such as smooth rocks, the wall of the tank and broad-leaf plants.  They are the mortal enemy to brown diatom algae.  Ramshorn snails are more adept at assisting algae removal from finer-leaf plants.  Other varieties of snails can prove useful as well.  All snails get along peacefully with goldfish.

While it is true that snails can be disease vectors to the fish, this is very rare – especially if you get your snails from a reputable breeder.  Snails kept and bred in captivity (rather than wild-caught) are far less likely to be harboring the parasites that would harmfully affect the fish.  Snails have been deemed as "messy," but in reality they only produce what they take in.  Snails have the important advantage of breaking down organic waste into a form that is more easily consumed by the beneficial bacteria in your tank.  It has been my experience that the larger your algae problem, the more snails you will need to make a dent.  Some are concerned about the snails eating plants, but healthy plants naturally repel snails.  Most snails only eat plants that are dying or if they are starving.

Goldfish eat snails, which can be both a drawback and a benefit.  The drawback is any snail that is too small will be lunch.  But the benefit is that this keeps the population in check, and by growing out snail eggs to adulthood in a separate space, you can replenish them as needed.

Algae eating shrimp, such as the popular Amano shrimp, are hit and miss, depending on the size and ability of the goldfish to find them.  Some hobbyists report keeping them together without issues.  Others find the shrimp are always depleted until they go extinct from their tank due to the fish picking them off.  Having larger shrimp and smaller fish seems to be the best combination to avoid shrimps going missing in action.

Catfish such as the Otocinclus have a ravenous appetite for algae, but (as with plecos) in some cases they may pick on the goldfish.

A magnetic algae scraper is a fun, easy to use algae cleaning tool that can be employed as often as needed.  Magnetic algae scrapers come in two varieties: one for glass and one for acrylic.

*Acrylic Algae Scraper*

As a goldfish keeper, you will probably encounter some form of algae.  The more light the water gets, the more green algae is likely to grow.  Planted tanks will usually have a coat of green algae, which the goldfish enjoy grazing on and helps oxygenate the water during the day.  While there are many different kinds of algae, most of them are a welcome addition to a goldfish tank even as they grow on objects in the tank and make a tasty snack.

*Glass Algae Scraper*

Cleaning the outside of the tank is necessary to rid it of those pesky dried water drops that occur most often after a water change.  A slightly damp paper towel can be used to remove them, followed by a soft cloth to dry any leftover water.  Mineral deposits can become a nuisance as they build up on the rim (and sometimes other areas) of the tank with time, and the only way to totally remove them is to remove the fish, empty the tank everything inside it and soak them in white vinegar water for an hour before scrubbing them off by hand with a sponge.  You will need to be sure to thoroughly triple-rinse away all the vinegar before putting fish back in though, so your pH doesn't plummet.  Salty water will also create an unsightly white crust around the top of the tank and tank equipment, but it is somewhat easy to remove with a tough cloth or stiff sponge and some elbow grease.  Remember to take into consideration what your tank is made of while cleaning it to avoid scratches.  Acrylic can scratch easily, so rough sponges or pads shouldn't be used for it.  The good news is the scratches can usually be buffed out with an acrylic cleaning kit.

# Feeding

Your goldfish's health is influenced in a very large part by what and how much it eats. Diet can make your fish sick or healthy, overweight or trim, dead or alive – it's that important to them. Sadly, the average goldfish diet is a far cry from a correct and balanced meal for goldfish, and as a result leads to many problems. So, let's learn how to feed your goldfish properly to avoid running into them.

## What kind of food should you feed?

In the wild, goldfish eat pretty much anything that won't eat them. They don't specialize in one particular thing. Their natural diets are actually quite high in protein as they forage for insects, worms and other small living organisms. Feeding the same thing exclusively over and over again is not a good long-term diet for your fish, even if it has a lot of nutrients in it.

That said, you will want a *"staple diet"* that makes up the base of the fish's diet. It will provide the protein, fat, vitamins and minerals the fish needs on a daily basis. On top of that is the *"additional diet"* where the fish gets the variety it needs to keep its digestive system working right. Contrary to older works which say goldfish are primarily vegetarians and need little protein, it has been found that low protein for goldfish can cause malnutrition and improper growth. However, too much protein can lead to obesity, so that must be taken into account.

So, what should make up the staple diet? Though flake food is a popular choice, I advise avoiding it. It clouds water, falls apart right away and can contribute to swim bladder problems. It is also difficult to tell exactly how much the fish is getting.

Whatever staple food you choose, it is very important that it is made of only good quality ingredients. Cheap foods often have a poor nutritional profile due to the quality of the ingredients being compromised. This is evident in the first few ingredients being a filler ingredient, such as soybean products, wheat products or corn, rather than seafood protein like whole fish meal. Such foods can compromise the short and/or long-term health of your fish, as well as result in dirtier aquarium water. When a fish is given poor nutrition, they are prone to getting fatty liver disease. Other conditions can also result from malnutrition or low-quality ingredients.

My advice is either use good quality *gel food* or *pellets* as a diet staple because they contain the all-too-important protein.

Slim-bodied fish do not seem to have nearly the propensity to digestive disorders with regular flakes, but I would encourage you to choose one of the better quality flake brands on the market for a greater chance of a healthy, long-lived fish.

*Repashy Super Gold*

Gel food is nutritious, moist, easy to digest and helps prevent swim bladder disorder and you can make it yourself.  It will not cloud water.  You can also put a chunk in the water and the fish will eat on it for a long time, mimicking their natural scavenging habits through slow digestion.  In fact, if you have fish prone to swim bladder I would highly recommend the use of a quality gel food over pellets.

The disadvantage of gel food is that it can be a bit more of a hassle.  You have to keep it in the fridge and it doesn't last more than 2 weeks in there.  Also, you or someone else has to be there in person to feed it.

Of the commercially available gel foods, I recommend Repashy Super Gold.  It uses high-quality ingredients formulated specifically for the dietary needs of goldfish and is especially suited for shorter-bodied fancies who are prone to swim bladder problems.

Pellets are long lasting, nutritious and can be put in an automatic feeder Quality brands will not cloud water.  However, they are drier unless they are soaked first, as some owners like to do, and then if they are soaked they can't be put in an automatic feeder.  It is regarded that high-quality sinking pellets do not need to be soaked.  There is evidence that the correlation between floating pellets and swim bladder problems is a myth, and that it is actually the quality of the ingredients that is the direct link.  Poor quality ingredients are hard for goldfish to digest and lead to excess gas in the GI tract, as well as buoyancy problems.  Bad brands cause swim bladder disorder and other health problems, such as fatty liver disease.

*Pellets*

Slim-bodied breeds are not as delicate, though even they can get swim bladder or other health problems from a poor diet (it is not recommended to feed them the typical junky brands).  Another pellet brand, Omega One, can be a healthier option for them without breaking the bank.  The makers of this pellet made efforts to ensure the ingredient profile emphasized digestible and nutritious ingredients first (like whole fish) and minimize starches, binders and fillers.

A good plan might be to alternate between the two types of food for a staple diet, but you will have to find what works best for you and your fish.

## Choosing a Quality Staple Food

I do not advise using pellets or gel food brands that have wheat, soy or corn in the first ingredients (or to be the very purist, ideally none of these at all). They are cheaper to produce but can hurt the sensitive swim bladder of the fancy goldfish. Goldfish cannot digest grains or soy easily and this can lead to swim bladder problems. They also will cause more issues with water quality, as the complex carbohydrates are excreted undigested, and then become a magnet for bacteria (leading to dirtier water).

Wheat flour and wheat gluten are all "code words" for wheat. Wheat germ may be alright as a source of fiber (the germ is the exterior hard shell). Whole fish meal or specifically mentioned fish (whole salmon, whole herring) is better than just fish meal because they are using the better parts of the fish to make it, rather than just any of the parts. Protein ideally should be plant or marine animal derived, such as shrimp, squid, krill or fish. As a rule, the food should include a good percentage of high-quality protein.

Feeding adult goldfish a low quality, high protein percentage food around the clock can lead to fat accumulation in the organs and swim bladder trouble. This is because they aren't growing anymore and don't burn as many calories. Likewise, young goldfish will not display good growth if they do not have high protein. Keep in mind that a goldfish does most of its growing in its first year of life.

Whether you choose pellets or gel food to feed your fish, it is important to use what is in the container for no longer than 6 months. If it has been over 6 months, it is time to toss the food. The reason for this is because after 6 months food can go rancid and the vitamins in it have all but gone. At that point, you may as well be feeding your fish cardboard. This can be dangerous to your fish as they can start to suffer from vitamin deficiencies, especially Vitamin C.

**The Raw Food Diet**

Something I've been experimenting with on my own fish that has shown good results is the raw food diet. Processed foods are usually heat-treated, which destroys the enzymes needed to completely digest it.

So what do you feed to make sure your fish has the nutrition it can't get from veggies? Bloodworms and fresh earthworms make excellent choices. They have the amino acid profile that suits the goldfish's needs wonderfully and are both what the fish would eat in the wild. You even can culture both at home. If you can get them, daphnia can also be an excellent food source. Be careful not to overfeed. Tubifex worms should be avoided due to the higher possibility of them transmitting disease to your fish.

I keep my earthworms in a shoebox-sized Tupperware container. To set up the worm bin, I first sprinkled a layer of crushed eggshells on the bottom, followed by some dead oak leaves. On top of that I placed some medium sized rocks to help with aeration at the bottom of the bin. The rest of the bin is then filled with dirt. Food scraps can then be fed once a week by placing them underneath the surface of the dirt (exposed to the open air they may dry out or grow mold). The box requires weekly watering to keep the soil moist but my goldfish have a constant supply of fresh, healthy earthworms. It should be placed in a cool, dark area such as a basement and covered with a perforated lid (I used tin foil with holes poked in the top).

*Fresh Earthworms*

To feed them, all you need to do is shake off the loose dirt and chop them into little pieces (if your fish are small). It can take a while to get over the "ew" factor if you're not accustomed to the task, but the reward of watching your fish gobbling them down outweighs that, in my opinion. Nutritious and delicious, right?

California blackworms are also a great source of nutritious live food for goldfish. These can be cultured at home in just about anything. They have a good amount of protein (43-59%) so they are fantastic for young growing fish or sick fish needing a nutritional pick-me-up. The more nutritious of a diet the worms eat, the more nutrition they will provide to your fish. I use a turkey baster to harvest and feed.

Bloodworms can also be cultured at home. You don't know what kind of conditions that bloodworms at the pet store were grown in, so there are some benefits to raising them at home. Growing them is easy – simply set a pan of water outside and add some soil or meal (such as flour, crushed fish food, or algae-rich green water – the best) for them to eat. In a few days, little bloodworms will start to coat the inside of the pan. To harvest them, simply scrape the insides with a fine net.

Raw shrimp can be an excellent food source for goldfish, as it is marine-based and full of good quality protein. Blending gelatin (dissolved in hot water prior to mixing) with raw shrimp in a blender can be done to produce a tasty treat.

Bits of fish (preferably raw or broiled without oils or spices) be a tasty treat. Shrimp, salmon or cod are good examples.

Veggies should be placed in the tank uncooked or dethawed and allowed to soften up enough for the fish to chew. I would not recommend microwaving your fish's food if at all possible.

If you do feed a pre-made food, such as a high quality gel food, perhaps consider not using boiling but hot water to set the gel. Feeding raw foods is as a treat at least 2 times weekly as a substitute for the processed foods is a great way to provide your goldfish with a well-rounded diet.

## Adding the Supplements

In addition to a staple diet of pellets given to the fish several times daily, it is important to also supplement. Variety in the diet is important. It makes sure the fish gets all the nutrients it needs, as well as helps keep that digestive track moving.

Now, for the additional diet, be sure to use both vegetables and live foods to supplement (assuming you feed a processed staple diet rather than a raw food diet, you will only need to supplement with veggies). Raw vegetables or shelled & diced frozen petite peas (fed sparingly) or green beans are a good choice for adding other vitamins and minerals. Good live food choices include blood worms, earth worms and brine shrimp fed twice weekly. These can be found online or at local fish stores.

**Veggies:** You don't typically use these other foods to replace the staple diet, but make sure the fish has something to munch on between meals and provide fiber. Fiber is what helps the fish's digestive track keep moving and prevents swim bladder trouble. Veggies are just the thing to add in. Some of the harder veggies can be blanched to soften them up prior to feeding them to the fish. (Blanching means dipping it in boiling water for about 10 seconds to soften it up a bit.) Dark greens such as lettuce, kale or spinach are important for vitamin intake, while cilantro, carrots and beets (naturally color enhancing), zucchini, squash, sparing amounts of avocado (high fat, don't blanch), cooked pumpkin, cucumber (peeled) and just about whatever veggies you have in the fridge left over are all good choices. Broccoli offers nutritional benefits but should be fed very sparingly as it can easily foul the water and lead to gas in some of the more delicate fancy goldfish.

Goldfish are foraging creatures and should be provided access to leafy greens around the clock. This helps prevent boredom and satisfies their natural craving to munch around the clock.

One tip that has been very useful for both me and to other hobbyists is the use of a veggie clip. This ingenious little device sticks on to the inside of the tank and holds the food in one place so it doesn't float all over the place or get caught in the filter intake. You also always know when it is time for a refill. Be sure not to leave any veggies in the tank for more than 24 hours as they can start to rot.

*Veggie Clip*

Remember that while veggies are fed in addition to the staple diet, they do not replace the pellets or gel food at any time, unlike higher protein foods like live foods or peas can. Peas are the exception to the rule because they are surprisingly high in protein. Also, if you have live edible plants like Elodea or duckweed, you can go more lightly on the veggie supplements.

**Live Foods**: Brine shrimp and bloodworms are a couple of the more popular and widely available live foods to substitute for a feeding of pellets or gel food. They are a source of quality protein and are good for the fish's digestion. You would feed them as an occasional replacement of your diet staple.

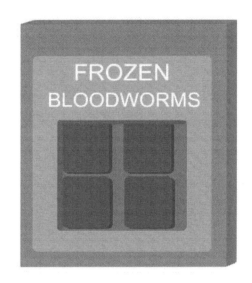

I do not recommend the use of freeze-dried bloodworms, no matter how convenient or cheap they may be, as they are very dry and do not sink. Even after soaking they still contain a lot of air bubbles, which do not need to be going into your fish's digestive track.

For those trying to pinch their pennies (or don't want to have to go shopping) earthworms are a must-have. They are easy to cultivate, harvest and prepare – and best of all, the fish love them. They are extremely low in pathogens, making them very safe. I purchase my earthworms online and store them to feed my fish as-needed.

*Fresh Earthworms*

To feed them, all you need to do is shake off the loose dirt and chop them into little pieces (if your fish are small). It can take a while to get over the "ew" factor if you're not accustomed to the task, but the reward of watching your fish gobbling them down outweighs that, in my opinion. Nutritious and delicious, right?

## How Often Do You Feed?

You wouldn't want to eat your breakfast, lunch and dinner all at the same time, would you? Goldfish will have health problems if they are forced to eat the amount of food they need daily all at once. Several feedings throughout the day are a much more natural eating pattern to goldfish.

They are physically designed to be grazers. They do not have a true stomach and food can get impacted in their gut, which can be very dangerous.

Because an enclosed and "pest-free" aquarium does not supply the ideal grazing environment for fish, we have to create that ourselves.

But how often you feed first of all depends on the temperature of the water because fish will not need as much food or burn as much energy in cooler water.

| Temperature | State | Times to feed each day |
|---|---|---|
| 32-43°F | In hibernation | Do not feed |
| 44-54°F | Partly hibernating | Do not feed |
| 55-64°F | Between hibernating and active | 1 time |
| 65-75°F | Spawning young fish | 2-3 times |
| 76-86°F | Growing young fish | 2-3 times |
| 87-97°F | Slowing growth | 2-3 times |
| 98-100°F | Max temperature | 1-2 times |

Due to having busy schedules, many people choose to make use of an automatic feeder. As said before, an automatic feeder will only work with dry foods such as pellets, and you will still want to use at least one of those feedings for providing supplements like veggies and live foods. (Be warned that your goldfish will no longer be as excited to see you and instead will hover around the feeder waiting for it to drop the food.)

*Automatic Feeder*

Your stocking and water change system must be able to accommodate the amount of food you put in. If your tank is sparsely stocked or stocked within the recommended guidelines it's okay to feed more in order to grow out younger fish. However, in a smaller space with more fish waste accumulates faster and can foul the water too quickly. To feed several times daily with a much great stocking level, you will need to compensate with more water changes. You will need to be observant of your water and remember that the more you feed the more you need to clean the tank.  If things start looking dirty or your fish start acting or looking poorly, it is probably time to reduce the number of meals.

## How Much to Feed?

There are specific formulas for figuring out how much food your fish needs each day, but it is based on the weight and age of your goldfish.  Because it is not practical for most people to be weighing their fish so often to figure out how much they need to be feeding, it is easier to use the time-based formula rather than the weight-based one because the fish's size will naturally influence how much they can eat in one period.

For the average fish keeper (one not intending to spawn the fish or grow out fry) feed fish twice a day **all they can eat in 30 seconds at a time**. If they start to look too lean, feed more. If they look too fat, feed less. You must use your eye and it may require some trial and error.  You will be able to tell if your fish is overweight if you lay off feeding but the fish's stomach area doesn't slim down.  Obesity in goldfish is dangerous for them and can lead to a host of problems and will shorten the fish's lifespan.  Uneaten food must be removed right away.

It is important to consider the age of the fish.  As with protein, younger fish will need a higher percentage of food each day in proportion to their size than older fish.  This is because their metabolism is higher and they are growing faster so their demands for food go up.  Feeding them less than they require can result in malnourishment.

If your fish are in a lightly stocked pond, reduce the quantity of the food you are feeding but keep the number of feedings the same.  This is because they have access to more food around the clock than aquarium-kept fish.

## Overfeeding and Sick Fish

What and how much you feed your fish has a massive impact on not just your fish itself, but the overall health of the aquarium. The simple fact is many hobbyists – knowingly or unknowingly – are overfeeding. Feeding our pets is a large part of what makes the hobby so enjoyable. We express our love to them with it. But the sad truth is that, in respect to food, more fish are killed with kindness than the lack thereof.

In the wild, goldfish and carp would go through a hibernation period where they shed all of their excess body weight they put on in the plenteous seasons. But in the home aquarium, the temperature stays relatively stable and food typically remains abundant... too abundant. Overfeeding causes fat accumulation in the body. This excess fat makes the fish sickly, lethargic and eventually dead.

Too much food causes a drastic problem with dissolved and undissolved organics as well as bacterial imbalance. What do I mean by this? The water becomes overrun with too much rotting debris. This leads to a surge of bacteria that try to consume the rotting material. This leads to the fish getting sick as the bad bacteria count skyrockets, overwhelming their immune system with sheer numbers (dose response).

What is the solution to an overfed, overweight fish and a bacteria-ridden aquarium? Fasting + water changes.

Fasting is a weapon we have in our arsenal for our fish's health. It is often the only way to recover an overfed, sick fish back to vitality. Fasting affects the entire nitrogen cycle. When you stop feeding, ammonia input is greatly reduced. If you are struggling with an uncycled tank, withholding food can do the trick of keeping your fish safe through the delicate time. 3-4 weeks without protein food is recommended. The fish will not starve; it will burn off the excess fat reserves. Gradually reduce the amount of food each day to avoid a sudden "drop-off."

Fasting can also be a great way to address swim bladder issues related to overfeeding or feeding the wrong kind of food.

## Vacation Feeding

If you plan on going on vacation, you can use a vitamin case to divvy up each staple diet portion for each day to prevent the sitter from overfeeding the fish accidentally. (Be sure to hide all the extra food). For leafy veggies, you can use plastic bags marked with the date to serve.

Another option is to use an automatic fish feeder. A good recommendation is to practice using the feeder for a couple of weeks before going on vacation so you can monitor the food output and correct anything if need be.

Slow-release vacation feeders can harm the water quality while you're not around unless you have tried them before. They are not necessary and can do more harm than good, fouling up the water.

If you do not have someone who can sit for you and you will not be gone for more than a week or two, the fish will be fine without food for that long. Simply add some fresh kale or other veggies to the tank prior to leaving so the fish have something to much on for a bit. Just be sure to perform a large water change before leaving. The biggest danger is not a hungry fish, but an overfed one causing fouled water.

## Growing Your Goldfish

Watching a small fish mature is so rewarding, isn't it?  Many goldfish keepers prefer to acquire small fish and nurture it themselves rather than buy a larger fish up front.

Here are some ways to help your goldfish get bigger:

1) **Smaller, more frequent meals** – Instead of one larger meal a day, breaking it up into several smaller meals throughout the day can yield improved growth.
2) **High quality food** – A good diet plays a massive role in growing big fish.  Higher quality ingredients of good brands of fish food provide more bioavailable nutrients.  Also adding other amino-acid and protein rich live foods such as bloodworms or earthworms can be beneficial as well.
3) **Water changes** – Water changes removes growth hormones from the water that can slow or inhibit the growth of your fish.  It also ensures good water quality, which is essential for a growing fish.  Water changes also help keep down the waste and debris from extra feeding.
4) **Warmer temperatures** – Raising the temperature to between 75-80 degrees F (some enthusiasts recommend water temperatures as high as 82 degrees F for the most growth) speeds up the metabolism of the fish and makes them grow faster than in cold water.  This can make the fish not live as long if the fish does not go through a period of cold temps.
5) **Aged water** – If you can, aging your water can offer better growth of your fish.
6) **Lots of space** – More room can lead to faster growth.  After all, fish kept in ponds constantly achieve larger sizes in shorter amounts of time.

**My Goldfish is Not Growing!**

Goldfish that don't seem to grow may be facing a few challenges.  Here are the common reasons:

1) **Water quality** – Poor water quality is probably the number one reason goldfish do not grow quickly if at all.  There is considerable evidence that high nitrate levels inhibit the growth of fish.  Filter media that reduces nitrates can greatly help.
2) **Improper diet** – Next to water quality, issues with the diet can inhibit growth.  Changing to a high-quality food (with high protein content for young fish) can be just what your fish needs to reach its full potential.  Improved coloration will probably be noticeable as well.
3) **Undersized space** – A greater volume of water allows for better water quality and more room to exercise.  Exercise plays an important factor in muscle development and growth.
4) **Stunting** – Depending on the conditions a fish was kept in, perhaps even prior to when you acquired it, you may have a stunted fish on your hands.  A stunted fish is permanently damaged due to improper husbandry.

5) **Genetics** – Aside from environmental conditions, the biggest influence on a goldfish's size is their genetics.  Sometimes you can do everything right, but your goldfish might still be a midget, or naturally tend towards being petite.  Midgets are naturally present in many spawns of goldfish fry and remain small for life.  It is important to remember that not all goldfish, especially the fancy ones, will achieve a large comparative size.

6) **Poor health** – Your goldfish may not be healthy.  A sick fish will not grow as it should as it is expending its resources toward trying to survive rather than thrive.

## Goldfish Lifespan

How long can your goldfish live?  Some goldfish have made headlines worldwide for living past 40 years.  Is that the realistic expectation owners should have, or are you being a bad pet parent for not being able to keep your fish alive that long?

The truth is, just like most people don't live to be over 100, most goldfish won't live to be over 40 – even the hardier breeds.

The closer the goldfish is to its original form (meaning slim-bodied breeds such as the common or comet goldfish), the better chance it has of living a long time.  The oldest goldfish in the world are consistently undersized, which points to a possible connection between a size and longevity.

While other factors such as the quality of your husbandry of the fish will greatly determine how long it will be able to live, sometimes it comes down to genetics.

The more modified the breed of goldfish is, the shorter the fish tends to live.  While much appreciated for their appearance, their exaggerated forms cause them to be prone to a variety of issues and are more sensitive to stress.  There is much less room for error when keeping fancies than hardier breeds.

It seems (on average) most fancy goldfish do not live past 10 years.  Some fancy fish do outlive that, but they tend to be the exception rather than the rule.  The average lifespan for these varieties, assuming the fish has proper care, ranges between 5-7 years.  The Asian fish farmers like to say that the fancy goldfish is like a delicate flower.  It grows and blossoms until it reaches its full height of beauty, then fades.  The fancy goldfish has been transformed by hundreds of years of selective breeding from the humble, mud-colored carp into a creature that is very physically far removed from its ancestors, and the tradeoff is that their life expectancy is shorter.  The same can be said of many other domesticated animals.  They are far less capable of dealing with stressors such as medications, shipping, low quality diet, marginal water quality, temperature fluctuations or even pond life.

Slim-bodied breeds are typically considered to be elderly after they reach the 10 year mark.  Why do most of these hardier varieties not live to 20, or beyond?  Some speculate that this may have to do with the stressful conditions of many being salvaged from feeder fish tanks at pet stores.  Many of them carry dormant diseases in their system waiting to strike when the fish gets weak or sick.

Goldfish who go through winter hibernation can live even longer.  It is as if they hit the pause button on their lifespan during that time.  The lowly common goldfish seem to be the most long-lived and resilient of all goldfish varieties.

# Section 3: Collecting Goldfish

Now we come to the climax of enjoyment in the goldfish keeping hobby: getting your fish!  Picking out your goldfish is always exciting.  There are a few more things you should know ahead of time that can help to lay a solid foundation for your goldfish keeping journey.

## Where to Get Your Goldfish?

There are three main ways to acquire fish, each with their own sets of pros and cons.  Obviously, there are room for exceptions but for the most part the pros and cons are pretty accurate for all places:

**Chain pet stores**

*Pros*: Usually the most affordable (for the cost of the fish itself), local, see the actual fish in person, take it home the same day

*Cons*: Lack of more exotic breeds, high risk of getting diseased fish due to lack of quarantine, fish often sold the same day they arrive without time to rest, high risk of getting bad advice from ill-informed and/or inexperienced workers, more stress for the fish due to multiple stops in transit

**Independent fish stores**

*Pros*: More knowledgeable workers, improved chance of getting healthier fish, local, see the fish in person, take it home the same day

*Cons*: Typically have more tropical fish than goldfish (so not as much selection), more stress for fish due to multiple stops in transit, may or may not quarantine

**Online**

*Pros*: Buy directly from breeders or importers, some are quarantined, some are high quality, lots of variety and selection

*Cons*: Typically more expensive for the cost of the fish, must depend on photos/videos rather than getting to see the fish in person

Out of all of these options, my personal opinion is that buying goldfish online is by far the best way to go, though wherever you choose to shop is ultimately up your discretion.

Goldfish that are shipped between several intermediaries have weaker immune systems because of this stress and are more likely to contract diseases. For most pet stores, ordering high quality fish causes their losses to be too high. They have to carry inexpensive and low-quality fish in order to make a profit, and in many cases these fish are or will soon be sick.

The quarantining process can also be inconvenient, requires the use of a variety of treatments and a good eye for diagnosing health problems to effectively eradicate the common pathogens. For those reasons, many hobbyists prefer to purchase fish that have already been prophylactically treated for disease and quarantined in advance.

If at all possible, for the very best chance of success I recommend that you **avoid pet stores or fair fish altogether**. Many fish don't survive the pet store – and the ones that do are almost always contaminated with some disease. Even if you manage to remove all the parasites and escape the treatable bacterial infections, there's still the significant possibility of mycobacterial disease that can show up a good while after you purchase the fish. This means they have a greater chance of not living their full life out, even with good care on your part. Sometimes they die from just all the stress they've been through, no matter what you do. It's hard to get attached to them and only have them perish no matter what you do.

Local breeders consistently afford healthy, strong, resilient fish that have been well-cared for. As an added bonus, they also afford access to some of the rarer varieties of goldfish.

## How to Purchase Healthy Goldfish

Goldfish keeping poses enough challenges on its own. Even if you don't care that much about the beauty or rarity of the fish (which is a large part of what makes the hobby enjoyable) it is probably a good idea to start off with absolutely healthy fish to avoid running into complications later. Unless you are very confident in your nursing abilities, it is usually best to avoid purchasing a fish you can tell is not healthy. Here is a quick checklist to have on hand:

- Is the dorsal fin upright while the fish is not swimming?
- Do the fish look perky, or sit lethargically on the bottom? A healthy young goldfish is always on the move in search of food.
- Do you notice abnormalities such as red spots, degeneration or bloody streaks on the fins, white spots, or gasping for air at the top? It is recommended to avoid sick fish unless you are very confident in your nursing abilities.
- Are there other sick or dead fish in the tank? If a tank has floating fish in it, do not buy fish from that store. Most pet stores have one central filtration system which circulates all the water, which spreads any disease.
- Is the water clean?
- Have the fish just arrived at the store? New imports may contain some fish that suddenly die from the stress of importation.
- Do the workers seem knowledgeable about goldfish?

Online companies will ship the goldfish of your choice directly to your door. Be prepared to cover shipping costs, which can be considerably higher for Expedited (overnight) shipping verses Priority (two-day) mail. Some sellers will only do overnight shipping while others only do two-day, and yet others will give the buyer the choice. I have found Priority mail to be cost-saving and is perhaps preferred for very young fish. However, the less time the fish are in transit the less stress.

 Check out our website to find where you can buy goldfish online.

*Goldfish for Sale*

## Choosing Your Type of Fish

Here are some factors you will want to consider when it comes to selecting fish for your setup:

- **Location**: Where are you going to be keeping the fish? Some breeds are best viewed from the side, whereas the fancy tails of others (take the Tosakin, for example) go to waste unless you are looking down at the fish. Also, more delicate varieties are not hardy enough to endure outdoor temperatures or evade predators. Of the fancy varieties, the Fantail is most able to tolerate the challenges of pond life.

- **Body Shape**: It isn't recommended to mix slim-bodied goldfish with fancies. It makes for disharmony in the tank having some fish swimming like crazy all over the place and others moving slowly. Not only that, but you will have issues with the fast, strong swimmers getting all the food.

- **Size**: Getting a big fish to begin with might be a good idea if the space isn't very large where you will be keeping it. That is because the fish will grow more slowly. Other people prefer to start with young fish and watch them develop by giving them ample room. As a side note, be sure not to mix fish that are very different in size to avoid bullying and/or one fish getting all the food.

- **Breed**: In general, fancy goldfish are very gentle-natured and get along fine (when it isn't spawning season!), but if incompatible fish are put together (such as less modified breeds with more heavily modified ones such as those with bubble eyes or really long fins) you could potentially run into issues.

## Acclimating New Fish

When you get your new fish, the best way to introduce them to the tank or pond is to float the bag in the water for at least 20 minutes until the temperature is matched. If you are putting the fish in a pond, be sure not to float the bags in an area where there is direct sunlight as this can cause the water to rapidly overheat.

During this time you should leave the bag sealed. After the time is up, you can open the bag and use your hand to quickly transfer the fish from the bag to the tank. As soon as the air hits the water the ammonia in the bag will become highly toxic, so you will want to work quickly. And that is also why it is advisable not to try adding water from the tank to the bag to adjust the fish. Be sure not get as little water from the bag into the tank as possible during the process.

Your new goldfish will most likely need some time to recuperate. It is normal for them to sit at the bottom, perhaps breathing rapidly for a while and looking stressed, but this should subside after an hour or so and the fish should then become curious about their new home.

Even if you have already gone through the fishless cycling process before getting your fish, the beneficial bacteria colony will have to readjust because of the new fish and the different kinds of toxins they introduce. This is a time when things can easily go wrong. It is recommended to follow a heavier water change schedule at this time to avoid any "glitches" such as an ammonia or nitrite spike.

Also, do not feed at this time. Feeding can shock the fish and cause issues with overloading the filter. Wait until 24 hours are passed. When you do feed, start gradually and in very small amounts. They won't starve until then and overfeeding at this time is a real danger and one of the most disastrous mistakes at this delicate time.

# Quarantining New Fish

**The Importance of Quarantine**

The nightmare of having an entire collection of fish wiped out by the addition of a single infected new one is one I've experienced firsthand. I don't want anyone to have to go through that, so I think it important to add a section in here on proper quarantine procedures.

I have a new respect for the importance of quarantine after my own experiences with buying new fish. I now firmly maintain that all new fish need to be quarantined, regardless of where you bought them or how reputable the seller is. To do otherwise may work out sometimes, but it is a big risk that can jeopardize your entire collection (especially if you are getting fish that have not been quarantined).

I used to think that if the fish looks healthy, then it is healthy. The truth is, a fish can look and act perfectly healthy and still be carrying a load of parasites, many of which are not visible to the naked eye. This is because most fish, unless they have been bred by a local breeder, have been shipped from place to place before they get to your house. They are stressed and exposed to these parasites in their holding tanks. Such fish may be fine for the first few weeks or even months, but as the parasites continue to multiply then suddenly the fish may become sick.

Plants and any other live creature should also be quarantined and/or treated to remove parasites if they have been grown or placed in an environment containing fish. Quarantining plants through simple isolation for 28 days at a temperature between 78-82 degrees F will help ensure no pathogens will transmit to your fish, as their life cycle will run out before they can find a host. I have also used MinnFinn as a plant bath for Anubias at concentration and duration recommended for fish without ill-effects. It is not approved for other creatures, such as invertebrates, which should be isolated for 3-4 weeks. This will allow the "hitchhikers" to die off without a host.

**How to Quarantine**

How you quarantine depends on the source of your fish. I classify them as "clean" or "questionable."

Your quarantining process varies depending on where you source your fish from, but all fish need to be kept separate from the main tank for at least 2-4 weeks, healthy or not, unless you don't have any fish already. Why? Because even healthy fish go through stress during the shipping process. Stress makes them weak and vulnerable to unfamiliar pathogens that might be in your tank, which your existing goldfish are already used to. They need a period of time to "rest up" and get their strength back before joining the others.

Fish from fish stores and importers who do not treat and quarantine their fish before shipping need a bit more attention than just the separation process. It is safe to assume these fish already have some parasite load. They need to be treated for internal and external parasites that could infect your other fish. Using a microscope is one of the best ways to confirm that the fish is pathogen-free before introducing them to the main tank after treatments.

If you buy your fish online or from an importer, as many readers do, it is useful to determine whether or not the seller does a quarantine period on all their fish with prophylactic treatments to target all common goldfish diseases (more on that later). Many if not most importers do not do this and will only medicate fish if they look sick before sending it out. Some may say they quarantine, but their process does not comprehensively address the spectrum of diseases and only targets a few of the major ones.

If you buy from a breeder, the best way to form a quarantine plan is to ask them how they ensure their fish are free of pathogens. A good one will use microscopy techniques to make sure their fish are clean and may not even need to use treatments to rid their fish of diseases because they are home-bred.

No matter what kind of fish you are quarantining, there are some basics for both processes. It is important to start with a sterile tank, be it brand-new or totally disinfected if used. To disinfect a used tank, spray the surfaces with 3% drug store hydrogen peroxide and let dry, and/or fill with vinegar water for at least 20 minutes, with 1 cup of vinegar per 10 gallons.

The quarantine tank needs to be kept very clean throughout the process through water changes and preferably cycled beforehand with bottled ammonia. A poorly maintained quarantine tank can often be more stressful to fish than simply adding them into your main tank. I don't recommend using bacteria from an existing tank until the very end of the quarantine period because it could harbor pathogens. If it isn't cycled, you will need to do more water changes, with more needed the smaller the tank is. It is ideal to use a tank that follows regular stocking guidelines, but it is not always possible in all cases.

If the tank is undersized, more frequent water changes will be necessary. I recommend no smaller than 5 gallons per fish and doing 50-100% water changes daily for that stocking level. For normal stocking levels, 50% every day or every other day is usually fine. Test the ammonia levels daily and dose with Prime to ensure the fish don't encounter New Tank Syndrome.

During quarantine, fish should not be fed in the first 24 hours and sparingly thereafter, as any filter established using bottled ammonia will be fragile and an uncycled tank even more. Cross contamination must be avoided between your existing tank and the quarantine tank, so it is a good idea to avoid sharing equipment. If you must share equipment, sterilize it first through a vinegar soak using the ratio above.

**Quarantining "Clean" Fish**

The quarantine time for a trustworthy seller who already treats prophylactically should be 2-4 weeks.

Why do you need to quarantine a clean fish? As anyone who has been on an airplane knows, traveling can be stressful. It is even more stressful to be put in a small space in the dark for many hours to be jostled around. This stress leads to a low immune system. Even a healthy goldfish needs time to rest up before being introduced to a new tank with existing fish. Your existing fish could be immune to pathogens your new fish have never been exposed to.

Keep in mind that a small number of parasites will not kill a fish as quickly as poor water quality.

There are also rare strains of dangerous viruses that can show up on otherwise healthy fish during quarantine, which are becoming more prevalent with imports of fish. If the fish starts showing signs of one of these problems or dies in quarantine, the loss is isolated to just the quarantine tank and you can protect your other fish without worrying about contamination.

All of this said, I still recommend taking gill and body scrapes of all "clean" fish before adding them to your existing tank. Even some sellers that say their fish are disease free have been found to send fish that somehow or another have picked up something that could have potentially infected the buyer's collection if not caught early. It is always better to be too cautious than to take a risk with all of your pets' health.

However, if you are getting your first group of goldfish from one trustworthy seller and you don't have any existing fish (assuming your tank and equipment is sterile), you do not need to quarantine in most cases as you don't have existing fish to protect.

As an added cautionary measure, some folks like to add a fish with little sentimental value into the quarantine tank before adding the quarantine tank's inhabitants into their display tank. I personally don't do this but don't question that it works for some people.

**Quarantining "Questionable" Fish**

I'll be honest with you, I'm not 100% against buying your fish from a pet store or maybe a private importer IF you do it properly – and if the fish appear relatively healthy to start with. Let's face it, sometimes we find a fish we fall in love with that way. Maybe that's all we can afford – after all, the alternative isn't exactly cheap for most people. (Of course, the cost of the fish will likely be dwarfed by the cost of the medications needed to clean it up.)

But there are some things in the fine print you need to be aware of.

These other sources have no quarantine and treatment procedures. That means even if the fish looks and acts healthy to the naked eye, it could be carrying a mild to severe load of pathogens. I believe it is safe to say that pet store fish tanks are swarming with invisible pathogens, and most goldfish are carrying at least one. These typically will rear their ugly head shortly after your new fish is introduced to your display tank and can quickly infect all your existing fish before you know it (hence why we quarantine).

One formidable disease that evade detection in quarantine is Fish TB. Nearly all other diseases can be detected or prophylactically treated in a matter of weeks, but Fish TB is often a slowly progressing disease that can lurk in hiding for 90 days or longer. Sometimes the fish live their whole lives with it just fine until they get old, weak or stressed. But it gets worse... many pet stores have problems with TB. By purchasing fish from them, it's important to recognize that there is a chance your fish is contaminated – even if it appears fine when you get it. These fish can be potential vectors of the disease to your established aquarium even after a full 30 day quarantine.

During quarantine, you have the opportunity to observe your new fish for signs of problems. It is so much easier to have those problems happen in a separate area than your display tank/s. Sometimes nothing shows up until the 2-week mark.

Quarantining a questionable fish is going to look a bit different than quarantining clean fish. You will want to treat them prophylactically for all the common "hitchhikers" before you add them to your display tank with your other fish.

Again, if you don't have other fish, you don't have to use a separate quarantine tank. You also will want to quarantine longer. **4 weeks** is the absolute minimum, with longer being better. That will give you time to go through the treatments, watch for disease, and ensure the pathogens have had enough time to be properly treated. Many pathogens, such as ich, have a longer life cycle and are only susceptible to treatment at certain times.

What does this mean for you? It means you will need to do a series of what is called prophylactic treatments on your new fish during quarantine in order to get rid of those bugs. Will the fish have all these pathogens to start with? Probably not. They may only have one or two. Without a microscope, you don't know exactly what it is in many cases. I recommend treating for all common pathogens right away – don't wait until a few months later when you notice your fish aren't doing as well as they used to.

While many commercially manufactured chemicals are available on the market today used to quarantine fish, I think the most natural route can be just as effective while being less hard on the fish. Not only are chemical treatments stressful, but most are carcinogenic for both the fish and the owner and may even contribute to a shortened lifespan according to some veterinarians:

> "The lifetime barrage of chemicals to which we expose our fish could be contributing to a high incidence of cancers in ornamental fish."[4]

*Microbe-Lift Herbtana*

Carcinogenic drugs such as Praziquantel (used for flukes) and toxic formaldehyde-based Formalin (used for ich and other ciliated protozoans) can all be easily and safely replaced with hydrogen peroxide and peracetic acid based MinnFinn, which is non-carcinogenic and environmentally friendly. Not only is it safer for the fish and you, but it is far more cost-effective than buying several medications.

*Microbe-Lift Artemiss*

Here is my recommended quarantine procedure:

*Colloidal Silver*

- For the first 4 days, I recommend letting the fish rest and boost the immune system with alternate applications of Microbe-Lift Herbtana and Microbe-Lift Artemiss. 1 tsp of colloidal silver (diluted to 10ppm) can be used for antiviral and antibacterial properties. Dose the water with a good probiotic bacteria supplement to maintain a low bad bacteria count in the water and help the fish recover after its journey. Unless you see something crop up, reserve stronger treatments until after the first 4 days so the fish doesn't get overly stressed. If disease shows up then proceed to treat. Microscope scrapes are recommended during this time to pinpoint exactly what the fish has.
- I then recommend using 5 treatments of MinnFinn to target flukes, costia, chilodonella, trichodina and external bacterial infection-causing organisms. This will be done over the course of 10 days. For the last 5 days during the end of the MinnFinn treatment, treat internal parasites with a 3% Epsom salt feed as described in the internal parasites section.

*Supplement*

---

[4] Dr. Erik Johnson, goldfish vet (quoted in *Fancy Goldfish: A Complete Guide to Care and Collecting*)

- Next it is time to perform a 10-14-day long <u>salt</u> 0.5% treatment primarily targeting ich at 82 degrees F.  Salt should not be mixed with any other treatments. Follow the instructions in the ich section.  Raise the salt gradually.

*MinnFinn*

*Aquarium Salt*

- If the fish are looking good at this point, it is recommended to introduce some filter media from the established tank.
- At the end of quarantine, it is a good idea to raise the temperature up to 86 degrees F by 1-2 degrees per hour and hold it there for 2 days, then reduce it over another 2 days.  This is intended to kill heat-sensitive strains of Aeromonas bacteria.

At this point, the only ciliated protozoan parasite that could still be left behind would be velvet.  Velvet is not as common in goldfish as it was once thought.  However, if all of this has been done and there is somehow velvet left untreated, copper could be employed.

*Seachem Cupramine*

Copper is immunosuppressive, suppressive to the liver, and rather harsh on fish in general, so I don't really like using it unless it's absolutely necessary.  Of the brands of copper treatments available, Seachem Cupramine is recommended for its less toxic, longer-lasting form.  Copper will harm plants and invertebrates, so these must be removed prior to treatment.  There is some controversy regarding whether or not a glass tank that has been treated with copper will ever be safe for invertebrates again, as it can linger in the substrate and silicone.  Some recommend using Seachem Cuprisorb to clean up the residual copper from the aquarium environment.  It should not be used until 48 hours of dosing with Seachem Prime.  Given the drawbacks of this medication, I would recommend confirming the fish truly has velvet through microscopy before using it, if at all possible.

Finally, you will want to keep a close eye out for anchor worm or fish lice.  If you notice either one of these during quarantine, you will need to add additional time onto your quarantine period to treat for them as well.  Please see the treatments section for recommended methods of control.

It will also be important to keep an eye out for bacterial infections and treat accordingly once the parasites have been dealt with.  These can rear their ugly head at the tail end of a parasitic infestation or simply from the stress of shipping.  Keeping the bacteria count in the water low through water changes and probiotic bacteria supplementation will help your fish to resist infection.

# Goldfish Communities & Aggression

## Goldfish as community fish

Goldfish are schooling fish by nature. As such, there is some question as to whether you should keep one in solitary confinement or not. Do goldfish get lonely? My personal opinion is that most goldfish should not be kept alone. They seem to be happier in the presence of those of their own kind. Companionship is an excellent antidote to boredom; something animals kept in captivity are prone to. As their owners, it seems kindest to try to prevent this if possible. Of course, I would add that relieving boredom should never come at the expense of the health of the first fish by overcrowding them or adding a fish that has not been quarantined first.

To some extent, getting a friend or not might depend on the fish. Some fish just seem to prefer to be alone and will remain permanently hostile to any tankmates. Of course, this is not common behavior for goldfish (which are peaceful community fish as a rule), but every fish has a different personality and there certainly are exceptions to the general rule.

## Issues with aggression

In general, goldfish are community animals and are very peaceful fish towards other goldfish. That said, aggression is a problem many goldfish keepers find themselves facing at one time or another. Aggression is characterized by pulling on another fish's fins, biting, chasing around and "nudging." Aggression causes stress on the victim. Once aggressive behavior starts, it can be hard to break the habit. There are multiple factors that can contribute to aggression, some of which are relatively simple to remedy. Here are some of the main reasons goldfish may not be getting along:

- **Overcrowding**: A significantly overcrowded aquarium can place stress on the fish, making them feel crowded and edgy.
- **Spawning time**: This behavior is especially prevalent in ponds during the spring and summer months. Considerable damage can be done to females in the spawning process, and some owners like to separate them until the frenzy is over. It may be worth noting that allowing the fish to spawn without interruption might help prevent egg-impaction.
- **Territorial**: A goldfish that has lived alone for a long time may not adjust well to having someone "move in" to their turf. This may or may not subside in time.
- **Sickness**: Goldfish seem to know instinctively when another goldfish is not well and may show aggressive behavior toward the sick fish. Perhaps this is a way in nature that disease is kept under control. Of course, there are still anecdotal stories of "compassionate" goldfish who seem to be nicer to the sufferer, so perhaps it isn't always a "dog-eat-dog" world.

- **Significant size difference**: A much larger fish could be more prone to picking on a much smaller fish. That said, small fish may bite at larger fish. Mixing size is not usually a problem unless the size difference is great enough that the littler fish can fit in the mouth of the big one and get eaten.

- **Breed-specific aggression issues:** Slim-bodied, athletic fish may tend to pick on more clumsy fancy goldfish. Some of the more heavily hybridized varieties, such as Bubble Eyes, Broadtail Telescopes, Celestial Eyes and perhaps some Ranchus could have issues competing with even the fancy varieties that can swim and see better, such as Fantails, Orandas and Ryukins.

- **Personality:** Some fish may be just more inclined to "throw their weight around" to get the most food. This can sometimes be seen in a batch of siblings where one is growing much bigger than the others. Goldfish are smart creatures and often learn to come back for more once they get a bite from another fish. For such fish, temporary separation in a floating basket (time-out) or the use of a tank divider as a longer-term solution may be useful.

# Section 4: Dangers to Goldfish Health

The goldfish is a remarkably hardy fish, and the fancy ones (though admittedly more delicate) can be surprisingly resilient - considering how much modification has been done to them in terms of their body shape and fins.

But like any pet, goldfish aren't made of iron. They are living creatures that have some basic needs like you and I. There are certain conditions that make them thrive, but there are conditions that cause them harm too. As owners we need to be aware of those harmful conditions and do our best to avoid placing our goldfish in them.   You are the one they depend on, you are responsible for their well-being.  They need you.  Maybe that's part of why we keep goldfish – the pleasure of being needed and considered vital to the life of another – but with that pleasure also comes a burden.  There will always be a measure of responsibility involved.

But by doing things the right way your burden will be a lot lighter and your fish will thrive as a result.  You just have to make sure you get off to a good start and avoid the pitfalls that can lead to issues with your goldfish's health. These potential dangers include:

- **Overfeeding**:  As we covered in the feeding section, goldfish who get more food than they are supposed to have are in for a lot of trouble internally as their organs become filled with fat and they become overweight.  But not only is overfeeding dangerous to the fish themselves, it puts the entire tank system in jeopardy.  This is because any uneaten food and the large amount of waste overload the filter.  Normal water changes aren't enough to keep things under control, and as a result, the ammonia can rise suddenly and make the fish seem sick or die.  Constant problems with water quality or sick fish can actually be caused by overfeeding.  Some people want their fish to be fat because they think it's cute or they want them to grow.  This is not a good approach.  Obese, sick fish aren't cute or able to grow how they should, and fish that are overfed quickly become unhealthy and have a shorter lifespan.
- **Tank dangers:**  The delicate eye sacks of more hybridized breeds such as the Bubble Eye can burst if scraped against a point or sucked into the filter intake, and the protruding eyes of the Telescope have been known to come completely off.  Other tank dangers such as water quality and high bad bacteria counts are important to avoid.
- **Parasites & Disease:** You can do everything right as far as tank setup and maintenance goes, but if a parasitic infection goes unaddressed, all your efforts will be in vain.  In a closed aquarium, parasites can multiply to massive numbers to the point where they actually kill the fish.  The secondary bacterial infections that follow can also be lethal.  Having a proper quarantine procedure can help prevent all this from happening to begin

with. Some diseases are very hard or even impossible to prevent or treat. Others can kill quietly, going unnoticed without careful observation until it results in death within a matter of days.

- **Stress:** Like you and I, goldfish are prone to getting stressed, even if their water quality is fine. Being chased around with a net or other objects (even being chased by other fish), rough handling while being moved from one place to another, or constant changes in their location or environment can all put strain on them. Effects of stress include a weakening of the immune system, making the fish more vulnerable to disease. Extreme cases of stress can cause shock and death. It's really important to minimize handling and other things that can cause stress so this doesn't happen. Sudden drastic changes in temperature or other conditions are also dangerous – consistency is an art that must be mastered.

- **Improper Care:** Probably one of the *biggest hazards* goldfish face is directly in the lap of the owner. When goldfish are overfed or their setup is not suited to the fish or their waste load, that quickly leads to health complications and (in the worst cases) death.

# Water Poisoning

We talked earlier about the importance of water quality and maintaining proper water parameters for goldfish.  But when those parameters get off, the fish displays unusual symptoms and the distressed owner often jumps to the conclusion that their beloved pet has a disease.  When a fish is unwell, the first question to ask is, "What condition is the water in?"  Only if the water is in good shape can the fish have the chance of being in good shape.

When their fish isn't acting well, many fishkeepers assume their fish has a parasite and needs medicine.  But the symptoms of water poisoning can be exactly identical to the symptoms of a pathogen.  Adding medications to toxic water often spells death for the inhabitants of that tank.

If you suspect that your fish is incurring issues with water quality, or for that matter if you are concerned that your fish is not acting or looking like its normal self, I recommend changing 50-90% of the water immediately and keep doing that every day to every until things are back to normal.  Large water changes are the best way to remove toxins in the water during an emergency, if your water source is good.  Aging and aerating the water prior to changing the water is very much suggested.

Also, it is a good idea to withhold food until the water conditions stabilize.  Adding food puts additional strain on a system that is already out of balance.

A reminder: if you are using a test kit and even if your water is "testing fine," don't go by the test results – go by the health of the fish (assuming you have ruled out parasite issues and no new fish or plants have been introduced).  Remember, we only have access to standard quality kits that can don't measure bad bacteria count.

These are the most common causes of water-related issues:

## Ammonia Poisoning

Ammonia poisoning is common in tanks that are new and/or have not been properly cycled.  Ammonia poisoning can also occur in established tanks that do not have adequate biological filtration or a surplus of food.

Signs of ammonia poisoning include the following symptoms:

- Clamped fins
- Black smudges (which are healing burns)
- Sitting on the bottom of the tank
- Lethargy

- Loss of appetite
- Gasping at the surface
- Repeated "yawning"
- Ragged fins, splits in fins
- Bloody streaks in fins
- "Flashing" or scratching on objects/surfaces in the tank
- Missing scales (from flashing)

These symptoms can also be caused by other problems with the water or parasites. Testing the water is recommended to confirm if ammonia is the cause.

Ammonia can be brought down by doing large water changes of 90%. The additional use of an ammonia binder, such as Seachem Prime, in addition to a high-quality ammonia-consuming bacteria supplement such as ATM Colony Pro. These should be dosed every 48 hours or as needed (test the water daily to confirm).

*Seachem Prime*

## Nitrite Poisoning

Nitrite poisoning causes a condition called "brown blood disease" because it makes the red blood cells of the fish unable to carry oxygen, resulting in brown-colored blood. Symptoms are similar to ammonia poisoning.

*ATM Colony Pro*

- Red patches (blood hemorrhaging)
- Flared gills
- Clamped fins
- Flashing
- Red belly (typically in advanced stages)

Maintaining 1 teaspoon of salt per 5 gallons of water can help alleviate the caustic effects of nitrite poisoning. Ensure plenty of aeration for the fish, as the damaged gills will have a harder time taking up oxygen from the water.

## Nitrate Poisoning

Too much nitrates in the water causes the blood vessels of the fish to dilate and can lead to many different symptoms.

- Buoyancy trouble (bottom sitting, floating)
- Bulging veins
- Lethargy

- Decreased appetite
- Streaky-looking skin

If your nitrate levels are above 30ppm and your fish are acting unwell, it could be an issue of high nitrates and lots of partial water changes are recommended (too large of a water change could shock the fish).  The application of liquid chlorophyll may help counteract the adverse effects of high nitrates.

## Low PH or PH Crash

A pH crash can wipe out an entire tank or pond overnight.  The smaller the volume of water, the more prone it is to having the pH be unstable.

The pH of goldfish blood is 7.4.  When the water pH is much lower or higher than that the fish is forced to work very hard to try to keep their blood pH where it should be.  To them, a low pH feels like being submerged in acid.  Sudden death can follow a rapid pH drop.  A goldfish suffering from a low pH or pH crash commonly show the following signs:

- Gasping and/or hanging at the top of the water
- Reduced activity or lethargy
- Suppressed appetite
- Excess slime production
- Slime coat shedding
- Death

Dissolved organic matter can cause the pH to dip very low.  A low pH can kill the biological filtration, beginning with Nitrobacter (the bacteria that consumes nitrites) and then Nitrosomonas (the bacteria that consumes ammonia).  This leads to a large nitrite spike followed by a large ammonia spike.  This burns the gills.  Any plants may be damaged or fried.  Surviving fish exposed to high ammonia and/or nitrite levels need to be immediately transferred to fresh water.

It is important to use a buffer to bring the pH back within the recommended range as fast as possible during a pH crash.  Normally, adjusting the pH should be done slowly and in small increments, but the advantages of correcting the low pH quickly far outweigh the drawbacks in such an emergency.  A massive water change is recommended.  If you have a commercial pH buffer on hand, you could dose according to the directions instead if you for some reason could not do the water change.  The household staple product, baking soda, (at 1 tsp per 10 gallons) pre-dissolved in tank water is also a way to raise the pH quickly in a pinch.

Because the filter has been reset, it will be necessary to do lots of large, frequent water changes and start over with a fish-in cycle. Please see the secret cycling shortcut section for tips on safely making it through this delicate time.

Finally, fish that survive a pH crash will be extremely stressed and prone to secondary infection. Feeding an antibiotic food may be a good precaution to take.

## Oxygen Deprivation (Anoxia)

This is rarely a problem in setups that have some kind of filtration. There are tests that can be used to measure how much oxygen is in the water for those who are especially curious. If the fish is...

- Surface gulping
- Breathing rapidly
- Showing lethargy

...it may be that your oxygen levels are too low.

Solution: Adding an air stone or filter can quickly remedy the situation. Oxygen is reduced in cases where the temperature is too warm (over 90 degrees). Cooling the aquarium by adding ice packs, frozen water bottles or a fan blowing on the water's surface can help.

The use of salt can decrease available oxygen in the water. Certain medications or combinations of medications can do the same thing. This should be taken into consideration when treating a fish and the aeration increased as much as possible without blowing the fish around too much in the current.

## High pH or pH Spike

While alkaline water does not harm goldfish directly (in fact, goldfish can do quite well in alkaline water), a high pH (above 8.8) causes ammonia to be far more toxic. This can be an issue in new, uncycled tanks with a high pH.

Concrete ponds that have not been properly sealed can leach high levels of lime into the water, causing death of the fish.

## Supersaturated Gas Poisoning

This is a condition prevalent where there is an aerator on the tap or the water is not agitated enough. It seems to be often an issue with the tank or pond being filled directly with deep well water. Deep well water is under pressure and is much colder, causing an increase in gasses.

You might observe:

- Pockets or bubbles of air on the skin
- in conjunction with air bubbles covering the surfaces in the tank
- in conjunction with bulging eyes
- in conjunction with buoyancy trouble
- in conjunction with "burping" through the gills or mouth

If you have trouble with supersaturated gas from the tap, I would recommend that you start by removing the aerator from your sink and agitate the water before adding it to your aquarium. This can be done by stirring or pouring the water from a tall height. Then, use the aging and aerating water techniques described in the water changes section going forward.

## Hydrogen Sulfide

Hydrogen sulfide, while not technically a water parameter, is a form of sulfer that is not good for goldfish. It sometimes causes a "rotten egg" smell. It can come from well water or (most commonly) plain gravel substrates – that aren't frequently cleaned and have no live rooting plants – where excessive numbers of anaerobic bacteria are living in a low-to-no dissolved oxygen environment. The disturbance of such substrates can lead to a sudden, concentrated release in hydrogen sulfide as the pocket explodes, which can poison your goldfish. It can also gradually leach into the water from areas of buildup, leading to disease and health problems.

Removing hydrogen sulfide is best done by aging and aerating well water (if using) and redoing the substrate (please see the section on gravel for more information on how to do this).

## Heavy Metals

Some water can contain heavy metals. To know which metals are in your tap water, it is a good idea to obtain a report from your water company. Some heavy metals are essential to life in trace amounts. However, large amounts can lead to toxicity. Other heavy metals, such as mercury and arsenic, are very harmful in even low amounts. Copper is a heavy metal that is far more toxic at a low pH. Well water may contain a high amount of iron which can cause gill irritation, but can be removed from the water through an aging and aerating process.

*Auro Liquid Gold*

Some commercial water conditioners can remove heavy metals from the water, as can reverse osmosis filtration. Plants have the ability to take up heavy metals and remove them from the water column.

## Salinity

Salt, as a temporary tonic or treatment, can do wonders for many goldfish ailments. That said, salinity is a water parameter. As such, too high of a salt concentration or too long of living in it can cause problems for goldfish.

Water that has been softened with the use of salt can cause considerable excess salt in your water. Such exposure to strong concentrations of salt can cause harm to goldfish (specifically the liver) over extended period of time, as they are not brackish water fish. If your water is softened, it is a good idea to consider the use of a salinity meter to determine the salt content of your water and bypass if necessary. This is especially important if you ever need to treat your goldfish with salt for any reason. If you don't know your water salinity to start with, adding more salt on top of what is in the water to begin with can harm you goldfish.

## High Dissolved Organics

Dissolved organics are created by rotting food and decaying plant or fecal matter. Some small amount of dissolved organics is normal in any system. On the other hand, high levels of dissolved organics can cause a large bacteria count in the water, some of which are opportunistic. A high bacteria count in the water drastically increases the risk of bacterial infection and other sickness in fish.

Evidence of high dissolved organics include cloudy water and bubbles that persist on the surface of the water. No test kit currently exists for dissolved organics, though a TDS meter can provide some level of indication.

Keeping your dissolved organics low is best done through careful feeding, regular water changes and prompt removal of dead plants in a system. Increased biodiversity can help break down the organics in the tank. Uneaten veggies should be replaced every 24 hours to avoid rotting material sitting in the tank. Adding new fish to a tank can cause high dissolved organics to spike, necessitating frequent water changes.

## Chemical Contamination

Bug sprays, household cleaning agents, air fresheners and other chemicals can contaminate your Bug sprays, household cleaning agents, air fresheners and other chemicals can contaminate your aquarium as the vapors land on the surface of the water and also through any air pumps that take air from the room for your filters or air stones.

There is also the possibility of contaminating your fish's water when you reach your hands in the tank for maintenance or interaction with your fish. Be sure to wash your hands very well before putting them in the tank if you use any conventional lotions, soaps, perfumes, nail polish, shampoos, sanitizers or wipes.  Many of these contain toxic chemicals that can harm your fish.  If you can still smell it on your hands after washing, it is not gone.  My personal recommendation is to use all-natural, non-toxic products for your hands and skin to help reduce this risk – better for you and better for your pets.

Again, some decorations or accessories you place in the tank may contain chemical coatings that could leach into your water over time.  Even the paints on gravel can gradually break down and contaminate your water.  By being very careful with what you put in your aquarium, you can help protect your pets from toxins.

# Other Miscellaneous Dangers

## Temperature Swings

For most people, temperature is not much of an issue. Goldfish are pretty flexible, but sudden drastic changes can harm them by shocking their system, causing stress or death. When the temperature skyrockets, such as during a heater malfunction from lack of a surge protector, there is less oxygen for the fish, so some of the symptoms will be those of oxygen deprivation.

- Labored breathing
- Buoyancy trouble
- Listing to one side
- Bottom sitting

Slim-bodied goldfish have been known to survive extreme swings in temperature, provided they occur gradually. The key is to bring it back to normal as soon as possible through the use of cooling or warming the tank.

Very cold temperatures can prove harmful to fancy goldfish varieties. They tend to do better in warmer temperatures with minimal if any temperature fluctuation.

## Aeromonas Alley (Outdoor Fish)

After a long winter and fasting, goldfish kept outdoors are very weak. As spring approaches and the water warms to the 47-62 degree F range, Aeromonas bacteria are multiplying but the fish's immune system is low and isn't as active yet. On top of that, the biological filter is not active yet, complicating the situation. Parasites can bring on infection even faster. This can lead to ulcers and internal infection.

Some advocate administering medications to prevent the fish from being infected. This can cause complications as meds can interfere with the biological filter becoming established.

There is a natural approach, which is to help get the fish out of Aeromonas Alley as fast as possible without causing undue stress to the fish.

Once the temperature starts warming up to 47F, raising the temperature using a pond heater by 1-2 degrees daily until the water gets to 65 degrees F. Only after temperatures above 55 degrees F do goldfish start building their immune system.

*ATM Colony Pro*

Begin feeding very sparingly while the biological filter is still establishing. During this time, you can use water changes and beneficial bacteria filter colony supplements to control ammonia and kick-start your cycle, as well as keep dissolved organics to a minimum.

*KoiZyme*

Many fishkeepers are finding success using a probiotic supplement to reduce these high bad bacteria counts in the water during Aeromonas Alley. The beneficial bacteria in KoiZyme offer a means of approach to control bad bacteria by outcompeting them for food. If you keep fish outdoors, this option could prove to be lifesaving for them.

## Jumping Out

Jumping out is often an indication that the water quality is not where it should be. However, during spawning a fish may leap out of the water in the course of the chase, or a fish dealing with parasitic attack. Athletic slim-bodied fish may jump out even when nothing is wrong! The longer the fish remains out of the water the smaller its chances of survival become.

You will know it is too late for the fish when you see:

- Cracked skin
- Sunken in eyeballs
- Gray eyes

If there looks to be hope, after returning the fish to well-aerated tank water you can try gently opening the gill covers. Note that if the fins dried out during the fish's time out of water they will probably fall to bits and they won't grow back.

## Getting Dropped

This happens in the process of moving fish from one area to another. A thrashing fish can fly out of a net, your hands or even shallow container while being m oved to the floor (usually several feet below). If the fish survives the fall after being returned to the water, they may show the following symptoms:

- Bleeding or redness where the fish landed
- Listing to one side
- Fright
- Not moving

Place the fish by itself in a dark, calm tank with plenty of clean water. Do not feed and do not disturb the fish for a couple of days to recover. After that time you can resume feeding and, if the fish has returned to its normal self, return it to the main tank. Avoid the temptation to add salts or medication as this will stress the fish.

## Electrocution

In the modern aquarium hobby technology has its perks, but it also has its downfalls. Electric current can suddenly charge into the water when using standard electrical aquarium equipment near the tank in certain situations. A fish that has been immediately shocked may suddenly show the following three symptoms:

- Kinked back while swimming
- Buoyancy problems
- Flipping upside down sometimes

In cases of immediate electrocution, some level of damage will be permanent, it is just a question of how much. Kinked backs are incurable.

Preventing electrocution involves making sure the water line never goes too far below submersible heaters which are (ideally) shatter-resistant. Unplug any equipment before performing a water change. And obviously, never place air pumps in the tank (or any other equipment not intended to be submerged) and never use a light over open water.

Something should also be said about electrical leakage into the water. This is a real problem and can be difficult to detect unless you either have fancy equipment or a really good handle on identifying fish behavior. That is because the levels of electricity aren't high enough to immediately kill or maim the fish, but it will cause issues regardless. It messes with their lateral lines (what helps the fish navigate in the water and sense vibrations). The fish are then being subjected to something that to us would feel to us like a deafening noise day and night without rest.

Symptoms of low electrical leakage include unexplained:

- Hiding in corners or dark spaces
- Confusion, disorientation
- Huddling in groups
- Darting around aimlessly

Note that these symptoms can also be due to bothering the fish from bright lights or excessive water current.

Heaters are a prime culprit for leaking current. Many of them are made cheaply and wear out even with proper care on your part. Be sure to purchase quality heaters and do not submerge the dial on top of manually set heaters, even if the box says the heater is submergible. That is the prime spot where water gets in and starts to cause problems. If you suspect electrical leakage, unplug the heater and other equipment immediately. In a few hours the fish should start returning to their normal selves.

## Injury

Injury to goldfish can happen as a result of spawning behavior, an encounter with a decoration in the tank or a host of other causes. Depending on the severity of the injury, you may see a wide range of symptoms including:

- Loss of appetite
- Hiding and isolation
- Bleeding in the case of a wound

Clean water is very important when an injury occurs because opportunistic bacteria will seek entry into the goldfish through that wound and cause infection. Clean water will keep the bacteria at bay and the goldfish's immune system uncompromised. Very deep wounds that expose muscle tissue may require sutures to prevent the fish from bleeding to death. A veterinarian who sees fish may be best to ask for this procedure.

Most wounds do not require any other steps than very clean water, calm and a good diet. However, in cases where the wound is deep, or you see the muscle of the fish, antibiotics may be necessary. A healing wound will fade; one that is becoming infected will get redder and should be treated. A 0.3% salt solution may help reduce osmotic pressure from the wound and prevent electrolyte loss.

Bubble Eye goldfish are prone to getting their delicate eye sacks popped by water change or filtration equipment. Pom Pom goldfish with large nares are also at risk for getting their pompoms torn off. Submersible pumps or filter intakes can inadvertently suck in the sacks or pompoms, causing injury. For these breeds, it may be necessary to remove any objects that could catch or damage these delicate features. In addition, covering the filter intake with a sponge can help prevent injury.

The good news is that the eye sack or pompom should grow back given time and clean water, though it will probably not return to its original size.

## Rock Blockage

Tanks with gravel pose the threat of choking to goldfish. As bottom-feeders, goldfish are constantly nosing about the bottom of the tank searching for food. If there is gravel, they will try to pick it up in their mouth as they forage. They take it in and spit it out. This is natural behavior for them, but gravel is the perfect size to get stuck in their mouth or throat as they do this.

Fish have rock blockage can show the following signs:

- Repeated yawning
- Unable to close mouth
- Head-standing
- Not eating
- Sitting at the bottom (advanced case)
- Death

Shining a flashlight down the throat of the fish can help identify if there is an object lodged further down the back of the fish's throat.

It is possible to successfully manually by capturing the fish and removing the rock with tweezers, but the issue can recur until the gravel is removed.

## Aggressive Tank Mates

Keeping other types of fish in with goldfish can lead to issues with aggression or injury that can stress your fish, possibly to the point of death.

Plecostomus and other algae eaters are notorious for trying to suck on the tasty slime coat of goldfish. They often do this during the night and the behavior can go unnoticed for a good while.

Spawning is a time when the chasing behavior of the fish can lead to stress and damage of female goldfish as well. Torn fins, missing scales and exhaustion can all come about from spawning. It is especially important to remove any objects the fish could get hurt on during this time. It is recommended to separate females that are becoming distressed due to constant chasing. The risks of injury are higher if the male is considerably larger than the female.

## Egg Binding

Egg binding can pose a serious threat to some female goldfish. Egg bound goldfish are characterized by abdominal distention (often asymmetrical) with a relatively firm belly. A female goldfish may swell with eggs that, if left unreleased, may become infected. Internal infections can spread quickly, leading to mortality.

Females do not need males present to expel their eggs and can do so even if living in an empty tank, though there is some thought that the nudging of males is more effective at getting the eggs released. Sometimes females may become egg-bound even in the presence of males if they are not sending the proper hormonal signals needed to induce spawning. Increasing the photoperiod and warmer temperatures may give the fish the final push they need. However, some may still not respond. Why are the hormones not functioning in the fish properly to send the signals at the right time, despite a conducive spawning environment?  Such may be the case for older female goldfish.  For young female fish that are egg-bound regardless of the proper environmental conditions, my personal theory is that the water may have some hormone-disrupting contaminants, such as pharmaceuticals that interfere with the fish's pheromones, bug sprays, heavy metals or other chemicals leaching into the water.

As with any problem, prevention is the best treatment.  A steady, warmer temperature (approximately 78 degrees to 82 degrees F) is likely to reduce the risk of an egg-bound female.  Females that appear to be carrying a large load of eggs, with or without the presence of gross abdominal distention (assuming infection has not taken place), may benefit from periodic manual massaging with the thumbs toward the vent.

Withholding food for 4 weeks has been suggested as a means to encourage the fish to reabsorb the eggs.  If the fish does not improve, a veterinarian may be able to administer hormonal injections to induce spawning or provide further diagnosis for the fish.

# Section 5: Health Issues & Disease
## Diagnostic Techniques
**8 Questions to ask When Something is Wrong with Your Fish:**

1. **What are your water parameters?** Improper water conditions can lead to caustic stress on the fish. Test the water for ammonia, nitrite, nitrate, pH, GH and KH and ensure they are at the recommended levels for goldfish.
2. **What is your feeding and maintenance schedule?** Feeding more requires changing the water more. If you are overfeeding, this can lead to high dissolved organics in the water, which can cause disease.
3. **Was the fish quarantined and treated for common goldfish diseases?** If you got your fish from a supplier that does not ensure the health of the fish, you will have needed to do this yourself.
4. **Have you added any new live things to your tank recently, such as plants or invertebrates?** If you didn't quarantine these first, they could carry disease to your tank.
5. **Do you share equipment with another tank in your house?** Cross-contamination between tanks can lead to disease.
6. **Was the fish recently weakened or stressed due to overcrowding, shipping or moving?** Stress can lead to issues that will often resolve with clean water and time.
7. **Do you age and aerate your water, mineralize it and remove toxins?** Most tap water contains a variety of contaminants that can irritate goldfish. Water that is free of contaminants but has no minerals can cause deficiencies in goldfish in some situations. Water that has not been aged and aerated does not have any bacteria in it which goldfish are used to.
8. **Where do you get your fish from?** Imported fish can sometimes carry parasites, bacterial diseases rare or unusual viruses.

## The Goldfish Physical
When you aren't sure what is wrong with your fish, a good place to start is with performing a physical examination of the fish.  Here is how to do that:

1) Check the body of the fish before removing it from the aquarium.  Be on the alert for any red marks from possible anchor worms or lice infestations.
2) Hold the fish upside-down at the surface of the water, trying to keep the head of the fish submerged to reduce thrashing.
3) Examine the gills of the fish. By gently prying open the gill cover with the thumb nail.  The gills should be a bright cherry-red.  Areas of discoloration or streaking can indicate bacterial

gill infection.  Brown gills indicate a nitrite or chlorine problem in the water. Pale pinkish gills can indicate a bacterial gill infection, medication toxicity, anemia (perhaps due to parasites) IHN virus (the fish will be dying), or organ failure (if the fish shows other signs of organ failure such as dropsy, bloating or septicemia).  If the gill filaments are stuck together, this could indicate parasites on the gills.  The fish will have a hard time getting oxygen from the water in that case.

4) Check the abdominal resistance.  A healthy abdomen will not feel mushy or hard.  A mushy abdomen could indicate egg impaction, organ failure, cancer, internal bacterial or parasitic infection.  Organ failure is currently not treatable.

## Microscopy

Like most people probably feel, I was intimidated for a long time about the thought of having or using a microscope with my goldfish.  But more recent experiences led me to believe that having a microscope on hand can prove an invaluable resource to have at our disposal.

Before you think yourself incapable of using such a tool, let me assure you that just about anyone who has been instructed on how to use a microscope can quickly pick up the basics. And here are some reasons why you should have one:

1) **Precision:** It is possible that you currently have or may end up having a fish that comes down with something you aren't sure of.  The symptoms of many different parasites appear to the naked eye to be identical when observing your fish.  For example, a fish that starts scratching, shedding slime and isolating itself could have a case of one of at least 5 parasites, several of which only respond to certain treatments.  With goldfish, there is no "one-treatment-cures-all" for disease and for many pathogens, time is of the essence when dealing with a sick fish.  If you try to medicate with the wrong treatment after treatment, the fish could meet its end long before you treat with the right one – not to mention go through considerable stress in the process.  Having a microscope means you can often know exactly which pest is most plaguing your fish and choose from a smaller range of the most effective treatments.  If the first one doesn't prove effective for some reason, you have some cushion.

2) **Protection**: I especially advise having a microscope if you purchase goldfish from goldfish suppliers who do not completely quarantine and treat their fish prior to sending them out – and especially if they do not use microscopy on their fish.  Even after you do prophylactic treatments on your fish, something could still slip by.  The treatment may have only eradicated most of the parasites but leave behind enough that the fish looks good now but could come down with sickness later – after you already introduced them to your main aquarium.  A microscope can help confirm whether or not your fish is ready to be introduced to your other ones.

The microscope you choose should have a minimum combined magnification capability of 1000X in order to see the smallest goldfish pathogens (specifically Costia). This number is the power of the eyepiece multiplied by the lens. So if your eyepiece is 10X and your lens is 40X, you will be using a 400X magnification. It is useful to have a built-in light so you do not have to rely on your environment to easily use your microscope.

*Microscope*

In order to use a microscope, you will need to be comfortable with handling your fish. If you are not comfortable doing so, it may be necessary to ask for veterinary assistance. Handling a fish when you are uncertain can lead to a shaky hand, which can cause accidental harm to the fish.

A mucus sample and a gill scrape are both important diagnostic tools, and it is advisable to perform both when diagnosing or examining your fish because some parasites may infect the gills exclusively.

1) For a mucous sample, it is necessary to hold your fish at the surface of the water upside-down in your left hand (if you are right-handed). Keeping the head of the fish under the surface of the water can help with thrashing. Holding the plastic or glass cover slip (plastic is preferred because it won't break as easily, harming you or your fish) in your right hand, gently slide the flat edge of the slip at a 45 degree angle along the fish. The best areas to scrape are the area underneath and beside the pectoral fin, the area on the stomach in front of the pelvic fins, and the ends of the tail fin. Immediately compress the cover slip onto the glass microscope slide and view the sample within 5 minutes (after that some parasite varieties will die and be unrecognizable). Please note that during the capture process, if you chase the fish around too much and wipe away the slime, it will be difficult to get enough mucus from the fish to examine with the microscope.

2) For a gill scrape, you can hold the fish as before with the head under the water upside-down at the surface. Using your left thumb, carefully and gently lift the gill cover of the fish from the top to expose the gill filaments. Insert the cover slip underneath the gill cover and, with mild downward pressure, slide the slip along the gill filaments. You should have a small amount of pinkish slime on the cover slip. Place a drop of tank water on the glass slide before compressing the cover slip to better view the parasites.

Of course, this procedure puts some level of stress on the fish, which is more of a concern if your fish is already very sick. The other side of the coin is that treating for issues that the fish may not have when its condition is already progressed will also put stress on the fish. Each fishkeeper will need to determine the best way to go for their particular case.

Once you are viewing the preparation through the microscope, be on the alert for movement. You will want to watch for creatures that are swimming around – the still mucous may contain darker blobs which are usually just organic debris. Costia will swim in tight circles. Flukes will poke around like earthworms, though they occasionally hold still. Many other parasites rotate around.

## The Hospital Tank

If you notice one of your fish is sick, it is usually a good idea to isolate that fish in a hospital tank. The primary reason for this is because a sick fish can be a "swimming hotel" of pathogens. As the other fish are continually exposed to the high level of pathogens from this sick fish, their immune system can eventually be overwhelmed and they, too, can come down sick. This is called dose response. Isolation of a sick fish is useful for bacterial issues, though the root cause will need to be identified or the other fish will likely succumb to the same thing at some point.

Another reason in support of isolation is to avoid having other goldfish in the tank start picking on the sick fish.

For parasitic infestations that do not happen in quarantine (the best place for them), the entire tank will need to be treated, regardless of how many fish are showing symptoms or not, because parasites can live in the filter or substrate and contaminate everything. In that case, a hospital tank is not necessary.

*Heater*

The hospital tank may or may not be filtered, but if there is no filter an airstone and frequent water changes are recommended – every 12-24 hours (depending on ammonia level after 12 hours) with aged, aerated water. A heater is also useful to have on hand for conditions that it would be beneficial for.

## Sudden Death

One day a goldfish can seem fine, the next it might be dead.  There are many reasons a goldfish might suddenly die without warning:

- New Tank Syndrome (in an uncycled aquarium)
- pH crash
- Ammonia or nitrite surge
- Rock blockage in the mouth
- Temperature extremes
- Shipping shock; fish that have just arrived at the pet store from being imported overseas
- Oxygen deprivation
- Bacterial gill disease
- Systemic bacterial infection
- Rancid food
- Toxic chemical contamination of the water
- If there really is no other explanation, cardiac arrest may be the cause

Prevention of the above (aside from factors out of your control) is the best way to ensure your fish don't suddenly die.

# Sterilization

If you have lost all the fish in a tank and need to start fresh, sterilization is very important. Introducing new fish to a contaminated tank overrun by pathogens is asking for trouble, so there are a few things you can do to push the "reset" button.

Bleach is a popular method, though I prefer to use more natural alternatives to this toxic chemical because I don't want to breathe the fumes. Not only that, but bleach does eradicate tuberculosis and mycobacteria.

Warning: do not boil the tank to disinfect it. This can ruin your aquarium as the silicone can melt. You can boil most filter media to thoroughly remove all bacteria, viruses or parasites.

*3% Hydrogen Peroxide*

Distilled white vinegar and hydrogen peroxide are two useful agents that can sterilize an aquarium on the cheap and naturally. Organisms cannot live in the low pH of the vinegar, and the peroxide eliminates them as well. For a tank full of water, use at least 1 cup of vinegar to 10 gallons of water and soak for 24 hours (leaving the filter running). Then the tank should be drained and everything thoroughly rinsed in fresh water until no more vinegar smell is detectable. It also doesn't hurt to run up the heat quickly to 90 + degrees F for 24 hours, as long as there are no fish, invertebrates or plants in the tank.

For a dry tank or other equipment, use a spray bottle of peroxide to coat the surfaces and allow to air dry.

Please keep in mind that anywhere there is debris buildup in the filter, tank or other areas should be completely manually cleaned.

To sterilize anubias plants, one method is to spray them with 3% hydrogen peroxide and allow to dry for 10 minutes before rinsing with tap water. Other aquatic plants will probably not be able to handle the direct spray. If you do not want to take any chances after an outbreak of disease in your tanks, the safest method is to throw the plants out and replace them.

## Parasitic Infections

Parasites are a prevalent threat to goldfish health.  They are one of the primary reasons why new goldfish owners leave the hobby frustrated.

This is because the fish may start out seemingly healthy, but is actually carrying a load of parasites that, within the first few months, cause the fish to become sick and die for seemingly no reason.

The confused owner is trying to do everything they can to keep their fish healthy, but they end up failing because of something that goes undiagnosed until it is too late.

It is safe to assume that any imported goldfish comes with parasites.  This includes those at pet stores.  The best approach to dealing with these is during a quarantine process, as discussed previously.

While parasites pose a threat to goldfish health, the good news is that most of them are relatively easy to treat if you know what you are dealing with.

There is also a broad-spectrum approach that can prove useful if you don't know what you are dealing with – after all, most parasites are only visible at microscopic magnification.

There are two primary classes of parasites that affect goldfish: internal and external, each requiring a different approach to treatment.

## Internal Parasites

Fish that have a heavy load of internal parasites will often have long, white stringy feces and/or a wasted, skinny abdomen and act lethargic.

Intestinal parasites can include intestinal hexamita or worms.

Metronidazole (available as Metroplex) is a drug commonly used to rid fish of internal parasites, used as a medicated feed for 3 weeks. It should not, however, be used prophylactically or parasitic resistance can be built up, creating "super bugs."

*Metroplex*

There is also a cheaper, more natural, and safer method that is easy to use, and that is using Epsom salt feed. Even larger fish operations recognize the effectiveness of Epsom salt (magnesium sulfate) for internal parasites:

*Epsom Salt*

> "Mortality ceased with an application of medicated feed (magnesium sulfate at 3% of the feed)..."[5]

You can purge internal parasites in your fish by deworming with a 3% Epsom salt feed. Use 1 level tablespoon of Epsom Salt (15 grams) to 500 ML of distilled water. Use an eye dropper to add water to food until the food does not absorb any more. Feed twice daily for 5 days.

One benefit of Epsom Salt for intestinal parasites is that it is very gentle on the fish. Excess magnesium is easily be removed from the fish's body and the risk of organ damage from medications is eliminated.

---

[5] *The Israeli Journal of Aquaculture*, Bamidhah 57(2), 2005

## External Parasites

External parasites are very common among imported goldfish who have not been quarantined and treated before being sent to you. This includes fish from pet stores, chain stores and many importers.

After any parasitic infestation, which causes stress to the fish, it is common for bacterial infections to follow. Watch the fish closely for signs of secondary bacterial infection.  Many times, parasites will not kill a fish as quickly as these secondary infections, so preventing them should be foremost in your mind.  (Pristine water quality, KoiZyme and antibiotics are three things you do not want to be without.  KoiZyme should be used throughout treatment to prevent secondary infection.) Fighting secondary bacterial infections without eradicating the parasite that is causing them tends to be an uphill battle, with no amount of clean water or tonics proving to be useful until the root of the problem is resolved. If the fish already has a bacterial infection by the time parasites are identified as the underlying cause, no medications will help until the parasites are first treated. After that, the bacterial infections can be addressed, if they have not resolved already with treating for parasites.

*KoiZyme*

Correctly identifying external parasites is important.  Once water quality issues have been completely ruled out, parasites can often be the next logical possibility.

Behavior of parasitized fish may vary greatly, but commonly include flashing, flicking fins, clamped fins and hitting or rubbing on the tank walls or decorations.  Later stages may include isolation, lethargy and labored breathing.  Excess slime production is evidenced by cloudiness of the water and strands hanging off the fish. The fish may even lose interest in food.  Some fish may get small red spots or even ulcers as a result of the parasites.

Some parasites themselves are even visible to the naked eye, such as anchor worm and fish lice.  These are the easiest to diagnose.

Most of these parasite infections will resolve quickly with a few applications of MinnFinn.  MinnFinn is a safe, eco-friendly treatment that eradicates common external parasites on goldfish when the directions are followed correctly.  However, some parasites can escape even several applications due to its unique life cycle – one of which is ich.

*MinnFinn*

Ich

**Microscope Identification**

The presence of ich can often be observed without a microscope in the presence of the characteristic white dots, but appears at 100X magnification as a dark, ovular organism with a "U"-shaped interior. It rotates around using its very tiny cilia (legs). With good microscopy, you can see small black dots inside the creature that move around. These are the tomites, which will turn into more ich organisms preparing to re-infect the fish.

## Symptoms

Ich, or "white spot disease," is very prevalent in goldfish. Actually, fish can have ich without even showing a single white spot, especially with minor infestations. Other signs of ich include flashing, labored breathing, or redness of the skin.

## Mortality Rate

Moderate. Ich can kill the fish through suffocation of the gills if left untreated.

## Treatment

Ich is protected from bath treatments (treatments you add to the water) while under the skin of the goldfish, where the parasite spends a portion of its lifetime feeding on its host. That is part of the reasoning behind raising the temperature, which speeds up its lifecycle and makes it vulnerable to treatment.

Contrary to popular belief, ich is not always present in the aquarium, just waiting for your fish to get weak so it can attack it. Ich is introduced into aquariums via plants, contaminated water, new fish, etc. In the wild, ich does not do serious harm to fish because of the large volume of water. Most ich organisms never find a host and a fish can live fine with just a few parasites. But in the closed aquarium system, a large number of ich organisms can easily find a host and totally overwhelm the fish. One ich parasite can create thousands of baby parasites! Each re-infestation will be worse than the last. That is why it is important to quarantine fish, plants or invertebrates, as well as prevent cross-contamination between tanks with water or equipment.

The combination of MinnFinn and water changes can eventually eliminate the organism, but the process can be long and tedious and if the life of the fish is in serious danger (ich will eventually destroy the gills of the fish and suffocate it to death, as well as create considerable stress which weakens the fish) other treatments are advised. The following protocol using salt was recommended to me by Ken Fisher of Dandy Orandas, who uses this method with success at his operation.

*Aquarium Salt*

- Raise the temperature to 77-82 degrees F. It has been found that temperatures above 85 degrees F harms the reproductive cycle of the parasite, but can be too stressful when combined with salt. Increase aeration as much as possible (but not to the point where the fish will be stressed by the current). This is because oxygen is lower in warmer water, and also because ich clogs up the gills of the fish.
- For most cases, begin by salting to a 0.5% concentration (19 grams per gallon).  Add the salt gradually in 3 separate doses at 12 hours apart (2 if the fish are severely infected), then replenish the same concentration with water changes.  Dissolve the salt by stirring it in a bucket of water prior to adding it to the tank.  Salt is therapeutic to goldfish, who can lose a lot of electrolytes due to dehydration as they shed their slime coat trying to get rid of the parasite.  If the fish is shedding profusely, lots of water changes and/or mechanical filtration will be necessary so the water doesn't foul. *Salt will harm or kill plants.*  More severe cases (such as when the fish is having trouble breathing, exhibiting lethargy, refusing to eat) or more salt resistant strains may need a stronger salt solution. 0.7% (26 grams per gallon) or 0.8% (30 grams per gallon). You will need to carefully monitor the fish at higher salt concentrations.  Watch for signs of stress. It is normal for the fins to get "edgy" at higher salt concentrations, but blood in the fins is a warning flag that the fish is too stressed or the filter may be impaired from the salt, leading to ammonia or nitrite spikes.  Do a 100% water change and reduce the salt down.  A salinity meter can come in handy.
- Vacuuming the bottom of the tank twice daily is useful to remove the ich eggs and can speed up the progress of treatment.  50% water changes daily are ideal.
- Observe the fish for 4 days.  If no improvement is seen by day 7, increase the salt concentration for an additional 3-7 days until the ich is vanquished with careful monitoring.

Observe the fish closely during the course of treatment. It is normal for the ich to get worse before it gets better with the addition of salt. The ich should be eliminated at the end of 1 week, but ensure the salt remains in the system for 14 days total or you can have a relapse, and relapses are always worse. Very severe ich infestations may take as long as 3 weeks to resolve.  To be on the safe side, continue the salt 1 week longer than you see symptoms.

## Costia

**Microscopic Identification**

Costia is a very tiny parasite, perhaps the tiniest one.  It is only visible under the microscope at powers above 400X.  They look like swarms of clear, tiny, twirling commas.

**Symptoms**

The symptoms can vary between cases, such as gasping at the surface, labored breathing, flashing and scratching, or excess slime production. Little red dots or spiderweb-like hemorrhages can very often be seen under the chin of the fish, but also along the back. Red dots under the scales are more likely bacterial in nature rather than parasitic.

**Mortality Rate**

High. Costia is often a quick-killing disease, which means it needs to be caught and treated early to have the best outcome for the fish. Costia can be responsible for sudden death of fish. The parasite can even survive for a period of time even if dried out and can contaminate any equipment it comes in contact with.

**Treatment**

2-3 applications of MinnFinn is my go-to treatment for Costia.

## Chilodonella

**Microscopic Identification**

Chilodonella is a leaf-shaped parasite that most commonly swims in small circles. It appears to be filled with clear bubbles.

**Symptoms**

Fish with Chilodonella may show clamped fins, flashing, labored breathing, excess slime production, paleness or isolate themselves.

**Mortality Rate**

Chilodonella, like many parasites, can lie dormant for a long time until the fish become stressed. In cases where the infection is greatly progressed (indicated by gasping at the surface), high mortality is expected. Weaker fish may perish.

*MinnFinn*

**Treatment**

1-2 applications of MinnFinn.

## Trichodina

**Microscopic Identification**

This parasite appears under the microscope at low (100-200X) magnifications as a circular, gyrating "wagon wheel" organism.

## Symptoms

Trichodina can cause clamped fins, flashing and labored breathing.  The scratching can eventually lead to ulcers (characteristic of heavy infestations).

## Mortality Rate

Moderate.  Trichodina is more prevalent in dirty water or water high in dissolved organics.  Like many parasites, they become more of a problem in large numbers.  A strong outbreak can lead to a high mortality rate.  Clean water is especially critical to clearing up this parasite.

## Treatment

1-2 applications of MinnFinn.

## Flukes

### Microscopic Identification

Flukes are common in goldfish.  They are the largest parasite to see under a microscope – only 40X magnification is required to see them.  One will appear as a "wormy" looking creature with hooks at one end, which it uses to eat the fish.  They are very repulsive when viewed under a microscope.  Both body flukes and gill flukes are almost always found together and their treatment is the same.

## Symptoms

Fish with flukes may exhibit heavy breathing, gasping at the surface, isolation, clamped fins and scratching, ulcers and excessive slime.

The less common (and untreatable) brain or eye fluke cause the fish to swim in circles.  It is visible as a white speck in the eye.  These flukes require another host such as a bird or snail to complete their lifecycle (hence why it is more prevalent in ponds).

## Mortality Rate

Moderate.  Perhaps the greatest danger flukes pose to goldfish is the subsequent bacterial infection that comes from all the damage they do to the fish.  They can transmit bacteria directly to goldfish as well as leave them vulnerable to secondary infection.

## Treatment

Flukes are resistant to salt and several conventional chemical parasitic treatments. At one point, Praziquantel was the only widely-known remedy, but the active ingredients in MinnFinn are even more effective at killing flukes. 1-3 treatments are necessary, dependent on the species of the fluke.

There is no treatment for fish with a brain or eye fluke infestation.

## Velvet

**Microscope Identification**

Velvet looks like a still, pear-shaped organism at 100X magnification. Sometimes it has a "polar cap" at one end.

**Symptoms**

Velvet is sometimes known as "gold dust" disease because it makes the fish look like it has a coating of tiny, rust-colored flecks. Some cases can look similar to very heavy infestations of ich. It can be seen best by shining a flashlight over the top of the fish in a dark room. Other key symptoms may include scratching, lethargy, loss of appetite and weight loss, paleness, clamped fins and difficulty breathing.

**Mortality Rate**

Moderately high. Because it can appear to the naked eye very similar to ich, but will not respond to salt, it is therefore important to correctly diagnose because if the case is mistakenly identified as ich and treated as such, it can be too late to change treatments to get rid of the Velvet. Early detection is important for things to turn around. This disease can go unnoticed for a while if the spots are very fine.

**Treatment**

Fortunately, velvet is actually pretty rare in goldfish. Salt does not do much, if anything, against Velvet. Its elusive life cycle makes it tricky to treat with MinnFinn as well. Copper (Seachem Cupramine) is the treatment of choice. It should be kept in the system for 14 days. There is some evidence to suggest keeping the tank in total darkness can help to eradicate it, but this is not usually necessary. As with all copper treatments, it can be harsh on the fish and deadly to plants and invertebrates.

*Seachem Cupramine*

## Epistylis

**Microscope Identification**

This parasite has a bell shape with a long "stem" at one end.  Sometimes the hair-like cilia can be seen on the end of the bell shape.

**Symptoms**

Epistylis appears as a white fuzzy tuft sticking out from under a scale or wound on the goldfish.  It may also be found on the fins, especially the edges.

**Mortality Rate**

Low.  Only once the disease progresses considerably does it endanger the life of the fish.

**Treatment**

Fortunately, Epistylis is pretty rare.  Clean water is especially essential to clearing up this disease, as it thrives in filthy conditions.  Poor water conditions are, in fact, the main cause.  Salting to 0.3-0.5% can help to knock it back.

## Anchor Worm
**Microscope Identification**

Not necessary.  Visible to the naked eye.

**Symptoms**

Stick-like worms protrude from the fish, which can be brown, white, yellow or green.  The damage the worm causes to the fish can cause red areas.

**Mortality Rate**

Moderate.  Highly contagious and can infect perfectly healthy fish.  Secondary bacterial infections pose a great threat from this parasite.

**Treatment**

Anchor worm has a more complex life cycle.  Simply removing the worms manually and sterilizing the areas with hydrogen peroxide can help, but there is a chance of reinfection as the eggs (resistant to treatment) at the bottom will hatch.  Copper and many other conventional chemical medications are ineffective.

One method of control offers a more natural approach but does involve more effort on the part of the fish keeper.  You will need two clean buckets or Tupperware containers.  It is then possible to eradicate it by not only manually removing all of the worms, but then transferring the fish to one of the clean buckets or Tupperware tubs full of aged, aerated water salted to 0.5%. The salt will help stimulate the slime coat of the fish and help to prevent bacterial infection. The tank and filter must then be drained and everything that was in it sprayed with 3% hydrogen peroxide and left to dry out completely for several days. Plants can be replaced. This will kill the eggs and prevent re-infestation. The tank will need to be re-cycled. The next day, transfer the fish to the second tub or bucket. Drain and sterilize the first bucket or tub and airstone, refill with water, dechlorinate, salt and aerate for the next 24 hours. Repeat the alternating process for the next 10 days.

Salt at 0.3% and repeated applications of MinnFinn (3 days in a row) may bring the problem under control, but stronger treatments (such as those containing the active ingredient of Cyromazine) may be warranted if the case is persistent or if the hobbyist cannot or would rather not do the daily transfer method.

*Cyromazine*

## Fish Lice

**Microscope Identification**

Not necessary. Visible to the naked eye.

**Symptoms**

The fish may appear to have a spot of green algae about 1/8" long growing on it, but closer inspection may reveal this as a living creature to be moving about on the surface of the host. The fish louse has two eyespots and is shaped like a saucer. The fish may also scratch and flash considerably, trying to dislodge the parasite.

Advanced cases may cause red spots. Cases where no lice are seen may show scale loss, anemia, lethargy, flashing and excess slime.

**Mortality Rate**

Moderate to high. Cases can rapidly escalate, and lice can carry other diseases including fungus. The lesions may become infected by bacteria. Advanced stages of infestation can result in high mortality rates.

**Treatment**

As with anchor worm, fish lice are egg-layers. These eggs may re-infect fish after manual removal if not treated. Manual removal with tweezers and the same sterilization and the daily transfer protocol can be useful for fish that live in tanks. Salt to 0.3% can help protect against secondary infection while applications of MinnFinn can help do damage to the parasite.

Cyromazine containing products can help to bring the infestation under control.

## Hexamita

### Microscope Identification

Identifying Hexamita with a microscope requires at least 1000X power to see these tiny organisms.

### Symptoms

Fish with hexamita may exhibit lethargy, frayed fins, and produce excess slime.  Intestinal hexamita can cause weight loss and hole in the head (HITH) disease.

### Mortality Rate

Moderately high.  Fortunately, Hexamita is not a very common disease.

### Treatment

Feeding Metronidazole (Seachem Metroplex) medicated food for 3 weeks eliminates the parasite. Metroplex can also be added to the water column.

## Myxobolus Cerebralis

### Microscope Identification

Necropsy required to acquire brain tissue.  Under a microscope it appears as a 3-tailed spore.

*Metroplex*
*(Metronidazole)*

### Symptoms

This condition is often referred to as "whirling disease" as the parasite (lodged inside the brain and inner ear of the fish) interferes with the fish's equilibrium, causing them to swim in circles or head down.  A bent spine or brain damage may result.  Emaciation occurs in most fish as the condition progresses and feeding becomes difficult for the fish.

### Mortality Rate

Very high.

### Treatment

*Kanaplex*
*(Kanamycin)*

Many owners choose to euthanize for this condition. Only one treatment, Kanamycin, has been found effective in some rare cases, when treated for 3 months. May need to be combined with Furan 2 and Metronidazole. Surviving fish will always carry the parasite and may transmit it to other fish.

Avoid feeding tubifex worms to help prevent this condition.

*Furan 2*

# Bacterial Infections

In every aquarium and pond there are always going to be teeny, tiny microscopic creatures called bacteria. Some of these bacteria are opportunistic, meaning that they wait until another creature is susceptible to attack and then start using the nutrients of the "host" to grow and multiply.

You, as the aquarium manager, may be able to reduce their numbers, but they are never completely eradicated. They will always be in the tank; you can't get rid of them completely without killing of your fish in the process. But healthy, well-cared for goldfish don't come down with them because their bodies have a built-in defense system which fights off any invaders. This system is the strongest weapon a goldfish has to stay healthy. However, when the fish is stressed out by parasites, bad water conditions, improper diet, being shipped, cold temperatures, injury, poor treatment, or large numbers of nasty bacteria to start with in the water, that defense system gets run down and the fish ends up sick with all manner of problems from those bacteria in the water.

This is not the same as water poisoning, where toxins in the water burn the goldfish directly. When a goldfish comes down with bacterial problems it is something called a *secondary infection*. This sickness is triggered by something that weakened their immune system in the first place.

### Preventing Bacterial Infections

Your biggest objective as the fish owner (who obviously wants a healthy fish) is to make sure the fish's immune system remains as uncompromised as possible in every aspect. This includes ensuring enough tank space, the right feeding regimen and – most importantly, good water quality through filtration and water changes. This is called *preventative care*.

Preventative care is the best method because it saves you from having to backtrack and undo the damage caused by bad care. Many problems can be avoided by doing things right the first time, saving you stress and the grief of losing your pets (not to mention your hard-earned money).

*KoiZyme*

Of course, not all bacterial infections are completely preventable, especially those where fish have been stressed out through parasitic attack (though there are some things we can do to try to prevent at least some of those kinds of infections, provided the fish isn't too bad off to start with) or have been present in their immune systems since you purchased them.

Fish are prone to contracting bacterial infections post-shipping from the stress of the process,

*Vitamin C*

especially if they sustain any injuries. While the fish's immune system is low from the stress, any wounds can be a point of entry to the fish to cause infection. One method of prevention for this is to use a probiotic supplement that reduces the bad bacteria count in the water, such as KoiZyme. Vitamin C can also offer immune system support for stressed fish.

## Causes of Bacterial Infections

Bacterial infections are caused by outside stress on the fish. This could be low dissolved oxygen, poor water quality, dirty tank conditions, or parasite attack. If the water is perfect, you do not overfeed and have good filtration, there is no outside cause of additional stress, the infection may be from a parasite.

Only after the parasite has been eliminated can you tackle the bacteria infection, which can often resolve itself with time, low stress, lots of clean water and a nutritious diet (depending on the severity). If the infection is from another stressor, eliminating the stressor and ensuring pristine dietary and environmental conditions are the first step.

Some more sinister bacterial infections such as Fish TB are not caused by parasites or your care, but are transmitted by other fish to your fish at the pet store.

## Treating Bacterial Infections

Many times, given the right care, you will be amazed at how quickly things turn around even if the fish is showing signs of illness. By correcting the environmental conditions that are causing illness for your fish, you are removing the "roadblocks" to your fish being able to recover. And these "roadblocks" are in many cases what causes the problem to begin with. When you eliminate what caused the problem, the problem should go away, provided things aren't too far advanced. You may have to be more aggressive in your tank maintenance and perhaps administer some tonics, in an effort to make a conducive healing environment, but the result should be a fish whose natural antibodies are able to do their job and a fish brought back from the brink.

When dealing with a secondary infection there are times when, after a period of a corrected environment, the problem persists. In that case it may be necessary to resort to other treatments – but in cases that are not very progressed, only after it has been given that opportunity to heal itself.

Perfect parameters are a must – daily 50-90% water changes are highly advised (being sure to correct any issues from the water source, such as a low pH). Low dissolved oxygen can lead to sickness.

*Liquid Chlorophyll*

In most light cases, I would recommend adding liquid chlorophyll and salting to 0.3% salt – or 11 grams per gallon – (especially if the fish has ulcers or fin rot, though regular salt for dropsy is not advised), colloidal silver, KoiZyme and Microbe-Lift Artemiss every 24 hours and give it time. If the infection is internal, stronger treatments are probably warranted.

*Aquarium Salt*

It usually takes a week to see improvement. Very much like when you catch a cold; your body must go through the "fighting it off" process.

Very advanced bacterial infections can happen when an issue goes unresolved for an extended period of time. In cases where the fish has an advanced infection and is truly near death, it may be necessary to administer antibiotics in an effort to save the fish's life. Owners will need to use discretion when deciding if antibiotics are warranted for their case. Antibiotics are very much overused in the fish industry and should really only be used as the last resort, as they can lead to antibiotic resistant bacteria (superbugs) and are stressful to fish. Some medications can be dosed to the water directly (especially useful for external infections) or blended into a medicated feed with the use of a binding agent to prevent the medicine on the food from getting back into the water – provided the fish is eating.

*Colloidal Silver*

*KoiZyme*

The following diseases are common bacterial infections:

## Bacterial Gill Infection

When a fish starts acting sick, it is often a good idea to check the gills. To do this, once the fish is captured, gently use your thumb to lift open the gill cover, revealing the filaments beneath. The gills are best examined in good light. Bacterial gill infections are characterized by light red to pink colored gills or red gills that have discolored rotting areas on or on the edges of the gills, streakiness or white patches. The damaged tissue can cause death within 3 days.

*Microbe-Lift Artemiss*

**First Defense**

Salt is not recommended for this condition as it can impair the breathing of the fish. MinnFInn is effective against bacterial gill disease. 1-3 treatments are recommended.

*MinnFinn*

**Emergency Action**

Like Dropsy, Bacteria Gill Disease can be very serious and in severe cases where fish are dying off rapidly, bringing out the heavy duty antibiotics – Furan 2 (Nitrofurazone) followed by E.M. Erythromycin (if necessary) – may prove life-saving for the fish.

*Furan 2*

## Ulcers

Ulcers often develop from fish scratching themselves, usually beginning with a parasite such as Flukes. Bacteria then begin creating ever-expanding holes on the fish which can cause electrolyte imbalance. Adding salt to the water (0.3% concentration) can not only help the fish heal but helps prevent the loss of fluids from the fish's body into the water. As well as killing the fish through dehydration, ulcer-causing bacteria can penetrate into the body of the fish and destroy an internal organ.

*E.M. Erythromycin*

Red blotches or sores are often the beginning of ulcers. If caught early, these can be treated without antibiotics, provided what caused them has been addressed (i.e. parasites, poor water quality, etc.).

**First Defense**

Swabbing the ulcer with hydrogen peroxide, salting to 0.3% and then treating with MinnFinn is recommended. Perfect water quality (50-100% water changes daily are advised), colloidal silver, Microbe-Lift Artemiss or Melafix and salting usually brings these in check.

*MinnFinn*

It is worth mentioning that some have found KoiZyme at a double dose to be effective at healing ulcers.

**Emergency Action**

An antibiotic – Furan 2 followed by E.M. Erythromycin – is advised if the ulcer is progressed (you can see the meat of the fish) because the infection can be or may already be in the fish's bloodstream.

*KoiZyme*

Please be aware that ulcers do take time to heal, sometimes over a week, regardless of the treatment method.

## Pop Eye

This condition causes the eyes to bulge to the sides or have what appear to be sacks of fluid surrounding them. Pop eye is usually an indication of an internal bacterial infection behind the eye, though sometimes damage to the eye can result in swelling or bulging. This is especially true of only one eye is affected. If the pop eye is from damage to the eye, clean water and 0.3% salt are recommended.

It is important to note that most water-born antibiotics will not penetrate behind the eye of the fish where the infection is.

*Wild Oil of Oregano*

**First Defense**

My preferred method of control of this internal infection is feeding a natural antibiotic feed. You can soak pellets in diluted Wild Oil of Oregano for 10 minutes, then feed them directly to the fish (assuming it is still eating). Continue this treatment for 1 week. If the fish seems uninterested, soaking the food in an appetite stimulant such as garlic extract (but not to the point where it is mushy) may help.

*Kanaplex*

**Emergency Action**

Finally, as a last resort, Kanaplex (ideally administered as a medicated feed) can offer some means of control if the case is severe and/or coupled with dropsy or not responding to a week or two of natural therapies outlined at the beginning of this section.

## Fin Rot

The fins may have a milky appearance or white edges. As the damage progresses, the fins begin to erode.

**First Defense**

0.3% salt is advisable. For fish with only a single tail fin, swabbing the area with MinnFinn daily can prove beneficial. MinnFinn will erode the fins on thinner-finned fish used in this manner and 3% hydrogen peroxide twice daily would be gentler. Raising the temperature to 83 degrees F for 48 hours can do damage to the bacteria that cause this condition.

*MinnFinn*

**Emergency Action**

*Neoplex*

In cases where the rot has consumed much of the fins, antibiotics might be necessary to stop the progress of the disease and save the fish. Neoplex is a good first choice for treatment. If no improvement is seen after 3 weeks, switching to Sulfaplex or Furan 2 may be used for very aggressive cases or those that may prove unresponsive to Neoplex.

*Sulfaplex*

*Furan 2*

## Mouth Rot

Mouth rot is a bacterial disease where the fish starts rubbing its mouth on surfaces in the tank, including the walls. Eventually the mouth turns red. As the condition progresses the lips start to detach. In very advanced stages, the whole mouth might erode away, leaving only a hole. Like many bacterial diseases, mouth rot is often caused by parasites.

*Hydrogen Peroxide*

**First Defense**

For cases caught early enough, swabbing with hydrogen peroxide is a good start. 1-3 treatments of MinnFinn can help to eradicate the bacteria attacking the mouth, in addition to salt at 0.3%.

*MinnFinn*

**Emergency Action**

*Kanaplex*

Kanaplex dosed into the water column can help to bring severe cases of mouth rot back in check. "Not worse" is often a sign of getting better, and tissue can take a while to regenerate. If the case is resistant beyond 2 rounds, it is advisable to switch to Sulfaplex as the infection may respond better to different medications, depending on the bacteria involved.

*Sulfaplex*

## Columnaris (Cotton Wool Disease)

External Columnaris looks to the naked eye like a fungal infection but is actually caused by opportunistic bacteria. It thrives in warmer water. It may grow on the body or mouth of the fish, though white fuzz on the mouth could be caused by bacteria other than Columnaris. It can also affect the gills, causing pale or yellow discoloration on the filaments.

Signs of Columnaris infection include white threads on the mouth, red anal vent, white sores, red anal vent. In addition, internal Columnaris may cause swim bladder damage, leading to floating and eating bubbles.

Some believe that Columnaris is not necessarily tied to poor water quality with low dissolved oxygen and that it can flourish despite having clean water and aeration, and that it is rather a result of lack of minerals in the water. Other evidence suggests that this condition is almost always a result of parasites in conjunction with high dissolved organics in the water.

Columnaris requires a high-power microscope to diagnose accurately and can be tricky to identify. White fuzz can also be caused by the parasite Epistylis in dirty water conditions or fungal infections which appear as coarse strands of hair under the microscope.

*MinnFinn*

**First Defense**

1-3 treatments of MinnFinn is recommended for external infection (those with wounds). Wounds can also be treated topically by swabbing with hydrogen peroxide.

*Sulfaplex*

Columnaris can be an internal as well as external infection, so feeding an antibiotic food is advised if internal infection is suspected (evidenced by infection of the mouth without external signs).

**Emergency Action**

If the infection does not respond, Sulfaplex or Furan 2 are alternative treatments.

*Furan 2*

## Mycobacterial Diseases

Mycobacterial diseases thrive in water conditions with warm temperatures, low dissolved oxygen, high dissolved organics, and a lower pH. Such conditions can increase the chances the fish will get sick as the bacterial count skyrockets (dose response).

Some mycobacterial diseases are considered commensal (can be present in low numbers without causing problems, but can crop up when the fish's immune system is weakened from stress, poor living conditions or old age). The disease has been isolated from fish that did not show any clinical signs of illness and were able to carry it without being affected by it.[6] These infections are increasingly prevalent in aquarium fish. It is transmitted by fish who have consumed the feces of sick fish or cannibalized other sick fish. Virulent strains can be transmitted through the water itself. It is also transmitted directly by sick fish to their offspring. It is particularly difficult to eradicate once it gets hold on a system.

---

[6] *Mycobacterial Infections of Fish*, Ruth Francis-Floyd, Southern Regional Aquaculture Center, November 2011

There are many kinds of mycobacteria, and the symptoms of infection are often similar to other bacterial diseases such as Aeromonas, Columnaris or pseudomonas, but Mycobacterial diseases are not treatable with any commercial medication. It is solely the immune system of the fish that can keep them at bay.

Mycobacteria is to be suspected in fish showing chronic signs of disease. A history of antibiotics being ineffective for the fish may indicate a Mycobacterial problem. Many "mystery" deaths are often overlooked mycobacterial disease casualties. Depending on the cause of the outbreak, the fish may appear fine one day and be in critical condition the next, or it may gradually decline and perish. Fish that have been stressed or weakened are especially vulnerable, as are old fish.

There are no "typical" symptoms of Mycobacteria because the disease can manifest itself with a wide variety of physical symptoms and affect different areas of the body of the fish.

Symptoms visible to the naked eye may include any of the following:

- Wasting
- Skin lesions (may be deep or shallow pitting)
- Scale loss
- Reproductive problems
- Dropsy (fluid accumulation with scale protrusion)
- Abdominal distention (bloat)
- Scale protrusion (without abdominal distention)
- Pop eye
- Loss of appetite or attitude
- Abnormal behavior (if the brain is affected)
- Collapsed spine
- Chronic mortality in a population of fish
- Granulomas of the organs (only visible during necropsy)

Diagnosis through lab work cannot be conducted without euthanizing the fish. Tissue culture diagnosis sometimes, but not always, reveals microscopic granulomas in the organs of the fish.

**Treatment**

Because there is no known treatment for Mycobacterial infections and mortality rates are so high, it is recommended to euthanize all sick fish and any fish exposed to them and thoroughly disinfect all equipment as they are to be considered hazardous. Vinegar can kill Mycobacteria and

Tuberculosis.[7]  It is very rare for the immune system to beat back this kind of infection once it has taken hold on the fish.  Such a fish may recover for a time with antibiotics, only to succumb to a relapse once the antibiotics are withdrawn.

My experience (and that of many other experienced fishkeepers I have spoken with) has been that pet store fish have a strong chance of carrying and succumbing to this disease, whereas fish from independent breeders are far less likely to have issues with TB.  The conditions in pet store tanks (shared centralized filtration that often includes the feeder tanks, fish stressed from transport, gravel trapping waste, unremoved dead or sick fish) favor high numbers of Mycobacteria to proliferate and perpetuate infection to new stock.

*Fish TB*

Prevention by quarantine and good husbandry is the best way to ensure your fish does not perish from a Mycobacterial infection.  While not practical for the average hobbyist, those who have received a new batch of fish may choose to euthanize one specimen from the collection to check for signs of Mycobacteria before releasing fish from quarantine.  UV sterilization is highly recommended in the prevention and control of Fish TB.  Water-borne probiotics such as KoiZyme may be useful in preventing Mycobacterial infections by reducing the number of Mycobacteria in a system.  I like to use a bit of colloidal silver every so often in the water in my tanks that contain pet store purchased fish.

Because two kinds of Mycobacterium are transmittable to people (though this is fortunately very rare), it is recommended to avoid putting your hands with any open wound in the water if you suspect a Mycobacteria problem with your fish.  Those who are immunocompromised should avoid contact with these fish or their environment.

*KoiZyme*

## Dropsy

Dropsy is perhaps the most feared disease in goldfish keeping as one of the most difficult to treat.  This is partly because by the time the fish shows visual signs of dropsy, much damage has already been done to the internal organs of the fish.  There is usually a high fatality rate associated with it as a result.  But on the bright side, the earlier it is detected the better is the chance of recovery.

A fish with dropsy may or may not show pineconing scales, but it will become swollen.  The eyes may also bulge with the excess fluid.  Dropsy is a condition that happens when the fish is unable to regulate its fluids properly, leading to fluid retention.  Dropsy can be caused by 6 things:

---

[7] https://www.sciencedaily.com/releases/2014/02/140225101501.htm

parasites, secondary bacterial infection, diet, temperature shock, bad water quality or virus. Bacteria are not normally the primary cause of this disease, but the secondary. Normally the fish's immune system keeps them at bay, but if their slime coat is disrupted through stress of parasites or something else, it allows them to enter. In order to attempt to treat the dropsy, one must get to the root of the issue and do so quickly.

- Parasites weaken the fish by chewing away at the fish's slime coat, paving the way for bacteria to attack. They also damage their immune system, causing stress. Check to see if the fish has shown signs of parasites and treat with 5 rounds of MinnFinn if present.
- An improper diet can damage the organs, leading to fatty kidneys (kidneys control the fish's fluid intake). This kind of dropsy might have nothing to do with bacteria and treatment will be ineffective. A fish with kidney damage may swell without any pineconing, though not all swelling is due to dropsy (egg binding could also be a possibility).
- Temperature shock can cause the fish to pine cone, especially going from very warm water to cold water too suddenly.
- Poor water quality (such as high ammonia, nitrites, improper pH, etc.) stresses the fish, damaging organs or making them susceptible to secondary bacterial infection. High dissolved organics can contribute to a high bad bacteria count in the water, which weaken the fish through a dose response. Other toxins in the water can cause dropsy as well, such as heavy metals, contaminants or pharmaceuticals in the water source (hint: use Auro Liquid Gold), room sprays, bug sprays, perfumes or lotions contaminating the water from your hands, paint leaching from gravel or other toxins.
- Viruses can cause dropsy as they weaken the immune system of the fish. Colloidal silver in the water and garlic fed orally may prove useful. Viruses cannot be diagnosed with commonly available microscopes.

*Heater*

**Bacterial Dropsy Treatment:**

The following treatment will not help if the fish has untreated parasites, effects from poor diet, bad water quality or a viral disease. Those things must be resolved first. This treatment is extreme, but dropsy is one condition that warrants extreme treatment if the fish is to have a chance at survival.

*Metroplex*

- Use high heat (86 degrees F for 2 weeks minimum). The temperature needs to be raised quickly, 1-2 degrees per hour assuming the water isn't below 70 degrees F. Ensure good aeration as high temperatures reduce oxygen content in the water. The temperature must be lowered slowly (-2 degrees F per day) after the high heat treatment is done.

*Epsom Salt*

- Use Epsom salts in the water at 1/4 tsp per 10 gallons. The Epsom salts helps draw the fluid out of the fish.
- Feed an antibiotic-laced food (Metroplex).  If the fish will not eat, administer Metro to the water column directly.
- Dose the tank with Kanaplex and Furan 2 together during treatment.
- Change at least 75% of the water every 48 hours.

I normally do not recommend antibiotics – all too frequently overused for fish that do not really need them and can lead to superbugs – but in the case of dropsy, which is extremely deadly, I believe it is warranted.  Dropsy is a severe, often terminal condition can quickly kill fish before their weak immune system is able to do battle.

If you do not have access to Kanaplex or similar antibiotics that target the bacteria that cause dropsy, you may try feeding diluted Wild Oil of Oregano-laced foods. This option may prove as effective as Kanaplex while being safer for the fish, but there is a lack of studies to support it as a reliable treatment.  The fishkeeper will need to use their own judgment.

*Kanaplex*

*Furan 2*

*Wild Oil of Oreganov*

# Fungal Infections

Fish that have had a very low immune system or have had an injury can get a secondary fungal infection. Fungus can start growing on a wound when conditions are favorable. MinnFinn is an excellent treatment for fungal infections in goldfish, and the same protocol for bacterial issues often proves useful for fungal infections as well.

*MinnFinn*

*Pimafix*

The combination of 0.3% salt, Pimafix (antifungal) and MinnFinn provides a triple punch approach effective against fungal infections. You can also add an additional layer of colloidal silver which has proven itself effective, at least anecdotally, against fungus in fish.

*Colloidal Silver*

## Saprolegnia

Large areas of white growth can develop on very stressed or completely immunosuppressed fish.  Unless treated, these fish usually die.  Harmless fungal growth can occur when the fish has had an injury but may be otherwise perfectly fine.  Such fish may recover on their own with clean water and good care.

**First Defense**

If the water is very cold, raising the temperature may be a good idea.  MinnFinn (1-3 treatments) can help for cases where the fish are not active.

**Emergency Action**

Furan 2 can help recover extremely sick fish back from the brink of death.

## Branchiomyces

Characterized by holes (erosions) in the gill tissue and bluish or grayish streaks (dying tissue), this disease is prevalent in warmer temperatures with dirty water conditions with high waste loads and dissolved organics.  Diagnosis through microscopy is not usually necessary.

Clean water, increasing aeration, reducing the temperature and treating with 1-3 rounds of MinnFinn is recommended.

# Viruses

Viruses are becoming an increasing problem as more fish are imported. Some viruses may respond well to higher water temperatures, antiviral food such as raw garlic, and colloidal silver (which has antiviral properties) in the water column. Other viruses may kill a fish very quickly and can infect and destroy an entire tank or pond within a short frame of time.

*Colloidal Silver*

## Carp Pox

Carp pox appears as waxy-looking "warts" that can be white, pink, tan or bluish in color, usually the size of a pencil eraser.  It is most common in early spring or late fall in ponds.  The colder water temperature suppresses the immune system of fish living outdoors.  While contagious, mortality with carp pox is relatively low.  The condition can disappear on its own as the temperature gets warmer, and though it may return with cooler water, the fish's immune system should eventually learn to cope with the virus.  A 0.3% salt solution may prove therapeutic.

## IHN Virus

This virus can cause listlessness and death and has a high mortality rate.  It cannot be identified with a regular microscope and conventional medicine comes up short-handed.  Preventing the immune system from getting low is the best method to combat it.

## Lymphocystis

Lymphocystis shows up on fish (typically on the edges of the fins but can also show up on the body) as waxy, white to gray colored lumps similar in texture to cauliflower.  It is contagious to other fish.  14 days of treating the water with Seachem Paraguard can also help with reducing the growths on the fish, though it will not totally eradicate the virus.

*Seachem Paraguard*

## SVC (Spring Viraemia of Carp)

While virtually unheard of until recent years, SVC is a highly contagious and can be spread by sick fish and parasites.  It is prevalent in colder water.  Mortality rates are very high, but fish who survive outbreaks can become immune to it.  Some goldfish can carry this virus with or without symptoms.  Some symptoms can include darkened skin, pop eye, dropsy, pale gills, lethargy, loss of balance, hemorrhages, and protruding vent with yellowish fecal casts.  Raising the temperature may help but there are no treatments on the market for SVC.

The water that came in contact with the fish can harbor the parasite for up to 42 days.  Sterilization via pH extremes or UV light is recommended.

## GHV (Goldfish Herpes Virus)

GHV, like most viruses, can be carried by otherwise healthy fish that may come down with the condition during times of stress. Most goldfish populations carry this virus, be they domestic or imported. The most common symptom with GHV is anemia, evidenced by pale gills and even a pale head. Other cases may have rough skin caused by loss of slime and damaged gill tissue. Bringing up the temperatures into the mid 80's F can help control the virus as it is more prevalent in cold water.

Surviving fish will become carriers of the disease.

## Tumors

Maybe you've heard it said that tumors are impossible to get rid of without surgery, certainly impossible to truly cure. I used to think so myself, until I learned about the only tumor treatment cure that I actually witnessed working on my red and white Oranda goldfish, Kona.

Raw apricot kernels contain a vitamin called B17, a vitamin almost nonexistent in food today. It has cured thousands of both people and pets of cancer. It must be taken orally or injected (if you can obtain its injectable form, called Laetrile). I have not personally tried the injections, but the oral treatment worked on my fish because he ate the kernels.

*Raw Apricot Kernels*

This is exactly what I did:

> *Soak 1 apricot kernel overnight in water. Pound into a pulp with a mortar and pestle. It cannot be heat treated in any way or it will destroy the cancer-killing properties. Mix with equal parts ground fish pellets and pack into a cube. Divide the cube in 3 pieces for a larger fish and 4 pieces for a smaller fish. Feed the fish daily one cube – nothing else.*

I saw visible improvement within 1 week. Within a few weeks, it was totally gone.  I am not making any promises that it will work for your fish, but I personally believe it is an excellent treatment.

Some difficulties were that the fish did not enjoy the taste at all. It is extremely bitter. The bitterness comes from the active properties that make it such a powerful anticarcinogen. But if the fish does not eat it, or only picks off the pellet part, it will not get better. This is where I can see the injectable treatment method coming in useful if you have a fish that refuses to consume the apricot kernel. Definitely do not feed any other food if you are trying to get your fish to eat this, as it will not be hungry enough to make the effort.

This treatment can be used for internal tumors as external ones.

Where do goldfish get tumors from? For a while, I advocated the dirty water theory. But now in light of recent studies done on animal populations exposed to industrialized society vs. those that are not, as well as the carcinogenic substances that is added to most water supplies, as well as the toxic preservatives lacing processed fish foods (more on that in the feeding section), as well as many imported fish being bombarded with a plethora of toxic medications prior to being sold, I've changed my opinion.

Preventing tumors is best done through providing a diet and water free of toxic and industrial contaminants.

Some chemicals and medications are tricky to remove from water. Most commercial aquarium water treatments won't remove them all. Most aquarium filters on the market won't either. RO (reverse osmosis) water filtration units can, but you will need to heavily remineralize the water and may need to adjust the pH to make it suitable for goldfish. Switching from processed pellet foods to a raw food diet can also stop your fish from consuming carcinogenic preservatives.

Many if not most commercially available medications are highly, highly toxic and cancer-causing — a fact even stated on the labels. Fish that are exposed to such medications have a higher chance of developing tumors later. That is a large part of why I advocate using more natural remedies if possible.

# Swim Bladder Disorder

Swim bladder problems can fall into two classes: "floaters" (fish who struggle to get to the bottom) and "sinkers" (fish who struggle to rise from the bottom). Floating problems with the swim bladder are common. Initially, the goldfish may begin to lean to one side before inverting. The behavior is usually most common while the fish is resting. The fish may right itself when it sees its owner. Eventually it may spend most of its time upside-down. Ulceration can be a problem on floaters who have areas of their body exposed to air.

Fish who do this may be having trouble with their swim bladder, the organ that controls the fish's position in the water. The condition is sometimes termed as Swim Bladder Disorder, though the swim bladder function itself is not always the cause.

There are several potential causes of this issue, some of which can be complex.

1) Diet plays a direct role in the condition of the fish's internal organs, especially the swim bladder (the organ responsible for helping the fish rise or sink in the water). Unfortunately, the typical goldfish diet consists of too much high protein food, especially foods like low-quality flake food. Overfeeding even good quality food can lead to constipation. In the short term, basically what happens is the fish gets backed up and can't control its swimming, so it ends up floating. Another theory is that gas buildup is taking place in the intestines of the fish, causing the fish to flip over, which may have nothing to do with the swim bladder itself. Mechanical blockage of food in the pneumatic duct of the swim bladder has been reportedly cured by feeding green peas, which forces expanded food out of the duct and allows the fish to regain buoyancy control.

2) High nitrates can cause the swim bladder to have trouble regulating itself.

3) Damage to the swim bladder by chemical medications can impair its function for life (tranquilizers used to sedate the fish during shipping can play a role in this). The effects do not always show up right away.

4) Some fish are born with swim bladders that do not work properly due to deformity or a highly modified body type (such as egg-shaped breeds).

5) Toxins such as hydrogen sulfide buildup (common in gravel) can leach into the water, causing slow, eventually irreversible damage to the swim bladder. This should be suspected when the fish shows imbalance during or right after disturbing the gravel during cleaning.

6) Intestinal parasites or liver damage (perhaps from tuberculosis) can cause significant weight loss in the abdomen. This makes the fish lose its balance in the water as its head becomes heavier than its body, making it flip over and float.

7) Goldfish with egg impaction problems can start floating, especially if there is infection (causing excess internal gas).  This is not a problem with the swim bladder directly.

8) An older goldfish that has been fed improperly may have fat accumulations in and around the organs (including the swim bladder), which can disrupt normal swim bladder function.

9) A caudally displaced swim bladder can cause buoyancy issues.  This is to be suspected when a bulge by the vent is evident, in addition to trouble swimming correctly.  Swim bladder displacement can happen due to disease, but is often caused by an internal tumor pushing the organ out of place.

10) Sickness such as internal infections – viral or bacterial – can lead directly or indirectly lead to swim bladder trouble, be they floating (overinflation) or sinking (deflation) problems.[8]  Post-illness scar tissue or adhesions of the swim bladder to other areas may cause impaired control over the swim bladder.  Fish with a deflated swim bladder often have a flatter abdomen toward the back and struggle to rise off the bottom of the tank.

For overfed, constipated goldfish, the remedy is to fast the fish for at least 1 week, then switch to a diet of strictly fibrous foods (aka blanched veggies like broccoli, lettuce, kale, carrots, etc.) for another 2 weeks.  This will cleanse the fish's digestive tract.  It may be also necessary to look into switching the brand of pellet or gel food to a lower protein formula, especially if your fish is an adult (see the feeding section for recommended percentages).  Raising the temperature a bit may help too as it gets the digestive tract moving, provided enough oxygen is maintained in the water.  Giving the fish a pea with a grain of Epsom salt inside of it can act as a laxative.

*Epsom Salt*

If your nitrate readings are over 30ppm, it is recommended to perform several water changes to reduce it to under that level.  Adding liquid chlorophyll to counteract the effects of high nitrates on the fish can be useful.

Not much can be done for a fish with a damaged swim bladder due to chemical medications.

*Liquid Chlorophyll*

The same is true for fish that have born with a defective swim bladder or deformity that causes floating.

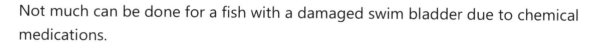

---

[8] Britt, Tara & Weisse, Chick & Weber III, E & Matzkin, Zach & Klide, Alan. (2002). Use of pneumocystoplasty for overinflation of the swim bladder in a goldfish. Journal of the American Veterinary Medical Association. 221. 690-3, 645. 10.2460/javma.2002.221.690.

If you suspect hydrogen sulfide poisoning, it is recommended to transfer your fish to another tank, remove all gravel and do a 100% water change before replacing the fish.

For internal parasites, treat as necessary.  There is no known cure for fish tuberculosis or liver damage.

Goldfish with egg impaction problems may benefit from raising the temperature, feeding Epsom salt in a pea, and an antibiotic food to help with any infection.

With fat accumulations, the damage is usually irreversible, except by surgery in which quartz stones are implanted in the fish's abdomen to weigh it down (this carries its own set of risks).

For a displaced swim bladder, an aquatic veterinarian may be able to correct the issue with surgery, though internal damage may be too progressed to reverse.

# Treatment Index

In this section, you will find a comprehensive list of recommended treatments for goldfish health issues.  I have divided it into two sections: natural treatments and commercial medications.

Some of the natural treatments can be combined with other natural treatments for more potent effects.  I have successfully used 0.3% salt, colloidal silver, liquid chlorophyll, Microbe-Lift Artemiss alternated with Microbe-Lift Herbtana together, alternated with treatments of MinnFinn in between to combat stubborn external bacterial infections.  This approach in this case was particularly effective when combined with daily 100% water changes.

However, not all combinations of either natural or chemical treatments are proven to be safe for fish and, unless indicated in the previous disease section or below, combine treatments at your own risk.

## Choosing the Right Treatment

Some antibiotics (both natural ones and chemical ones) only work for certain kinds of bacteria (gram positive or gram negative).  Advanced microscopy with the use of special stains is required to determine whether the infection is gram positive or gram negative, which is beyond the scope of this book.  It is usually safe to say that if the bacterial infection is not responding to a certain kind of medicine, be it a natural treatment or an antibiotic, that treatment is primarily targeting one kind of bacteria and the fish is dealing with the other kind of bacteria.  This means switching treatments to something that targets the other kind can prove effective.  It does not necessarily mean the first treatment itself is totally useless altogether, but in your case it may not help your particular infection.  That is why I prefer to have a variety of treatment options on hand in case the first option proves ineffective.

With some natural treatments targeting diseases that are bacterial in nature, such as Microbe-lift Artemiss, we do not always know if the formula specifics targets gram negative or gram positive infections.  Though again, we also may not know what strain of infection the fish has to start with.  If the fish is not too bad off, the fishkeeper has some more flexibility in their treatment approach.  If the first treatment doesn't help, switching to another one can be just the ticket.  But if the clock is ticking and the fish has a serious condition and/or is in very bad shape, there is little room for making the wrong choice.  In that case, a broad-spectrum approach for such a bacterial condition would be to choose a treatment that has been shown to target both rather than take the risk of using a treatment that only targets one kind of bacteria (the kind the fish might not have).

When should you try a natural or a chemical treatment?  As a general rule, natural treatments are ideal when:

- The fish has a minor to moderate issue and is still active
- The issue is caught quickly
- The fish has been through considerable stress already
- You are treating a ciliated protozoan parasite or flukes
- Chemical treatment for the condition is not possible

Chemical treatments are probably better when:

- The fish has not responded to 2-3 rounds of natural treatments
- The fish is continuing to decline, despite the natural treatments
- The fish has a moderate to severe or very dangerous issue
- The fish is in bad shape and will likely die unless there is a quick turnaround
- Natural treatments for the fish's condition are unknown

## The Medicine Cabinet

It is extremely important that every goldfish owner have a "medicine cabinet" of treatments on hand at all times for the same reason every family should have a first-aid kit.  There are many, many kinds of treatments and you do not always need to have all of them at your fingertips, but some basic ones should be available for immediate use in case something unexpected comes up.

Here are my top must-haves in my medicine cabinet:

1) **Salt** – Salt is an excellent treatment used for a variety of issues.
2) **MinnFinn** – An essential disinfectant and parasite killer.
3) **Melafix** – Antibacterial agent, useful for slight bacterial issues.
4) **Heater and airstone** – For an instant hospital tank.
5) **Kanaplex** – Broad-spectrum antibiotic useful for dropsy.
6) **Metroplex** – For treating hole in the head, hexamita, dropsy.
7) **KoiZyme** – Powerful natural bad bacteria reducer
8) **Wild Oil of Oregano** – Natural broad-spectrum antibiotic.
9) **Focus** – For binding Seachem powdered antibiotics in food.
10) **Furan 2** – Antibiotic for very sick fish or serious issues.

If you live in an area that is prone to power outages, it is a good idea to have a backup plan. Keeping a battery operated air pump on hand can prove lifesaving for fish that live in warmer water with low dissolved oxygen.

# Natural Treatments

## Aloe Vera

*Aloe Vera*

Aloe Vera contains many beneficial vitamins, minerals and amino acids. It is useful for fish who have recently been through the stress of shipping or suffered minor injury as it can help repair the damaged tissue of the fish.

You can make your own homemade, chemical-free version of Stress Coat using the below recipe:

**Dosage**

Use 1 teaspoon of aloe per 10 gallons of water. Pre-mix in a bottle of water prior to adding to the tank.

## Chlorophyll

*Liquid Chlorophyll*

Liquid chlorophyll has been used for health benefits in both humans in pets and the benefits are backed with much scientific evidence. Chlorophyll is necessary for almost all forms of life, goldfish included. In tanks where there are no plants it is a great dietary addition.

Some things Chlorophyll can help goldfish with:

- Combating nitrate poisoning
- Healing after injury
- Fighting tumors
- Fighting bacterial infections (internal & external)
- Preventing anemia after blood loss
- Boosting the immune system

To use it for fish, you can mix it in with their food (easier for gel food) and/or even give them a chlorophyll bath.

**Dosage**

Treat the bath water with 4 ounces of chlorophyll per gallon. Leave the fish in the water for no more than 20 minutes. Repeat twice daily for 7 days during treatment, refrigerating the water for up to 24 hours before discarding.

With so many benefits, you should seriously consider adding chlorophyll to your own diet too! For humans there are even more fantastic benefits such as eliminating free radicals and helping cleanse from cancer-causing toxins.

## Precautions

Chlorophyll may discolor the skin of light colored fish temporarily, so don't panic if your fish turns green during the bath.

### Colloidal Silver

*Colloidal Silver*

**Benefits**

Colloidal silver is one of nature's natural antibiotics.  It also has antiviral properties.  There have been several encouraging anecdotal accounts of fishkeepers who have used it to treat fish infected with fungal and bacterial issues.  It has been shown to be effective against even antibiotic resistant bacteria.

**Dosage**

Colloidal silver should be diluted to 10ppm before use.  1 tsp of 250ppm colloidal silver to 1 oz (approximately 6 tsp) of distilled water will give you a 10ppm solution.

This solution can then be added to the tank at a ratio of 1 tsp per 10 gallons every other day.  I have used 1 tsp of straight 250ppm colloidal silver per 10 gallons without adverse effects – if anything, it seemed more effective – but every fish may respond differently so it is best to start with lower amounts to see how the fish respond.

**Precautions**

Colloidal silver has few precautions.  It should not be used over an extended period of time as it can burden the liver.  It is a treatment that is difficult to overdose with in moderate amounts.

Colloidal silver is ineffective at killing parasites in the doses recommended for goldfish.

### Epsom Salts

**Benefits**

Epsom salt (magnesium sulfate) is a naturally occurring mineral which may prove useful when treating a fish dealing with internal fluid buildup (such as that caused by dropsy) or constipation.  Epsom salts can be given orally by wedging the grains into gel food OR added to the water directly.  It can be combined with most treatments without issues.

*Epsom Salt*

**Dosage**

Dose the volume of the tank at 1 teaspoon of Epsom salts per gallon (dissolved in tank water prior to dosing) and perform 90% water changes every 24 hours. Replace the salts you take out.

## Precautions

Be aware that adding Epsom salts can alter your GH.

## Garlic

Garlic has potent immune boosting, antibacterial, some antiparasitic and antiviral properties. Heat-treating garlic destroys much of its benefits, so it is recommended to administer it in its raw, uncooked form. It is useful for fish who are combatting various infections or are stressed.

Garlic is an effective appetite stimulant. It can be useful for enticing fish to eat that are picky eaters, as well as helping encourage sick fish that aren't interested in food to eat.

## Dosage

To create a water tonic, liquify 1 cup of water to 1 tablespoon of fresh, finely grated garlic in a food processor or blender. Dose the liquid at 1 tablespoon per 10 gallons of water. Perform a large water change after 24 hours before re-dosing.

This liquid can also be used to soak fish food in for oral ingestion. Garlic can also be fed in small pieces to the fish directly.

## Precautions

As a food product, garlic will degrade in the tank with time. Water changes with this treatment are advised. When added to the water, it has a pungent smell. By itself, it may or may not resolve parasitic infestations, depending on various factors.

## Heat

The value of heat as a medicinal treatment for goldfish should not be overlooked. For this reason I recommend keeping a good quality heater on hand, even if you normally don't use it on a regular basis.

## Benefits

Heat is useful for speeding up the life cycle of certain parasites, especially ich, in order to eradicate them faster. It can prove therapeutic when attempting to resolve some bacterial infections such as dropsy.

*Heater*

## Dosage

Not applicable.

**Precautions**

Warmer water carries less dissolved oxygen, though this is not usually an issue if the water is sufficiently aerated when applying heat. Goldfish with bacterial gill infections should not be subjected to heat in order not to further stress the damaged gills. The ideal range for treating certain parasites is 82-84 degrees F. Always monitor the fish carefully when applying higher temperatures.

## Apricot Kernals

Apricot kernels can be blended into fish food and used in an effort to reverse tumor growth in goldfish.

**Dosage**

To feed, soak 1 apricot kernel overnight in water. Pound into a pulp with a mortar and pestle. Do not cook. Mix with equal parts ground fish pellets and pack into a cube. Divide the cube in 3 pieces for a larger fish and 4 pieces for a smaller fish. Feed the fish daily one cube exclusively. Continue treatment until desired results are achieved.

*Raw Apricot Kernels*

**Precautions**

Tumors can kill goldfish, so if the fish dies during treatment it does not necessarily mean that the treatment is to blame.

## 3% Hydrogen Peroxide

Hydrogen peroxide is a useful disinfectant. It is great for spraying on the inside of a tank to disinfect it. It can also be used as a topical disinfectant swab effective against fin rot, mouth rot and some fungus.

*3% Hydrogen Peroxide*

**Dosage**

Use a Q-tip to apply the peroxide to the desired area.

**Precautions**

Be careful not to get it into the eyes of the fish.

## KoiZyme

KoiZyme is a completely natural probiotic additive used to reduce the bad bacteria count in the water. High bad bacteria counts are often the precursor to fish that are sick, and likewise sick fish increase the bad bacteria count in the water. This can inhibit recovery or contaminate other fish. By adding probiotic bacteria to the water that compete with the bad ones for food, their count can be reduced (which can aid in healing of sick fish). It can also be used as a preventative during times of stress, such as fish that have recently been shipped, injured or gone through a cold winter.

*KoiZyme*

**Dosage**

Dosage depends on the water temperature. It is difficult to overdose this product. Follow manufacturer's instructions.

**Precautions**

None.

## Melafix

Melafix has antibacterial properties. It is useful for preventing a variety of infections when parasites are active and treating existing bacterial infections that are gram-positive in nature. While many fish infections are gram-negative and may prove unaffected by Melafix, it is a safe treatment worth trying for a sick fish.

Melafix is manufactured by API Fish Care, but you can also make it at home. It is much more cost-effective to make it yourself, and you can use natural emulsifying agents instead.

*API Melafix*

*Recipe:*

1 tsp unrefined, cold-pressed and preferably organic cajeput oil (tea tree oil can be substituted)

1 tsp organic aloe vera gel

1/8 tsp unscented castile soap (optional emulsifying agent)

*Cajeput Oil*

100 tsp (33 and 1/3 tablespoons) distilled or dechlorinated tap water

*Directions:*

Combine all ingredients into a convenient bottle or jar with a tight-fitting lid.

*Organic Aloe Vera
Gel*

**Dosage**

Shake well before using.  Use 1 tablespoon per 10 gallons every 24 hours.  Melafix has a very long shelf life.

**Precautions**

None.

## Microbe-Lift Artemiss

The exact formula of Microbe-Lift Artemiss is unknown, but it seems to contain some essential oils with immune-boosting properties.  It can be helpful when treating bacterial infections, though I find it effective when used in combination with other treatments.

*Microbe-Lift
Artemiss*

**Dosage**

Follow manufacturer's instructions.

**Precautions**

None.

## Microbe-Lift Herbtana

Microbe-Lift Herbtana is the parasite formula version of this treatment.  As with Artemiss, I have not found it to be effective at eradicating parasitic infections when used alone for parasites with more complex life cycles such as ich, but it may prove useful against less resilient parasitic infections (especially when used as an immune system supporter) or when paired with other treatments.

*Microbe-Lift
Herbtana*

**Dosage**

Follow manufacturer's instructions.

**Precautions**

None.

## MinnFinn

MinnFinn is highly recommended for controlling a wide variety of external parasitic and bacterial infections. It is one of the only treatments available that effectively treats the common infections of goldfish. The ingredients are environmentally safe and will not cause cancer in your fish. It does not require water changes to remove it as it comes with a neutralizer that gets added to the water.

*MinnFinn*

For questions about the MinnFinn treatment, you can contact Paul, a fish pathologist of over 25 years and the mastermind behind MinnFinn.

> Paul A. Curtis
> AquaSolver LLC/ AquaFinn
> 2255 Seaquest Trail
> Escondido, CA 92029
> 760-518-8170
> www.aquasolver.com
> www.aquafinn.com

### Dosage

Goldfish should have a double dose of both the liquid and the neutralizer. Follow manufacturer's instructions.

### Precautions

Do not leave your fish during the 1 hour treatment periods and watch for the signs of stress described in the directions. Careful attention to the directions is required.

## Pimafix

*API Pimafix*

Pimafix is primarily used to treat fungal infections in fish. Its active ingredient is west Indian bay leaf oil, a natural antifungal remedy. Pimafix is manufactured by API Fish Care, but it contains (according to the product label) a carcinogenic additive. I recommend making it yourself, as it is more cost-effective and safer for your fish.

*Recipe:*

1 tsp West Indian Bay Leaf Oil

1 tsp organic aloe vera gel

1/8 tsp unscented castile soap (optional)

100 tsp distilled or dechlorinated tap water

*Directions:*

Combine all ingredients and shake well.

*West Indian Bay Leaf Oil*

*Organic Aloe Vera Gel*

## Dosage

Add 1 teaspoon per 10 gallons of aquarium water.  Repeat daily every 24 hours for 1 week or until desired results are achieved.

## Precautions

None.

## Salt

Salt is one of the most effective, inexpensive treatments we fishkeepers have at our fingertips.

It is useful for both killing off several kinds of parasites as well as helping fish that are dealing with a variety of bacterial infections. It is particularly excellent for the eradication of ich.

Salt is one of the most incorrectly dosed treatments, which has led in part to salt resistance in certain strains of ich. The good news is that goldfish are very adept at handling a good bit of salt in their water. It usually takes a very large amount to cause any stress.

Salt replenishes the lost electrolytes when fish are shedding their slime coat and acts like a healing tonic. For fish who are losing fluids due to an ulcer or other injury, it reduces osmotic pressure on the wound. It lowers the number of bad bacteria in the water and will not stain the silicone in your tank, unlike many commercial medications designed to do the same thing. And, as an added bonus, it is natural.

The kind of salt you use is important. Many salts available at the grocery store contain anticaking agents or have iodine added to them. These can hurt your fish and your bacteria colony.  Aquarium salt is safe for fish but can be expensive to treat a larger volume of water.

*Aquarium Salt*

A good fish-safe salt is Morton solar salt.  Morton solar salt comes in a large 40 pound bag and is very cost effective.  Be sure to get the kind that has no anticaking

*Himalayan Salt*

or antirust additives.  It is typically sold as 99.7% pure salt.  The other percentage is usually harmless minerals.

In my opinion, Himalayan pink salt is the best kind to use when nursing a sick fish.  It contains many trace minerals that goldfish use to stay healthy and may offer more benefits than regular aquarium salt.

## Dosage

When treating with salt, it is recommended to measure salt using a grams scale rather than with measuring spoons or cups because it is the most accurate.  Salt should be dissolved by stirring it in a bucket of tank water before adding it to the aquarium to avoid burning the fish.

- **0.3% (11 grams per gallon)** is the therapeutic tonic level of salt. It is ideal for external bacterial infections such as fin rot, ulcers or injuries, or preventing infection after damage or stress. It should be noted that using a 0.3% salt concentration to eradicate parasites can lead to salt resistance as it is largely ineffective for goldfish parasites.
- **0.5% (19 grams per gallon)** is the level that causes most ich infestations to succumb.
- **0.7% and 0.8% (26 and 30 grams per gallon)** are the higher concentrations used for stubborn, more salt-resistant cases of ich. These high levels of salt require careful monitoring of the fish to ensure they do not become stressed.
- **0.9% (34 grams per gallon)** is the maximum salt concentration to be used on goldfish.  It also must be used with caution and careful monitoring of the fish.

A salinity meter is a useful tool to monitor the exact concentration of salt in the water, but can be expensive.  Instead, a TDS meter includes salt in the total reading and can give you a rough idea of the amount of salt in the water when compared to your average tap water.

## Precautions

Salt levels that are used to eradicate parasites (0.5% and up) can cause fraying or splits in the fins.

Some damage to the fins may be inevitable in order to beat the disease, but considerable stress from high salt can cause holes in the ends of the fins, blood streaks in the fins or considerable gouges out of the edges of the fins.

If this is happening, the salt concentration is too much for the fish and should be adjusted to lower levels.

As with copper treatments, salt should not be used on tanks with plants or invertebrates in them, as it will harm or kill them.

The plants will need to be removed and either kept in a separate container for 4 weeks or disinfected before reintroducing them into the tank after treatment. Reintroducing plants without taking those precautionary steps can reintroduce the same disease you just got rid of right back into the tank and you will have to start over with treatment.

## Tank Transfer Method (TTM)

The tank transfer method was initially developed by the Chinese when they found that changing fish to fresh water every day could help the fish to overcome disease. The strategy is also used by marine fish keepers, who use it as a way to overcome ich in saltwater systems. It can be particularly useful for combatting many parasites, especially anchor worm and fish lice. As the fish naturally sheds its slime coat, any parasites or bacteria that come off are removed constantly to prevent re-infestation or buildup.

5 gallon buckets can be used, though more water volume is encouraged if possible. Tupperware bins can also be used. The 5 gallon approach works best for one fish in my experience.

1. Add an air stone to each bucket.
2. Add the fish to one bucket and any treatments, medications or a heater if using (you will need 2 heaters if using this method).
3. Allow the other bucket to age for 12-24 hours. If the ammonia is climbing in the fish tub after 12 hours, transfer the fish to the aged bucket. If not, wait another 12 hours and then transfer the fish.
4. Empty and sterilize the now fishless bucket and any equipment in it using hydrogen peroxide and vinegar, boiling water or bleach if desired. Triple-rinse. Refill with fresh water and proceed to age another 12-24 hours.
5. Before moving the fish again, feed them an hour beforehand. That way they should eliminate in the old bucket before being moved to the new one, keeping the ammonia level down. Add any treatments to the new water prior to moving the fish again.
6. Repeat this process for 10 days to 2 weeks, depending on the parasite's life cycle (if treating for parasites) or the progress of the sick fish.

## Vitamin C

Vitamin C is a very strong immune boosting agent for fish and people. Vitamin C can be provided through diet (red bell pepper is tasty for goldfish and is 5 times higher in Vitamin C than an orange) or by adding it to the water directly. Vitamin C can naturally remove chlorine and chloromines from the water.

Vitamin C can be purchased in powder, liquid or tablet form.

**Dosage**

Vitamin C only lasts for 8-9 hours, so it needs to be added morning and night.

It should to be added gradually to the tank using the following method:

Day 1: 5ppm

Day 2: 15ppm

Day 3: 30ppm

Day 4: 50ppm

Continue after day 4 at 50ppm daily for 10+ days. Another 7 days may be necessary in severe cases.

To figure out the correct ppm, multiply the number of gallons in your tank by the concentration you want to achieve. Example: 90 gallons by 30ppm = 2700mg Vitamin C.

*Liquid Vitamin C*

Alternatively, you can purchase buffered vitamin C in liquid form for your aquarium. Then you don't have to worry about pH fluctuations.

**Precautions**

It does lower the pH if it isn't buffered first, so you must have a test kit on hand. Check the pH before and after adding the Vitamin C and correct with a buffer if necessary. Carbon or any chemical filtration must be removed.

## Wild Oil of Oregano

Wild Oil of Oregano (WOO) is a highly potent natural antibiotic proven to be useful against both gram-positive AND gram-negative bacterial infections. Even better, it is non-toxic to the cells of fish (unlike commercial chemical antibiotics) and does not promote digestive flora imbalance. It kills bacteria by its active ingredient, carvacrol, which harms the cell membrane of the bad bacteria. It is worth noting that many farmers, including those in aquaculture, are turning to natural antibiotics

*Wild Oil of Oregano*

to help their animals with infections that are resistant to chemical antibiotic treatments. It is best obtained in its cold-pressed form. WOO also has been shown to have some antiparasitic properties.

## Dosage

Wild Oil of Oregano can be used to make a medicated feed (especially useful for internal bacterial infections) or dosed to the water directly. Some fish farms are adding it to their feed for its beneficial properties against bacteria. The amount of oil needed will depend on what kind you get.

When added to feed, pure WOO should be diluted in an approximate 1/3 ratio to olive oil (WOO should make up 1/3 of the mixture) as it is quite strong. You can also use pre-diluted WOO in capsule form (140mg). I have also had success with a 175mg capsule. Pellets can be rolled in this solution and let sit for 10 minutes before feeding to the fish. If possible, feed it directly from your hand to the fish's mouth to keep as much oil on the food as possible.

To make a water treatment, the following recipe can be used:

*Recipe:*

1 capsule of 140mg Wild Oil of Oregano (or 5 drops of pure Wild Oil of Oregano)

*Organic Aloe Vera Gel*

1 tsp organic aloe vera

1/8 tsp unscented castile soap (optional)

100 tsp (33 and 1/3 tablespoons) distilled or dechlorinated tap water

*Directions:*

Mix into an empty container and shake well. Add 1 teaspoons of this solution per 10 gallons of aquarium water. Repeat daily every 24 hours for 1 week or until desired results are achieved.

## Precautions

Observe fish for signs of stress and perform a large water change if necessary. May harm aquarium plants.

# Commercial Medications

I sometimes recommend the use of commercial medications in cases where the fish is afflicted with an advanced infection which could be threatening its life. Significant fin rot, ulcers, dropsy, or reddened belly probably all merit the use of such medications. Issues such as a fish sick from bad water quality, an active fish with a slight pink smudge on the body, a bit of fraying on the end of the fin, gasping at the surface without signs of infected gills or parasites probably would do best with a natural treatment. If these kinds of issues do not resolve with such treatments and good water conditions or continue to get worse, something else may be going on that, until addressed and resolved, will likely only result in the fish going downhill regardless of the type of treatment.

One common class of these commercial medications is antibiotics. They can be life-saving. There are some cautions that users should know before they administer them.

- One significant downside of antibiotics is that, regardless of the manufacturer claims, all of them will harm or hinder the biological filter to some degree. This can make maintaining good water quality, which is essential for healing fish, a challenge. A hospital tank may be a good option if a manageable number of fish are infected. Testing the water daily is advisable throughout treatment.
- Another problem is that antibiotic resistant bacteria (aka "superbugs") are developing due to the overuse of these medications by fish farms and some importers. This means that infections can stop responding to commercial antibiotic treatments, which can be dangerous to the fish.
- It is also worth noting that antibiotics affect the digestive flora (good bacteria in the gut) that both people and pets rely on for processing food and for a strong immune system. The effects on the digestive system by these medications are considered by many health professionals to be permanent and irreversible.
- Extra caution should be exercised before using any chemical treatment, as they are harsher on the fish than natural treatments and can do more harm than good if not carefully administered for the correct condition. Be sure you are treating for the correct issue to avoid undue stress.

My advice is only once all other causes of sickness have been ruled out and other avenues exhausted should medications be turned to, unless the fish is near death or has a serious condition.

The advantages of commercial medications are that more study has been invested into their effectiveness for certain conditions. For most of them, there is a "track record" of reliability we can look to for their ability to help a certain disease. The manufacturers have had some level of testing performed prior to making them available on the market. This can make them especially valuable to have on hand for cases where time is of the essence.

For convenience's sake, I have included only medications that are commercially available to hobbyists. Those that require a prescription to be obtained are best discussed with your veterinarian.

It is worth noting that many of the antibiotics that are (at the time of writing this book) available to the public may eventually be restricted where you live. This has already happened in several areas as a result of legal battles. Many aquarists are stockpiling these medications so they will have them on hand in case something goes wrong with their fish and they can't get access to them anymore.

## Copper

Copper is effective at treating several parasites, including ich and velvet. I recommend it as a treatment for the latter and use salt instead of copper to treat ich, as it is safer for the fish. Seachem Cuprimine is the brand I recommend.

*Seachem Cuprimine*

**Dosage**

Follow manufacturer's instructions.

**Precautions**

Copper harms or kills plants and must be tested regularly with a copper test kit during treatment. Immunosuppressive to the fish. Linked to liver damage.

## Cyromazine

Cyromazine is useful for the eradication of anchor worm and fish lice, especially in ponds where the transfer method is impractical.

*Cyromazine*

**Dosage**

Follow manufacturer's instructions.

**Precautions**

While toxicity of this medication is low, overdosing can be dangerous to fish. There is no treatment for poisoning from this medication.

*MinnFinn*

Alternatives include the combination of and 0.3% salt (though results may vary) or the Tank Transfer Method.

## E.M. Erythromycin

This broad-spectrum antibiotic medication is used for treating gram positive bacterial infections. It is formulated to address fin rot, bacterial gill disease, ulcers, septicemia and Columnaris.

*E.M. Erythromycin*

### Dosage

Follow manufacturer's instructions.

### Precautions

Carcinogenic. Can cause cancer in people and fish. Can cause irritation.

May use Melafix as an alternative.

## Furan 2

The active ingredient in API Furan 2 is Nitrofurazone. It is used as a broad-spectrum antibiotic for both gram positive and gram negative bacterial infections.

### Dosage

Follow manufacturer's instructions.

*Furan 2*

### Precautions

Nitrofurazone can linger in fish tissues after treating. Should not be combined with or used prior to treating with MinnFinn or death can result. Can harm the biological filter.

May use Wild Oil of Oregano as an alternative.

## Formalin + Malachite Green

Formalin is made of 37% formaldehyde. Sometimes it is combined with Methanol. It has been mostly used to treat parasitic infections and some fungal or bacterial infections. It may be able to reduce flukes. It may also pose an antiviral affect in the case of lymphocystis. The combination of a similar aldehyde (to formaldehyde) and malachite green have been combined in Seachem's Paraguard medication for a bit less toxic formula.

### Dosage

Follow manufacturer's instructions.

**Precautions**

Formalin reduces dissolved oxygen in the water.  Do not use Formalin in water over 80 degrees F.  Formalin can burn fish, especially smaller weaker fish.  Formalin will harm the biological filter.  Malachite green is a known carcinogen, along with aldehydes and this medication is gradually being removed from the market.  May use MinnFinn as an alternative.

## Kanamycin

Kanamycin (commonly available as Seachem Kanaplex) is a broad-spectrum antibiotic.  It can be useful when treating bacterial dropsy, as well as other bacteria-induced conditions such as pop eye, fin rot, and Columnaris.

*Kanaplex*

**Dosage**

Can be added to food or to the water column directly.  Follow manufacturer's instructions.

**Precautions**

Do not exceed recommended treatment time.  This can do more harm than good to the fish.

May use Microbe-Lift Artemiss or Wild Oil of Oregano as an alternative.

## Metronidazole

Seachem manufactures this as Metroplex.  Useful in treating Hexamita.  Sometimes used to treat internal parasitic infections or the very rare case of ich that reproduces under the skin of the fish with no free-swimming form.

*Metroplex*

**Dosage**

Can be added to food or to the water column directly.  Follow manufacturer's instructions.

**Precautions**

Metronidazole is relatively gentle but, as with all medications, should not be overused.

May try Wild Oil of Oregano as an alternative.

## Neomycin Sulfate

Neoplex can be incredibly useful for fin rot or fungal infections.  It is a broad-spectrum antibiotic that is especially beneficial for external bacterial infections.  If the infection does not respond in 3 weeks, switching to Furan 2 is recommended.

*Neoplex*

**Dosage**

Can be added to food or to the water column directly.  Follow manufacturer's instructions.

## Precautions

Do not mix with other antibiotics.

## Sulfathiazole

Sulfathiazole (commonly available as Seachem Sulfaplex) is an antibiotic that can be useful for treating conditions that are not improved by Kanaplex, such as fin rot, mouth rot and Columnaris.  It is also not quite as harsh as Kanaplex.

*Sulfaplex*

## Dosage

Can be added to food or to the water column directly.  Follow manufacturer's instructions.

## Precautions

As with any antibiotic, keep a close eye on water quality and check for signs of stress from the fish.

May use Wild Oil of Oregano or colloidal silver as an alternative.

# Euthanasia

Sadly, sometimes it's too late for the fish.  Too much damage has been done for them to be able to heal – damage such as internal bleeding, extreme fluid retention or organ damage.  In cases like these, the kindest thing may be to euthanize, as it avoids prolonging an inevitable death and causing further suffering.

How do you know if you should put your fish down or not?  It's a hard question to answer, because sometimes goldfish are able to make a recovery you would have thought impossible, so you don't want to act in haste.  After all, they can be remarkably hardy.

Some goldfish owners do not like to prolong the suffering of the fish that may die.  On the other hand, others prefer for various reasons to "let nature take its course" and do not interfere.  I will only say that in the end, all we can do is seek the best interest of the fish.  Their good should come before even our emotional attachments to them.

In some cases, it is safe to assume that the fish won't make it, such as when the fish is doing the "death curl" (inverting itself) and hardly breathing or has been refusing to eat.

### Clove Oil Method

*100% Clove Oil*

Some goldfish owners do not feel comfortable with the old-school freezing method of euthanasia out of concerns for potential discomfort of the fish.

Because injections of anesthetic overdose are not available to the average hobbyist, an alternative method is to use oil of cloves, which will peacefully sedate the fish so it can pass, completely pain free.

To perform euthanasia with clove oil:

1. Shake 10 drops of 100% oil of cloves in a small bottle of hot water until cloudy (larger fish may require more drops of clove oil).
2. Add the mixture to 1 quart of tank water or dechlorinated tap water.
3. Wait for 10-15 minutes, then transfer the fish and water to a Ziploc bag and place in the freezer or add 25% of Vodka to the water (1/4 cup of Vodka to 1 cup water) and wait 20 minutes (to be completely sure).  Skipping this final step can lead to a fish that later wakes up once the anesthetic effect of the clove oil has worn off.

What to do with the remains of your fish is entirely up to you, as the owner.  Some prefer to bury their goldfish in a paper bag or box in a special way.  In a garden or underneath a tree are common burial places.  By ensuring the fish is buried at least two feet underground, you can prevent the fish from being dug up by scavengers, other pets or rain that might wash away the soil.

# Symptom Lookup & Solutions

Wondering what mysterious issue is going on with your goldfish?  Here you can find a list of symptoms goldfish can have and what you can do for them.

There are some symptoms that are a result of injury, such as missing body parts or open wounds. Only suspect injury if your fish have been displaying aggressive behavior (such as during spawning) or you have decorations in the tank that can cause the fish to get stuck or jabbed. Injury can occur during shipping as well, though this is rare.

Others are actually genetic defects, such as outturned/flared gill covers, collapsed mouths, bent backs or missing fins.  Genetic defects will develop as the fish ages, regardless of how well you care for it.

It's important to recognize when something has suddenly changed and your goldfish isn't doing well before things get out of control.  That is why it is important to regularly inspect your goldfish for anything out of the ordinary on a daily basis.

So, let's get identifying!

## Bent Back

Also called Scoliosis, this is usually genetic but can also be induced through electrocution.  If the fish has been electrocuted it will never return 100% to its normal self and there is no course of treatment.

Additional causes for a kinked back can include adverse reaction to chemical medications, nutritional deficiencies of essential vitamins (especially Vitamin C) or amino acids.  These are to be suspected if the fish was not born with a bent back and electrocution has been ruled out.

**What to Do**

This problem is likely permanent, though changing to a more nutritious diet may slow the advancement of the condition.

## Black Patches

Black in goldfish can mean a few things.  If the black is new, it could be natural color change as the fish ages, though typically blacks go away rather than appear (being an unstable color).

However, it can be a sign that there was recently an injury of some kind, usually a burn.  Ammonia burns are characterized by a black, smudgy look on the fish.  The black is actually a sign of healing after the burn but can be an indication that the tank is not stable. Black smudges can appear after using chemical medications as a result of their caustic action on the fish. Fish who have recently been shipped can incur black spot from the high ammonia levels in the bag.

Much rarer is black spot disease, caused by flatworms carried by birds or snails (called metacercaria). This typically occurs in fish kept in ponds. The spots will "rupture" and leave a wound behind, which could be infected by opportunistic bacteria.

**What to Do**

Ensure ammonia and nitrite levels are at 0ppm. Time and clean water are recommended.

If you are suspicious about the black spots not being from burns, it is possible to try salt at 0.3% for 48 hours in ammonia-free water. If the fish does not improve, it could be black spot disease. Salt and water changes can help prevent infection. Removing snails will end the parasite's lifecycle.

# Bloating

When there is severe fluid imbalance in the fish, a goldfish can swell up enormously in their stomach area. You may also discover bulging eyes or prickled scales as well. Alone or with other symptoms, this is usually an advanced case of an internal Aeromonas bacterial infection. If the fish is very inflated, chances are that too much damage has already been done to the internal organs for the fish to function properly. Pale gills can indicate organ failure.

Ascites (swelling without lifting of scales) can point to a fatty liver, cystic ovaries or kidney damage of some kind, especially if the fish has stopped producing ammonia or gentle massage causes red-tinged fluid to be released.

Occasionally egg impaction is to blame, causing the bloat. Egg impaction is usually lopsided and may cause the scales to spread out.

**What to Do**

For fish with raised scales, treatment for dropsy is recommended.

For ascites, there are not many options beside surgery. If the gills are pale, it may be advisable to euthanize the fish as there is likely no possibility of recovery from this condition.

If a tumor is suspected, I would recommend trying the tumor protocol outlined in the health issues section.

Egg impaction may be resolved by allowing natural spawning behavior to occur by placing the female with other males in a warmer environment with a longer photoperiod.  If spawning does not happen naturally, there is probably a hormonal imbalance going on because the female is not sending out the pheromonal signals to the males to induce spawning behavior while continuing to produce a large amount of eggs.  A veterinarian may want to perform an injection of hormones to get the fish to spawn.  Gentle massaging towards the vent with the thumbs (for larger fish) may prove be useful to release some of the eggs.

## Bloody Veins

You may have noticed your goldfish's fins are looking red, and on closer inspection there is what appears to be red streaks in them.  This is easiest to see on the tail, and even more on goldfish who have white fins.

Red veins are not always a sign of a problem.  It is often very normal to see a little red veins in fish with long fins or white-colored fins.  In general, only when the redness is excessive is there cause for concern.

Stress of many kinds can cause redness of the fins.  This could be from septicemia internal bacterial infections, parasites or water quality problems.

For bacterial infections characterized by severe veining stemming from the base of the tail, adding salt or an antibiotic may prove beneficial.

Red veins mean the fish may be experiencing the effects of toxins in the water, often ammonia or nitrite.  The fish's blood vessels then break due to osmotic pressure.

Some long-finned varieties of goldfish have chronic issues with red veins in their fins or even patches or areas of the fins that show continual redness.  This has been referred to as "fin congestion."  Adding a UV sterilizer consistently seems to reduce this.  A bit of salt in the water (1tsp per 5 gallons) may also be therapeutic.  Finally, you may consider adding a soil underlayer to the substrate with a strong colony of live plants.  These help support good bacteria to help outcompete the harmful ones in the water.

**What to Do**

If the ammonia or nitrite levels are coming up over 0ppm, perform an immediate 90% water change and dose with an ammonia and nitrite binder such as Prime.  Continue to monitor the levels daily and adjust accordingly.  Correct the pH if necessary.  If these are all normal, perform a 50% water change and make sure

*Prime*

there is not an excessive amount of detritus in the tank or filter. The next step would be to consider your feeding schedule to ensure no overfeeding is happening. If there are still no problems as far as the water goes, you can biopsy the fish to check for parasitic infection and treat accordingly. If the fish has very bloody fins and does not improve with clean water and is confirmed to be parasite free, treat for internal bacterial infection.

# Bottom Sitting

A normal, healthy goldfish will be actively swimming around the tank, constantly on the move as it forages for food.

Fish that spend a considerable amount of time resting at the bottom of the tank could be dealing with a number of different things.

- **Swim bladder problems** can cause the fish to have difficulty swimming upwards in the tank, sometimes even scuttling along the bottom on their stomachs. This could be due to bacterial infection which causes the swim bladder to become filled with fluid, weighing the fish down.
- **A heavy load of parasites** can cause the fish to sit at the bottom, only swimming around just fine when they see their owner. This is because the fish feel weak, so they rest at the bottom of the tank. The fish may also show other signs of parasitism, such as red spots, red fins, flicking or excess slime production. Such a fish will eventually die if left untreated as the parasites multiply out of control.
- **Body exaggerations** on fancy goldfish, such as massive bubble eye sacks or long, oversized fins can weigh a fish down, making them tire easily and rather spend their time resting on the bottom. Such a fish may seem unhealthy but is simply just doing what feels comfortable. This is a setback of breeding for more unusual physical characteristics.
- Occasionally, **temperature extremes** may cause the fish to be lethargic. Very cold water especially will cause goldfish to sit at the bottom. This is common outdoors during winter months.
- **Internal bacterial infections** (such as mycobacteriosis) can cause the fish to bottom sit.

**What to Do**

For sinking swim bladder problems, treat for internal bacterial infection.

For parasitic infestations, check for costia and flukes with a microscope and treat accordingly.

For body exaggerations, nothing can be done other than ensure the water current is not too strong for the fish and the fish has a good, nutritious diet.

If the water is cold outside and it is winter for the pond, don't worry. The fish will return to its normal activity level when the water warms up in the spring.

Finally, consider mycobacteria as a cause.

## Clamped Fins

When goldfish don't feel well, they start to look droopy as they hold all their fins close to their body – most noticeably the dorsal fin. Fish that have parasites do this out of irritation and flashing often accompanies such clamped fins. High ammonia or nitrite levels – especially during New Tank Syndrome – are possible causes, but other water quality issues, such as a pH crash can be at play too.

This is not the same as the fish who has a folding top fin due to genetics. Very long dorsal fins that bend can be more difficult for the fish to hold upright even though the fish is perfectly fine.

**What to Do**

Test the water and correct if necessary. If this was normal, use a microscope to check for parasites. If no microscope is available, treat with 3-5 applications of MinnFinn followed by 2 weeks of 0.5% salt if no improvement is seen.

## Cloudy Eyes

Does your fish look like it has cataracts? Cloudy eyes, or eyes that have a white, foggy film over the lens, come as a result of burning or injury to the eye which causes the fish to produce excess slime (the white film). The damaged area can also become infected by bad bacteria.

This issue is most common with telescopes during the shipping process, who are prone to injury or scraping of their eyes more than other goldfish because their large eyes stick out farther. If this is the case then the fish will usually heal on its own quite quickly.

A goldfish, telescope or not, who has suddenly developed cloudy eyes in your tank is most likely an indication of burning from water quality problems. This issue can also happen when fish have been exposed to some chemical medications, causing whiteness on the eyes.

It is worth mentioning that old age can also cause the eyes of a goldfish to go cloudy.

**What to Do**

Test the water, then adjust ammonia, nitrite and nitrate levels back into the correct ranges if necessary.

If bacterial infection is the cause (likely if there is already perfect water quality and the fish have not been shipped recently), check for other signs of illness and then salt to 0.3%. Ensure the temperature is kept in the mid to high 70s and the water quality stays pristine. Applications of MinnFinn can help to resolve the bacteria causing the cloudiness. Finally, adding an antibiotic to the water may be advised, especially if the fish is not eating.

For cloudiness from damage to the eye by chemicals or ammonia, you can salt to 0.3%, aloe vera and ensure the water remains in perfect quality. Only time and clean water are recommended for recently shipped fish with cloudy eyes.

## Color Loss or Pale Skin

This is often just a natural effect of a change in environment (such as reduced lighting or a change in food) or losing color due to genetics. It is also typical of a fish who just woke up from their good night's sleep. In that case their colors typically return as they move around more in search of breakfast. No worries if any of these are likely.

However sometimes fish lose their vibrancy because they are either stressed out or don't feel well.

**What to Do**

If the fish has no other symptoms in addition to this, such as poor water quality, loss of appetite, milky slime coat or clamped fins, there is no need to do anything. Further diagnosis is needed if other symptoms are present.

## Coughing

Goldfish "cough" by rapidly opening and closing their mouth in what appears to be an effort to dislodge something from the gills. As with people, a cough now or then may be perfectly normal. But if it is more frequent and accompanied by other symptoms, illness is to be suspected.

Parasites that affect the gills (such as flukes and ich) can cause coughing. Fish TB can cause the fish to cough as its gill filaments become clogged, congested and vulnerable to secondary infection.

## Curling or Folding in Half

Known as the "death curl," fish who are nearing their end will sometimes lay at the bottom or hang at the surface of the water in this pathetic position, and typically refuse to eat, in which case it is safe to assume it will not recover and euthanasia is advised.

High nitrates can cause curling as a result of nitrate poisoning.

**What to Do**

If your nitrates are high, frequent small water changes are recommended to gradually bring them back into recommended levels.  The fish can greatly benefit from liquid chlorophyll added to the water.

*Liquid Chlorophyll*

## Eating Bubbles

Sometimes a goldfish may swallow bubbles, with or without spitting them out eventually after a bit of swimming.  Fancy goldfish seem to be particularly susceptible to this issue.

"Bubble gulping" is characterized by a rapid dart to the surface and snatching a big mouthful of air before the fish returns to the water body, where it may hold the bubble in its mouth for a while before spitting it out.

**What to Do**

Bubble gulping is typically the fish trying to clear its gills.  Test the water for all parameters and ensure there is not a high load of dissolved organics in the water.  Perform a gill examination to check for signs of bacterial gill disease and scrape for parasites.  An internal infection can lead to swim bladder damage or accumulation of scar tissue on the air sac.  There is a theory that the fish may grab bubbles to try to simulate the necessary and natural filling of air when the fish moves about in the water if the swim bladder isn't doing that on its own.

## Filmy Skin, Milky White Patches

This is a result of the fish producing extra slime, giving the fish a milky appearance.  Sometimes the fish will look to have white, filmy patches covering its body and fins.  The slime can even hang off of the fish or trail through the water.

The reason?  A low pH or other water quality problems (often a low pH) can cause the slime coat to shed.  If the pH is the problem, the fish may also be hovering near the surface of the water.

Parasites can also be the cause of shedding the slime coat as the fish tries desperately to rid itself of the attackers.

**What to Do**

Test the pH level and correct if necessary.  Adding 0.3% salt can help the fish recover from the pH burns.  Check for parasites with a microscope and treat as needed.

## Flashing & Itching

A fish who is flashing will suddenly dart wildly around, dashing themselves into things or rubbing quickly on the walls of the tank. They may even tilt to the side to quickly "roll" along the gravel. Again, clamped fins or flicking fins almost always accompany flashing. The fish is feeling irritated.

What causes flashing? Parasites or poor water quality (especially ammonia) are the two main causes. It's important to note that a fish may dart wildly around if startled or stressed out... this is not the same thing as flashing.

**What to Do**

Check that the water quality is within recommended ranges, especially ammonia, nitrite and pH levels. Chlorine or other chemicals in the water should be removed with the proper water treatment.

If the water is in good shape, parasites are to be suspected. Almost all parasites can cause some degree of flashing. Diagnosing with a microscope is recommended in order to choose the right treatment.

## Floating Upside Down

It can be a shock to look in your tank and see your fish belly-up, especially when you look closer and realize it is still alive. Floaty fish may not necessarily flip over completely, but may struggle to get to the bottom of the tank or even log-roll through the water as they swim (a sight to be sure!).

**What to Do**

See the section on swim bladder disorder for further diagnosis and recommended treatment options.

## Gasping for Air

Also known as "piping," surface gulping is a sign that the fish is not getting enough oxygen. If your water has a filter and/or bubble stone and not much dissolved organic matter, chances are it's not because you need more aeration in the water. The fish's gills are being strained in some way.

Water quality issues and parasites cause damage to the gills directly, making it harder for the fish to breathe properly. High dissolved organics can use up oxygen in the water. The fish feel like they are suffocating so they try to get air from the surface instead of from the water like they are supposed to.

Higher temperatures and the use of chemical medications can lead to not enough dissolved oxygen in the water.

**What to Do**

Ensure the water parameters are within recommended ranges and that there is not a lot of decaying material at the bottom or in the filter (uneaten food, plants, fish waste).  Doing a large water change is recommended, along with bringing the temperature down if it is over 80 degrees F.  There may be too many plants in the system; if so, manually removing some is recommended.  Finally, check for parasites or damage to the gills with a gill examination and biopsy.

## Gills Flared Out

This can be a genetic mutation (considered defective in fish that are not of the "Curl Gill" variety).  A common cause is gill flukes, which can cause the gills to swell open.  Bacterial gill disease can also cause this symptom.

**What to Do**

Perform a visual examination of the gills, then biopsy for parasites.  Treat as necessary.

## Gills Pale

Pale gills (the tissues underneath the gill cover) in fish is often an indication of blood loss.  There may be a heavy infestation of flukes attacking the gills.  Another possibility is organ failure (if seen in combination with other symptoms).  Finally, fish with the IHN virus show pale gills as they die.

**What to Do**

Perform a gill biopsy to check for parasites and treat as necessary.  Both organ failure and the IHN virus are not treatable.

## Green Dots

At first, you may think you see a speck of green algae on the fish.  But actually, these little specks are small, disk-shaped creatures that scuttle around on the goldfish.  Meet the fish louse.

These creepy bugs suck the blood of your pet by inserting a probe into its skin for its meal.  You will typically find them on the stomach, chin or base of the fins of the fish.  Fish with fish lice may also sport little red wounds where they have been "bitten" or dart around like crazy.

**What to Do**

Treat for fish lice as described in the treatments section.

## Hanging at the Surface

Clearly a sign that the fish isn't feeling well, there are two main reasons the fish does this. (And it isn't the same as a swim bladder problem.)

First, it may be the fish feels like it can't breathe properly. It is having trouble getting oxygen from the water and there is more oxygen near the surface. Check to see if the fish is also gulping for air – that is a giveaway that the gills are burdened. Please see the gasping symptom for further details.

If it isn't gulping/gasping but just hanging listlessly, the fish may be feeling weak from poor water quality, illness or an off pH. It will stop struggling to swim and float in a place where there isn't much current.

**What to Do**

Test the water parameters and correct as necessary. Ensure the tank is properly oxygenated if the fish is gulping at the surface.

You will probably want to check the gills of the fish for signs of bacterial gill disease, as well as perform a gill scrape to check for parasites.

## Head Standing

Causes for this can vary. Poor water quality is a likely candidate. Intestinal parasites that consume the body mass can make the head heavier than the rest of the fish, causing imbalance and head standing. If the fish is very tired, such as females after spawning, they might headstand. Gas or excess air in the gut can make the abdomen lighter. Kidney damage may also be a possibility.

**What to Do**

Test the water and correct if needed. Check for internal parasites by examining a fecal sample under the microscope for eggs. Consider separating a worn-out female from aggressive males. If the condition is related to diet, increasing fiber content and switching to a high-quality pellet, gel food or raw food diet is recommended. No cure for kidney damage exists.

## Holes in Gill Covers

Holes in the gill covers are a common sign of tuberculosis in goldfish. There is also a possibility of a bacterial infection attacking the gills or, in rare cases, a parasitic infection.

**What to Do**

There is no available treatment for fish tuberculosis. Please see the section on tuberculosis for further information. If the case is bacterial, antibiotics may help. Treat for parasites if necessary. If the fish survives, the holes will not close.

## Holes in Fins

This can be seen as pin holes in fins or gaps in the fins that may periodically close and reopen or remain open. Sometimes the area becomes a white spot before dropping out. This can to malnutrition of the fish. A fish starving for calories begins to utilize the tissues between the rays of the fins. This can happen despite being fed a good diet, as the gut is not able to absorb nutrients properly. The fish may also look thin or lose weight.

Malnutrition is usually caused by an intestinal worm problem or Fish TB. Treating with a dewormer is recommended first. In about a month with good feeding, the holes should heal. If unsuccessful, TB is to be considered as the cause.

Finally, parasites can cause pinholes in the fins as they chew away at the tissue and eventually drop out.

**What to Do:**

Check for parasites and treat as necessary. See the section on Fish TB for more details.

## Jerking

Jerking fish may seem to suddenly have been zapped with a bit of electricity and twitch without explanation. Fin twitching or flicking is also common with the presence of ammonia or because of surges during new tank syndrome. Parasites can cause the fish to flick its fins or jerk out of irritation.

**What to Do**

Ensure the water quality is optimal and examine the fish for signs of parasitic attack.

## Jumping Out

No, your fish isn't trying to commit suicide! A goldfish who has made the leap is usually trying to escape something, be it bad water or an aggressive tank mate during spawning. Irritants such as parasites can also cause jumping, sometimes attack of anchor worm or lice. Sometimes jumpers can survive if caught and returned to the tank soon enough.

**What to Do**

Check that the ammonia, nitrite and pH levels are in the advised ranges and correct if needed. If this is fine, check the fish visually for signs of parasitic attack and then biopsy for smaller parasites.

## Labored Breathing

A sign that the gills are stressed, this is most often caused by water poisoning, low dissolved oxygen levels (warmer water may be the case) or parasites. Labored breathing in fish must be addressed quickly to prevent death.

**What to Do**

Perform a complete water test to make sure there are no detectable ammonia or nitrite levels and that the pH has not sagged. Examine the fish for other symptoms and then perform a gill scrape to check for parasites.

## Leaning to One Side

Water poisoning is probably the primary cause of this condition – high ammonia, nitrite or nitrate levels. The next possible cause would be an infection of some kind which is weakening the fish, causing them to lose their balance. This could be bacterial, parasitic or viral in nature. Finally, lack of oxygen could be a possibility.

**What to Do**

Investigate the water conditions by testing for all the recommended parameters, then correct if necessary by performing water changes and ensuring proper aeration is provided. Biopsy the fish for parasites. Next, feel the abdomen of the fish to see if it is mushy and treat for internal infection if needed.

## Lumps

Usually tumors, these masses can range from the size of a pea to the size of a quarter or larger and can grow in size rapidly if conditions aren't corrected. They are typically black, white, or the color of the fish's skin.

In some cases, the lumps could be white and cauliflower shaped. This is Lymphocystis, which is caused by a virus.

Carp pox is a possibility if the lumps look like waxy warts the size of a pencil eraser, most commonly found on the edges of the tail fin.

Lumps or bumps that suddenly appear on the fish may suddenly rupture, oozing white. This is probably due to bacteria such as Columnaris (white center, red edges) or aeromonas (red center, white edges).

**What to Do**

Removing tumors can be possible with a quick snip if the tumor is attached by a small "string."

Please see the section on tumors or goldfish viruses for further treatment possibilities.

Salting to 0.3% can prove beneficial for bacterial lumps, as can the tank transfer method.

## Missing Scales

Extremely common in tanks that have not been properly cycled or cleaned, missing scales indicate the goldfish is scratching itself out of irritation (ammonia or nitrite can be the culprit). Damage to the fish's scales can happen as a result of spawning behavior, which removes some of the fish's protective slime coat and the scales can get dislodged. They do grow back if given time, a nutritious diet and perfectly clean water.

The more serious cause of this condition could be poridia, an uncommon protozoan infestation transmitted by birds to ponds. Check for white cysts in the gills. Another possibility is Mycobacterial infection, which can result in missing scales that seem to refuse to grow back.

**What to Do**

Test and correct any water quality issues if needed. It is also probably a good idea to make sure the tank does not have any rough decorations or objects in it that the fish might bump into. For myxosporidia, clean water is the only treatment. Mycobacterial infections are untreatable.

## Mouth Red or Rotting

This is a horrible bacterial infection that results from poor water quality, a high bad bacteria count in the water or parasites such as flukes. It often begins with the mouth area looking a bit red, then spreading and corroding away until the jaw is disintegrated.

**What to Do**

Correct any water quality issues that may be present and treat for mouth rot as described in the treatments section.

## Mouth Stuck Open

The fish may have gotten some gravel lodged in its mouth. If there is nothing in the mouth it can be a result of deformity showing up as the fish grows. Another possibility is an ulcer on the inside of the mouth.

**What to Do**

Look in the fish's throat to see if any gravel or other foreign object is lodged in the back and gently remove it.

## Mushy Belly

A mushy abdomen can indicate an internal bacterial infection, unreleased infected eggs, a damaged liver, internal tumors, internal parasitic infection or organ displacement.

**What to Do**

If the fish is acting well, feed a varied, nutritious diet. If it isn't, treat for internal bacterial infection with antibiotic feed. An X-ray of the fish by a fish veterinarian may help in diagnosing internal tumors. Organ failure is not treatable.

## Pale Color

Loss of color is often an indication of stress. A thick slime coat can lead to the fish appearing lighter in color than normal. Goldfish that have been administered steroids prior to being sold may pale out once they are no longer having such unnatural color-enhancement.

**What to Do**

Check the water quality and correct as needed. If that is fine, examine the fish for other symptoms such as excess mucus production (which could indicate parasitic attack).

## Popped out Eye/s

This is often an internal bacterial infection, resulting in fluid building up behind the eyes that causes them to stand out grotesquely. It is usually – but not always – accompanied with prickled scales (dropsy).

Another reason for bulging eyes could be damage to the eye, resulting in swelling, which will subside on its own.

**What to Do**

For an internal bacterial infection, an antibiotic feed is recommended.  If the popped eyes are accompanied with prickling scales, the condition may prove to be fatal to the fish.

## Pineconing Scales

Also called Dropsy, pineconing scales are most easily seen when standing over the fish, but a trained eye can detect it from the side.  The scales stand out as a result of fluid imbalance in the body, often from trouble with the liver or kidneys.

**What to Do**

While it used to be considered terminal in all cases, there have been some success stories.  However, in other cases the dropsy seemed to get better only to return later.  This is often because internal damage has been done to the fish because of Aeromonas bacteria, as is the case with most instances of dropsy.  The fish keeper is advised to use their own discretion with regard to attempting to treat or not.  Early detection is the key, when the scales are just beginning to lift.  The later it is caught the more likely it is that the fish won't make it.  See the treatment section on dropsy for more information.  Fish that recover may never quite be the same.

## Red Anal Port or Prolapsed Anal Port

Redness of the anal port in goldfish can indicate an internal bacterial infection, such as Columnaris.

A prolapsed anal port can commonly occur due to a diet high in indigestible fillers or female fish with a heavy egg load.  Anal prolapse can occur from manual stripping of the eggs from a fish.

**What to Do**

Examine the fish for signs of internal bacterial infection and treat as needed.

Feed only highly digestible, preferably raw foods for several weeks and then switch to a high-quality goldfish food with no fillers or grains.

Epsom salt in the water can prove beneficial to ease impaction.

Hand-stripping is not recommended for those other than seasoned breeders or those who have been instructed by one.

## Red Belly

Red belly is not a condition where a sore has developed on the belly (commonly caused by bottom-sitting and parasites or floating upside-down with the belly exposed to air).  This issue is diagnosed by redness showing through the scales along the underside of the fish. It is an ominous sign that the organs have been damaged by an internal infection.

**What to Do**

This condition is usually terminal. Antibiotic feed may save the rare fish.

## Red Hole in the Head

Fish with wens may sometimes get a very serious infection that begins as a dark red spot that gets larger as it erodes away. However, this condition is not restricted to fish with wens. It can happen to any kind of goldfish and even tropical or marine fish.

This infection is likely bacterial in nature (some say Staph bacteria is the cause) and is thought to be induced by external Hexamita parasites. It must be treated quickly or the fish can perish. Swelling of the body may follow as the infection spreads through the goldfish's system. Other symptoms may include lethargy, refusal to eat, white, stringy poop, anemia and red/prolapsed vent.

**What to Do**

Swab the area twice daily with hydrogen peroxide, 12 hours apart. Tank Transfer Method may be advisable. Daily treatments of water-dosed Metroplex (10 days) combined with Furan 2 (10-14 days) should be started immediately. The sooner this condition is diagnosed, the better is the prognosis for recovery. Raising the temperature to 78-80 degrees F can also be beneficial. If swelling is present, adding Epsom salt can help draw the fluids out. Swelling can indicate internal organ damage from infection.

*Hydrogen Peroxide*

*Metroplex*

## Red Spots

Typical of nitrite poisoning, red spots can be a sign of blood hemorrhaging on the body or fins. Poor water quality may be the culprit, and/or parasitic infection.

**What to Do**

*Furan 2*

Test the water and perform a biopsy to check for parasites on the fish.

## Shredded Fins

Not the same as fin rot. This condition causes the tissue between the fin rays to be eroded away. It can happen when the fish is exposed to poor water quality such as high ammonia or nitrite levels. Another possibility would be the parasite hexamita.

Shredding can leave the tail almost completely destroyed, and it may not fully repair.

**What to Do**

If the water is in good condition, check for hexamita with a microscope.

## Sores

Red sores, or ulcers, usually start as a red spot that begins to open and become very nasty. They can grow to the point where the muscle is exposed inside the fish and will eventually cause death through fluid displacement. They are an external bacterial infection usually on the body of the fish.

If the sore is red with a white rim, this is likely from *Aeromonas* bacteria.

If it is white on the inside and rimmed with red, this is likely from *Columnaris* bacteria.

**What to Do**

Make sure the water quality is as pristine as possible. Proceed to biopsy the fish for parasites with a microscope. After treatment for parasites is finished, treat as described in the bacterial ulcers section.

## Spitting out Food

The fish may eagerly gulp the food, then immediately spews the chewed up food back out.

If a fish is doing this, there is a chance that there is an ulcer in the mouth creating discomfort when the fish takes in food. There is also the possibility of a large gill fluke infestation. Another problem could potentially be a blockage in the gills or throat.

**What to Do**

Holding the fish upside down, check inside the mouth for signs of sores or foreign object. Check that the gills look healthy and do not have something lodged inside.

Finally, check for flukes or other parasites with a gill scrape and treat as necessary.

## Splits in Fins

Fins can get torn during shipping or from spawning behavior. Flukes can cause fins to split, as can poor water quality.

**What to Do**

If the water is in good shape, check for flukes with a microscope. Many times the splits will heal on their own; they line with black when healing and often seal shut given clean water and some time.

# Swimming in Circles

The fish may swim in loops or stand on its head as it spins in corkscrew fashion. Flukes (brain or eye) or Myxobolus Cerebralis parasites can cause fish to swim strangely in circles, as can neurological issues such as mycobacteriosis of the brain. Difficulty eating or skeletal deformities may result.

**What to Do**

By the time the fish is whirling, irreversible brain damage has likely taken place. Humane euthanasia is advised. Ensure birds cannot get to fish in the pond and remove snails.

# Tail Standing

A fish with exaggerated finnage (especially Veiltails) may often stand on its tail. This is because the weight of the fin is greater than the body mass of the fish due to its genetics.

Another possibility is a fish that is suffering from water quality deterioration. Finally, tired females may do this after spawning.

**What to Do**

Ensure the water quality is safe for the fish. Female goldfish that have spawned may do well to be separated from the others.

# Wasting/Weight Loss

Fish that are not getting enough to eat might start looking thin.

Wasting, despite eating, is often an indication that the fish is having internal issues and stress is being placed on them, such as an internal bacterial infection or parasites (wasting on younger fish is more likely to be a fluke infestation). A wasting fish will eat and eat and never seem to put on any weight. If things go unchecked eventually they may have trouble with their balance.

Poor quality food, fish Tuberculosis, cancer, or intestinal parasites such as intestinal hexamita or intestinal spironucleus can also cause wasting.

**What to Do**

Check for parasites with a microscope, then treat for internal parasites. Ensure you are feeding a high quality diet to your fish.

## Warts

Warts can come in many variations. Carp pox virus can cause waxy warts to appear on the edges of the fins and sometimes the body.

**What to Do**

See the section on goldfish viruses.

## White Edge on Fins

If there is red in addition to the white, ammonia or nitrite, high nitrates or a high pH may be to blame. Salt in the water can cause the fins to start getting ratty white edges. Another cause is bacteria. Water with a high bacteria count can stress the fish, in addition to getting attacked by bad bacteria. This is called fin rot, a condition that begins at the edges of the fins and moves upward, eating away (if it goes unchecked) until the whole tail is consumed. If it gets to that point it won't grow back. However, if caught soon enough and water quality is corrected the tail may blacken as a sign of healing and can begin to regenerate.

**What to Do**

Check and correct any water parameter related issues. If you are treating for parasites with salt, be aware that some level of fin damage may be inevitable. Ensure the water does not have high dissolved organic material (waste, decaying plants, uneaten food) and perform several large water changes in addition to cleaning the filter. Remove snails. If all else fails, try the transfer method.

## White Fuzzy Patches

Without access to a microscope, white fuzz can be tricky to identify, as many issues (Columnaris bacterial infection, Epistylis parasitic infection or fungus) can cause white cottony growths on the fish.

If it is fungus, it will look like course strands of hair under a microscope.

If it is Epistylis, it will appear as a moving, bell-shaped creature.

Columnaris may appear in conjunction with other symptoms, such as sores, and is not easy to identify even with a microscope.

**What to Do**

If the infection is fungal, treat accordingly.  See also the sections on Columnaris and Epistylis for diagnosis and treatment.

# White Spots

White spots on fish can be caused by a few different things.

If the spots look like grains of salt sprinkled on the body and fins of the fish, you may be dealing with an outbreak of ich.

If the fish has a wen (such as a Ranchu, Lionhead or Oranda), white spots in the wen only are usually nothing to worry about.

If the white spots are primarily located on the gill covers and pectoral fins of the fish, you are probably seeing breeding stars on a male.  Breeding stars may also appear in evenly distributed patterns on the body scales of the fish.  These too are perfectly normal.

Sometimes white spots are an immune reaction of the fish.  It can indicate hexamita (if localized to the lateral line) or mycobacteria (if on fins and/or body).

**What to Do**

Check for ich with a microscope and treat if necessary.  Rule out hexamita as a cause if the spots are along the lateral line.

# White Spots in Wen

Goldfish with wens (such as Oranda, Ranchu, Lionhead varieties) are prone to getting fluffy white bits of matter in the folds of their hoods.  This is thought to be benign debris that gets trapped in the cracks of the wen and starts to break down, or (for harder nodules/pimples) new wen growth coming in.  Microscopic biopsy does not detect fungus.  It usually goes away on its own.

**What to Do**

If no other symptoms are present, no treatment is necessary.

# White, Long Stool

Long white poop can indicate an internal parasite problem.  Sometimes the stool can be several times the length of the fish's body.  However, if you are feeding white foods such as rice, it may be nothing more than that.  If the poop is clear, long and thin with zigzag shapes, this could be reabsorbed eggs in a female goldfish.

**What to Do**

Check for internal parasites by squashing the poop on a glass microscope slide with a cover slip. If eggs are found treat for internal parasites according to the internal parasite treatment section.

# Won't Eat

If the fish is not eating and not eliminating, it may be constipated. If they are producing waste, consider internal infection as a possibility. Another possibility is the fish has a foreign object lodged in the throat. Fish nearing their end may lose their appetites.

**What to Do**

See the section on swim bladder disorder if the fish is not eliminating. Check if the belly is mushy to the touch. If it is, treat for internal infection. Try performing a large water change. If the fish is spitting food, check for parasites. Use a flashlight to examine the inside of the throat for foreign objects.

# Worms on Body

If you see little white (or brown or green or a different color) stick-shaped objects poking out of your fish's head or body, likely you have a case of Anchor worm on your hands.

**What to Do**

Treat for anchor worm as described in the parasitic diseases section.

# Yawning

Some periodic yawning is normal, but frequent yawning can be a warning that something isn't right.

Water quality issues can fry the gills of the fish, making it difficult to extract oxygen from the surrounding water.

The fish might have a rock stuck in its mouth. This is to be suspected if the mouth is seems stuck forming an "O" shape.

Parasites or bacteria infecting the gills can interfere with gill function, leading to yawning.

Finally, medications or toxins in the water (such as hydrogen sulfide pockets from gravel) can cause frequent yawning.

**What to Do**

Check that the ammonia, nitrite and pH are within recommended ranges. Examine the mouth of the fish for an obstruction with a flashlight. If further diagnosis is necessary, examine the gills of the fish for signs of bacterial infection and scrape for gill parasites. Finally, address any areas of hydrogen sulfide production in the aquarium.

## Yellow Speckles

Velvet can be diagnosed by shining a flashlight over the fish in a dark room. The fish may have velvety appearance all over the body or in patches.

**What to Do**

Use a microscope to check for velvet, then treat accordingly.

# Sources List

## Further Reading

See a list of recommended books by scanning the code.

*Books List*

## Websites

*Puregoldfish.com* is a website dedicated to furthering the goldfish hobby by providing information on a variety of goldfish topics

*Weloveteaching.com/puregold/care/care.htm* is a website with much useful goldfish information compiled by Ingrid Buxton and Jo Ann Burke

*DrJohnson.com* contains some useful, free information on goldfish and koi diseases

*Thegoldfishcouncil.org* is an international society of goldfish breeders and fanciers and a great way to connect with local breeders

# Conclusion

First of all, I would like to congratulate you for making it this far. The sad reality is that most people don't make the leap of faith to find out the truth about goldfish. They are fed misinformation and never understand they are doing everything wrong until it is too late.

As already mentioned, this book is the result of over 15 years of searching, probing, analyzing, experimenting and conversing with goldfish keepers around the world. It was hard but rewarding work, and I loved every minute of it. I still enjoy talking and writing about it.

You've learned a lot here. Now it's time to put your knowledge to use and watch your goldfish blossom under your confident care. You can now enjoy rather than stress out about one of the most relaxing and gratifying hobbies around, and your fish will thank you for it.

Lastly, remember that you're not left to play guessing games if you have any more questions. Don't be afraid to give me a shout out if you ever need any advice.

Happy fishkeeping,

Meredith

Made in the USA
Coppell, TX
08 March 2020